THE TEN MOST MISUNDERSTOOD WORDS IN THE BIBLE

BY ROBERT N. WILKIN

GES

John 3:16

Believe *Him* for Life

The Ten Most Misunderstood Words in the Bible

Requests for information should be addressed to: ges@faithalone.org

Cover Design & Typesetting: Holly Melton
Editing: Grant Hawley & Kyle Kaumeyer
Special Thanks: Pam Esteven & Bob Kenagy

Library of Congress Cataloging-in-Publication Data

Wilkin, Robert N., 1952-
  The ten most misunderstood words in the Bible / Robert N. Wilkin.
  ISBN 978-0-9788773-8-5
  1. Faith.   2. Hermeneutics.   I. Title.

Includes bibliographical references

Contents

Introduction

Why a Book on Misunderstood Words?

If we do not *understand* what God is saying, then we do not *believe* what He is saying. To believe something requires that we first understand it.

The truth is, there is a lot of confusion about certain words that occur in the Bible. This confusion is not merely among those in children's church. It isn't merely lay people, the people in the pews, who are confused. Even pastors, missionaries, professors in Bible colleges and seminaries, evangelists, and parachurch workers are often confused.

Why Ten Words?

I actually cite 21 misunderstood words in this book, ten in the body and eleven in an appendix. I picked ten for primary treatment since the book would be too large otherwise.

I picked these ten words because I believe they are the most misunderstood and because these misunderstandings are so detrimental to assurance, evangelism, and discipleship.

This Book Is Especially Helpful for Group Discussion

If you lead a discipleship group or a Sunday School class, this book can generate a lot of excellent discussion. Each chapter gives plenty of material for one or more lessons. A study guide has been provided for each chapter.

Families could use this to guide their family devotions.

I've spoken on these words all around the country and found that these presentations generated lots of great questions and comments.

Chapter 1
Faith

Introduction

It wasn't until after I was born again that I began reading Christian books that defined faith as something other than persuasion or the conviction that something is true.

Before I believed in Christ for everlasting life, when I was in a cult, I was convinced—that is, I believed—that one had to do more than believe in Jesus to be born again. I believed that to be born again one had to not only believe in Jesus, but also turn from his sins, commit his life to Christ, and follow Him. And I was convinced that to *keep* everlasting life one had to live a sinless life until death. Obviously this was an extreme view. But my view of faith itself was simple.

I came to believe differently through the ministry of Athletes in Action, a branch of what was then called Campus Crusade for Christ. Warren Wilke met with me four or five weeks in a row. Each time he would return to Eph 2:8-9, which reads, "For by grace you have been saved through faith, and that not of yourselves; it is the gift of God, not of works, lest anyone should boast." Warren was like a broken record week after week.

"Salvation," he would say, "is the gift of God. Salvation is not of works, lest anyone should boast. There is no ground for boasting because we receive salvation as a gift the moment we believe in Him, apart from any works at all."

Finally I became convinced. I came to believe that simply by faith in Jesus I was saved once and for all, apart from any works I might have done in the past or even apart from any works I might do in the future.

When I was on staff with Campus Crusade, and later when I went to seminary, I learned that many theologians and pastors who profess to believe in justification by faith alone, apart from works, do not define faith as mere persuasion.

What I found is that many who profess to believe in justification by faith alone actually believe more or less what I believed when I was in the cult group in Southern California. They believe that in order to be born again one must not only be convinced that Jesus is the Christ, the Son of God, but one must also turn from his sins, commit his life to Christ, and follow Him.

I wasn't convinced of this proposed understanding of saving faith. That is, I didn't believe that Biblical faith is some special kind of faith that includes repentance, commitment, and obedience. I saw this understanding of faith as a way in which someone could profess to believe in justification by faith alone when in fact he did not believe that.

If a person must believe in Jesus to have everlasting life, then he must know what it means to believe in Jesus to know if he has done it. Now that isn't a challenge if people know what believing in Jesus is. However, many have been influenced by radio and TV preachers, pastors, theologians, popular authors, and missionaries who have told them what I read about in seminary, that saving faith includes works. Thus one cannot be sure that he believes in Jesus since believing in Jesus is not a persuasion, but is instead a lifestyle.

In this chapter we will first consider many popular but quite misleading explanations of saving faith. Then we will conclude with an explanation of what saving faith really is.

Common Myths about Saving Faith

Myth: Saving Faith Is Different Than Regular Faith

Preachers and theologians can proclaim justification by "faith" alone and at the same time say that justification requires obedience, perseverance, commitment, and turning from sins. They do so by defining faith as including those things.

While working on my Master's thesis at DTS, I came across an article by Donald Dunkerly on hyper-Calvinism. Dunkerly said,

> I remember a seminary student who insisted at a conference that it is wrong to say to unbelievers, "God loves you" and "Christ died for your sins." When asked what he did with John 3:16, he replied, "John 3:16 is a very difficult verse. I would never preach from John 3:16."[1]

Dunkerly went on:

---

[1] Donald Dunkerly, "Hyper-Calvinism Today," in *The Presbyterian Journal* (November 18, 1981): 15. See http://theologicalmeditations.blogspot.com/2010/04/donald-dunkerley-on-hyper-calvinism.html. Accessed June 5, 2011.

I remember once hearing a prominent Calvinist preacher inveighing against decisionism and the immediate assurance of salvation that God sometimes sends.[2] "You must be saved for at least three years before you have accumulated enough good works to be sure that you are truly saved and not just a stony-ground-hearer," he said.[3]

Once we define faith to include commitment and obedience and perseverance in good works, John 3:16 is no longer an impediment to regeneration by commitment and obedience and good works.

Leading Bible teacher, John MacArthur, writes:

> Hebrews 11:1 faith is not like the everyday faith that we speak of. We drink water out of a faucet, believing it is safe. We drive our automobiles in freeway traffic, trusting that the brakes will work. We submit to the surgeon's knife and the dentist's drill by faith...The capacity for that kind of faith is intrinsic to human nature. But it is not the faith Hebrews 11:1 describes.[4]
>
> ...
>
> The *nature* of faith is different in the spiritual realm.[5]
>
> ...
>
> Saving faith, then, is the whole of my being embracing all of Christ. Faith cannot be divorced from commitment.[6]

Though he says that faith is the sole condition of justification, MacArthur, later in the same book, says:

> The gospel...does not call for a mere decision of the mind, but a surrender of the heart, mind, and will—the whole person—to Christ...*All* sinners...need to be confronted with God's demand that they turn from their sin to embrace Christ as Lord and Savior.[7]

---

[2] Dunkerly clearly does not believe that assurance is of the essence of saving faith. See the end of this chapter where I argue that at the moment of faith everyone has assurance because that is what we are believing Jesus for.

[3] Dunkerly, "Hyper-Calvinism Today," 15.

[4] John F. MacArthur, Jr. *Faith Works: The Gospel According to the Apostles* (Dallas, TX: Word Publishing, 1993), 42.

[5] Ibid., emphasis his.

[6] Ibid., 45.

[7] Ibid., 194-95, emphasis his.

People should, of course, reject any suggestion that Biblical faith is not really faith, but is something else.

If saving faith in the Bible is different than what we think of as faith, then isn't *all faith* in the Bible different than what we think of as faith? Wouldn't faith that Jesus is God be different than simply being convinced He is God? Wouldn't faith in the inerrancy of Scripture be different than simply being persuaded that the Bible has no errors in it? Wouldn't *all* Biblical faith include commitment and obedience and good works? No. Preachers are forced to take the impossible position that Biblical faith is always faith, except when it is referring to faith in Jesus for everlasting life.

It is extremely important that you see that this view of faith is wrong. Otherwise, you are open to being misled by well-intentioned yet wrong pastors and theologians and friends. If you become confused on this point, John 3:16 takes on a whole new meaning: "For God so loved the world that He gave His only begotten Son, *that whoever surrenders his entire heart, mind, and will to Him* should not perish but have everlasting life." Such an understanding of John 3:16 will not result in anyone being born again.[8] In addition, that view makes assurance of your eternal destiny impossible. You will go through life wondering if your commitment and obedience is sufficient. Every time you have a major argument with your spouse, curse another driver, or do anything which you confess as sin, you will wonder how a fully surrendered person could do *that*.

What follows are 1) different ways in which people attempt to support this idea, and 2) declarations from Scripture that saving faith is really the conviction that Jesus guarantees everlasting life to all who simply believe in Him for it.

Myth: Saving Faith Is Not Intellectual Assent

Another way of saying that saving faith is different than everyday faith is to assert that it is not intellectual assent. Everyone recognizes that everyday faith is indeed intellectual assent.

Most people believe that George Washington was the first President of the United States. They find the evidence persuasive. While they probably wouldn't think to call that belief *intellectual assent*, that is what it is. It is intellectual and it is assent, or agreement.

---

[8] Whatever God means by "believing in Jesus" is what one must do to have everlasting life. If we don't do what God requires, then we will be eternally condemned, no matter how well intentioned we are and no matter how much we find our way to be right for us (cf. Matt 7:21-23).

Most people in Christianity today do not actually believe that justification is by faith alone apart from works. Thus they either must say that justification requires faith plus works, or they must insist that saving faith is not intellectual assent, but that it includes commitment and works.

At the website *Stand to Reason*, Gregory Koukl writes concerning the difference between what he calls "true biblical faith" and what he calls "mere intellectual assent" as follows:

> If people tell you they already believe in Christianity, but you suspect something amiss, ask, "Are you willing to be baptized? Are you willing to stand up as an adult in public and confess your faith and trust in Jesus Christ, and to publicly identify yourself with Christ's Church?" If they're not willing, I suspect their so-called faith is just intellectual assent, not saving faith.
>
> Willingness to be baptized helps separate the sheep from the goats, spiritually speaking. It distinguishes those who have a genuine faith in Jesus Christ from those who are merely giving intellectual assent to the doctrines of Christianity. *True biblical faith entails action and identification.* If one acts to publicly identify himself with Jesus Christ and with His people in baptism, then he's probably moved *beyond mere intellectual assent.*[9]

Myth: Saving Faith Is Heart Faith

Similar to the charge that saving faith is not intellectual assent is the idea that saving faith is not *head faith*, but instead is *heart faith*. Never mind that there is not a single verse in the Bible that uses the expression *heart faith*, nor is there a verse that mentions or denounces *head faith*. This sounds catchy and it has become popular in Evangelicalism.

Yet the Biblical evidence demonstrates that this supposed distinction between head faith and heart faith is really a mind game.

First, the Scriptures never refer to the *head* as the source of thinking or feeling. In addition, the word *head* is never associated with faith in the Bible.

Second, of the two remaining words, *heart* and *mind*, the Scriptures often use them interchangeably. Both refer to the inner self where one thinks and believes and feels.

---

[9] Gregory Koukl, "Curing the Intellectual Assent Problem," http://www.str.org/site/News2?page=NewsArticle&id=5194. Accessed June 24, 2010. Emphasis added.

Third, the mind is not viewed as being inferior to the heart in Scripture. We are to "be transformed by the renewing of [our] *mind*" (Rom 12:2). There is nothing inferior about the mind in that verse.

Similarly, Paul exhorted the Ephesian believers, "Be renewed in the spirit of your mind" (Eph 4:23). Paul spoke to the Corinthian believers of having "the mind of Christ" (1 Cor 2:16). Luke said that the Lord "opened [the disciples'] understanding [literally, *mind*], that they might comprehend the Scriptures," that is, the Old Testament Scriptures, concerning His death and resurrection (Luke 24:45-47).

Imagine what human beings would be like if God had not given us minds to think.

Believing in Christ is the sole condition of everlasting life. There is no such thing as special types of faith called *heart faith* and *head faith*. Saving faith doesn't include commitment, obedience, or turning from sins. It is merely the conviction that Jesus is speaking the truth when He says, "He who believes in Me has everlasting life" (John 6:47).

Myth: Saving Faith Is More Than Believing Facts

Since intellectual assent (i.e., head faith) is believing facts, then it logically follows that if saving faith is different than intellectual assent, it is more than believing facts.

If saving faith is not like everyday faith and is not intellectual assent, then why say that it *includes* intellectual assent? Why not simply abandon the idea of believing facts altogether?

Actually, many today *are* abandoning the idea of believing facts when it comes to saving faith. In the emerging church, for example, becoming a Christian occurs when one has *an encounter* with God. Believing in Jesus is *an encounter, an existential experience*, that is not dependent on believing certain facts.

James Danaher is the head of the Department of Philosophy at the Nyack campus of Nyack College, a Christian and Missionary Alliance school. A faculty interview of him was posted at the Nyack website in November of 2006 when I wrote a paper on the postmodern concept of conversion.

Under the heading, "My conversion to a life in Christ," Danaher said:

> I had an experience with the Lord when I was eighteen, but it was an experience and not a conversion into a radically new and different life. Twelve years later, I had another God experience but again without the kind of surrender that marks the beginning of a transformed life. God was faithful still and, two years later, with a third experience, there was

a surrender and the beginning of a transformation that has continued for the past twenty-five years.[10]

Of course, many Evangelicals today are uncomfortable with abandoning the believing of facts altogether. Their concern is not with intellectual assent and believing facts, *per se*. Their concern is that more is needed than believing facts.

We are back at the core problem. People today do not believe that justification by faith alone is true. John 3:16 is a problem verse for them. Many wish to replace *whoever believes in Him* with *whoever behaves in Him*.

If saving faith is more than believing facts, then one cannot have assurance of his eternal destiny by any cognitive method. That is, one cannot say, "I believe in Jesus, therefore I have everlasting life."

A Calvinist can say, "I *intellectually* believe in Jesus." But since, in his understanding, saving faith is more than believing facts, he's not sure if he has true saving faith (and everlasting life) or not. As he looks at his works, he wonders, *Do my works prove I have true saving faith?* He isn't sure. He's concerned, because he realizes that he falls short much of the time.

Myth: Saving Faith Is an Ongoing Commitment to Obey

Even though the idea of commitment to obey is foreign to the idea of believing, once people divorce saving faith from belief, commitment to obey seems a reasonable part of saving faith. Many verses in the Bible can be shown in which people were or were not committed to serving God. Even though none of those verses show that such commitment is saving faith, or that it is a condition of eternal life, that isn't necessary. As long as one can show that faith is the condition of eternal life and faith is not really faith, then anything can be the condition of eternal life.

The citations already given demonstrate the popularity of the belief that saving faith includes commitment to obey. Many more references could be given.

For example, Curtis Crenshaw, a graduate of my *alma mater*, Dallas Theological Seminary, writes:

> One who claims to know Christ as Savior but does not bow to Him as Lord is deceiving himself. He has the kind of faith

---

[10] This testimony is no longer on the Nyack website (http://www.nyackcollege.edu/fs/personnel-listing) under faculty. When one clicks on the James Danaher faculty profile, his testimony is no longer present. However, in November of 2006 when I accessed the website the testimony was there as cited here.

James says the demons have (2:14ff.), which is a knowledge of Him without obedience. Such professors—and that is all they are—deceive themselves into hell. Genuine faith necessarily manifests itself by obedience; otherwise it is a veneer, only skin deep, a façade. The sinner trusts in the *whole* Christ with his *whole* soul, mind, will, and affections.[11]

Alan Day writes that "the main issue" in terms of being born again is being "committed to Christ."[12] He continues, "Easy believism reduces faith to mere intellectual assent. I fear that many in the organized church today have 'believed' in that sense and yet still never been born again."[13]

The late famed pastor and author James Montgomery Boice similarly wrote:

The minimum amount a person must give is *all*. I say, "You must give it all. You cannot hold back even a fraction of a percentage of yourself. Every sin must be abandoned. Every false thought must be repudiated. You must be the Lord's entirely."[14]

One of the leading New Testament scholars of our day is Darrell Bock. In a recent book called *Recovering the Real Lost Gospel*, he says this about saving faith:

By far the most common way to summarize the proper response to the gospel is to talk about *faith* [emphasis his]. The simple definition of faith is trust. The idea is so fundamental to Christianity that we often refer to Christianity as "the faith." Faith is an idea worth probing. For one thing, *it is not static* [emphasis added]. That is, *we do not have faith in a moment; it is an ongoing state* [emphasis added]. That is part of what tells us that the gospel is about more than a transaction. An act of faith initiates our new relationship with God, *but faith is not a one-time act; it keeps going* [emphasis added]. When we equate faith with belief, we are talking about an

---

[11] Curtis I. Crenshaw, *Lordship Salvation: The Only Kind There Is!* (Memphis, TN: Footstool Publications, 1994), 59, emphasis his.

[12] R. Alan Day, *Lordship: What Does It Mean?* (Nashville: Broadman Press, 1993), 19.

[13] Ibid., 20.

[14] James Montgomery Boice, *Christ's Call to Discipleship* (Chicago: Moody Press, 1986), 114, emphasis his.

ongoing faith, *not merely a moment of intellect assent* [emphasis added]. That is why trust, or reliance, is a better synonym than belief. *This faith means that we are open to God and responsive to Him. Without that responsiveness, faith is not faith* [emphasis added]."[15]

This way of looking at saving faith certainly motivates people to get to work and to give to the ministry of the local church. If only people with an ongoing commitment to Christ, people who are continually open to and responsive to Him, will spend eternity with Jesus, then church people better demonstrate their commitment by working hard in their local churches or else they will prove that they don't *really* believe. "Without that responsiveness, faith is not faith." People who want to avoid the lake of fire need to get to work, because saving faith is committed, obedient, and persevering.

Myth: Saving Faith Always Perseveres

As the above citations show, according to most Evangelical scholars and pastors today, saving faith perseveres in two senses.

In the first place, saving faith, understood as commitment to Christ, perseveres until death. It must be ongoing. Commitment to obey that is not followed by actual obedience certainly would not satisfy this understanding of saving faith. In fact, even a few years of actual obedience would not meet up to this standard of what saving faith is. One must persevere in obedience to the end of life in order to spend eternity with God in this way of thinking.

A person could be committed for a time and then stop being committed. Many preachers teach that it is naïve to think that a person can get off the hook that easily. What God clearly wants is endurance in the faith (cf. 2 Tim 2:12; Rev 2:26). If such endurance is either a part of saving faith, or a guaranteed result of it, then only those who persevere in good works until death will escape eternal condemnation.

In the second place, saving faith, understood as including the belief of certain facts about Jesus, cannot fail. Thus if a person who professes faith in Christ ever stops believing the fundamentals of the faith, he proves he was never born again in the first place.

This contradicts the clear teaching of the Lord Jesus. When the Lord interpreted the Parable of the Four Soils for His disciples, He said that the second soil "believed for a time and in time of temptation fell

---

[15] Darrell L. Bock, *Recovering the Real Lost Gospel: Reclaiming the Gospel As Good News* (Nashville, TN: B & H Publishing Group, 2010), 98.

away" (Luke 8:13). That the belief spoken of here is saving faith is clear in context (compare Luke 8:12). And earlier, when the Lord told the parable, He indicated that the seed in the second soil "sprang up" (Luke 8:6). A plant does not spring up out of the ground unless the seed under the ground has already germinated. That is, the new birth had already occurred. The second soil believed for a time and then stopped believing. Paul also tells of believers who suffered shipwreck regarding the faith (1 Tim 1:18-20; 2 Tim 2:17-18).

We are born again the moment we believe in the Savior who will never deny His promise to the believer (2 Tim 2:13). We are not saved by perseverance in obedience or having eternal faith. We are saved by faith in the Savior who is eternally faithful to His promise.

Myth: Saving Faith Is Unknowable

If saving faith is not like everyday faith in the ways already mentioned, there are several undesirable ramifications. One is that it is impossible to be sure of your eternal destiny since you can't be sure that you believe in Christ. This leads to a definition of *assurance* that is less than certainty.

To be assured of your eternal destiny, for most Evangelicals today, means you are *confident* that were you to die today you'd *probably* go to heaven.

If saving faith is not being persuaded that Jesus guarantees everlasting life to all who simply believe in Him, then the basis of assurance is our works, not our "intellectual assent." And since our works are not perfect (Rom 3:23; 1 John 1:8, 10; 3:2), our "assurance" is like a person who has one-third of the lottery tickets. He knows he has one chance in three of winning the lottery and the millions. But he also knows that he has two chances in three that he won't win.

Back in 1991 I debated Ken Sarles at Dallas Theological Seminary (DTS). At the time Ken taught historical theology there. We debated the issue of saving faith on back-to-back days for an hour at lunch in front of several hundred DTS students. He took the position that saving faith is more than believing facts. He admitted in the debate that it is impossible to be certain that you are born again. When I asked him on a scale of 1 to 100 how sure he was that he himself was regenerate, he said he was 99 percent sure.

I wondered at the time, and I still wonder, if a person might think it is highly probable he is born again when he is conducting a theological debate or preaching or evangelizing, yet might have serious doubts about his regeneration after he loses his temper and says something he regrets to his wife or one of his children. Surely his "assurance" dips south of fifty percent. What would happen to his assurance if he had a bit too much to drink? Another dip would occur. No one who looks to his works for assurance, no matter how godly, can avoid being concerned about going to hell. Fear of hell thus becomes a major motivation to obey and live for God. Put another way, this way of thinking causes a person to try to work hard enough so that he goes to heaven and not hell.

Myth: You Don't Really Believe *Until* *You Get in the Wheelbarrow*

There is a famous evangelistic illustration that many people use. I used this illustration myself before I came to see that it is a bad illustration of faith.

Blondin was a tightrope walker who literally strung a wire between the U.S. and Canada across Niagara Falls. He took a wheelbarrow across and then asked, "Who believes I can take a man across in this wheelbarrow?" Many in the crowd were shouting, "I do. I do." Then he pointed at one man and said, "Okay, then. Get in the wheelbarrow." The man refused. According to the illustration he didn't *really* believe because he didn't get in.

There are many variations of this illustration (e.g., the chair, the lifeboat, the airplane). The point of all of them is that believing in Jesus is more than simply believing in Jesus. That sounds odd to me even as I write it. I hope it sounds odd to you.

Believing in Jesus, according to many Evangelicals today, requires getting in the wheelbarrow, chair, lifeboat, or airplane. And what does that translate to in terms of what we must do to be born again? Typically the way one *gets in* is said to be by repentance, commitment, and obedience.

None of these illustrations are found in the Bible. Indeed, while there are figurative representations of saving faith in the Bible (e.g., eating the bread of life, drinking the water of life, seeing the Son of God, coming to Jesus), none of them are remotely like these examples. Indeed, these illustrations actually *contradict* the Biblical pictures of faith and the result is that people become confused about what they must do to have everlasting life.

See John 11:25-26 and the Lord's question, "Do you believe this?" Jesus never asked anyone to pray a prayer, walk an aisle, get in a wheelbarrow, or do anything in order to believe in Him. These are man-made distinctions that inadvertently deny justification by faith alone.

Imagine yourself as an unbeliever hearing that you must get in the wheelbarrow to be born again. What is your question? *What must I do, then, to get into the wheelbarrow?* There is no literal wheelbarrow to get into. So how does one *get into faith in Jesus?* Now we are back at commitment, obedience, and perseverance. And what is the proof you are in the wheelbarrow of faith? It is your imperfect works.

Drop this illustration and all like it unless you wish to teach works salvation.

Myth: Saving Faith Is a Gift of God

Calvinists often say that unbelievers are like cadavers and that they are incapable of believing until they are born again. Hence they reason that regeneration must precede faith. Let me repeat that. Calvinists say that a person is first born again and then later he believes in Christ.

It is in this light that Calvinists say that saving faith is a gift of God. First He gives life; then He gives faith.

This whole idea sets the words of the Lord Jesus on their head. Jesus said that it is the one who believes in Him who has life, not the one who has life who then believes in Him. While life is received the moment one first believes, clearly there is never a moment when an unbeliever has life. Well, that may be clear to me. But it is far from clear for many Calvinists.

Some Calvinists today go so far as to say that the new birth precedes faith not only *logically* (which is a common Calvinist claim), but also *in time.* Thus a person may have been born again for months or years or even decades before he comes to faith. One Calvinist, Stephen Smallman, said he knew of a man who was born again 65 years before he came to faith in Christ.[16]

Smallman explains that the new birth is like physical conception and the coming to faith is like physical birth, which occurs nine months after conception:

> Unlike a physical pregnancy, the length of which is fairly fixed, spiritual pregnancy goes on as briefly or as long as it takes God to bring us to faith and repentance...Once we finally come to vital faith, we can look back and see God's hand at work [i.e., regeneration] long before we believed.[17]

In this view the only people who can believe are people who are already born again and even then born-again people are not able to believe until God gives them that gift. Assurance is tricky in such a

---

[16] Stephen E. Smallman, *Spiritual Birthline: Understanding How We Experience the New Birth* (Wheaton, IL: Crossway Books, 2006), 22-23. See also pp. 24-28.

[17] Ibid., 27.

system because assurance is not found in believing in Jesus for everlasting life, since in this view believing is not a condition of everlasting life, but a result of it. Nor is everlasting life found in believing certain facts about Jesus (e.g., His substitutionary death, bodily resurrection, deity) since for most Calvinists faith is commitment, obedience, and perseverance. Thus, assurance in this system is found in looking at one's life and determining that it shows that the new birth and faith—and repentance as Smallman and most Calvinists are careful to add—have occurred. But because no one's life is perfect, certainty of one's eternal destiny is impossible in this system.

This view of saving faith being a gift of God is based on a faulty premise that leads to a faulty conclusion.

The idea that unbelievers are like cadavers is not Biblical. Nicodemus came to Jesus (John 3) and asked perceptive questions. Jesus answered those questions, which would be a foolish thing to do if He were talking to a cadaver. Jesus even rebuked Nicodemus, saying, "Are you the teacher of Israel, and do not know these things?" (John 3:10). The Lord expected that Nicodemus should already have grasped these things, though he was not yet born again (John 3:3-5).

Cornelius, in Acts 10, is another example. This unregenerate man (cf. Acts 11:14) received a visit from an angel. Unlike a cadaver, he understood and believed what the angel said and he sent for Simon Peter. When Peter came, Cornelius understood and came to faith in Christ because of what Peter said, and when he believed, he was born again (Acts 10:43-44).[18]

The Truth about Saving Faith

Having revealed and shown to be false many views of saving faith, it is time that we turn our attention to what faith, and saving faith, really is.

Most North Americans believe that George Washington was the first President of the United States. Why? The answer is simple. Most know the evidence and find it persuasive.

---

[18] See also Acts 10:35, which indicates that unbelievers sometimes work righteousness. Even Isa 64:6 teaches that unbelievers do righteous acts: "All our righteousnesses are like filthy rags." Isaiah says that humans—and he is not distinguishing here between regenerate or not—do righteous deeds, but that those deeds are worthless in reaching God by our works. Only by faith in the Messiah can anyone have right standing with God.

While a small number of conspiracy theorists do not believe the U.S. landed men on the moon, most people on the planet believe that we did. Most find the evidence to be overwhelming.

Almost everyone finds the evidence that JFK died in 1963 to be believable.

People believe that which the evidence persuades them is true. That is what belief is. It is a conviction, based on available evidence, that something is true.

Belief is not something we conjure up by strength of will. The key to believing something is the proof in favor of it. Faith is not really a choice. You don't choose to believe anything. Either you believe that two plus two equals four, or you don't. You can't *choose* to believe it. When the evidence that something is true persuades people, they believe it. When the evidence is insufficient, people don't believe it.

That's the way juries work. After listening to all of the evidence, each juror believes one of three things about the defendant: he's guilty, he's innocent, or he may be either guilty or innocent but I can't tell from the evidence. You couldn't *choose to believe* that he was innocent or guilty. You could *vote* against your convictions, but that would be acting dishonestly, contrary to what you believed. The only way you could move from belief to unbelief or the other way around is if you came to perceive the testimony differently.

Of course, two people can look at the same evidence and draw different conclusions because they have different opinions on whether the evidence is trustworthy. But the point still stands; we are guided by our perception of the evidence. We believe evidence that we perceive is true. We don't believe evidence that we perceive is false.

Therefore, faith is not a decision. It is the conviction that something is true. Let's now look at precisely what one must believe to be born again.

Jesus Guarantees Eternal Life to All Who Simply Believe in Him[19]

Faith in Christ is sometimes called *saving faith*, since the Bible teaches that all who believe in Jesus have eternal salvation. There are many things that Jesus promised. When the Lord Jesus spoke of those who *believe in Him*, He was talking about those who believe in Him for something specific. He made a promise and those who believe His promise have what He promised.

Jesus explained that saving promise to His friend, Martha:

---

[19] For further information about faith and saving faith, see our website (www. faithalone.org).

Jesus said to her, "I am the resurrection and the life. He who believes in Me, though he may die, he shall live. And whoever lives and believes in Me shall never die. Do you believe this?" She said to Him, "Yes, Lord, I believe that You are the Christ, the Son of God, who is to come into the world" (John 11:25-27).

For years I thought that verses 25 and 26 were two different ways of saying the same thing. I thought Jesus meant that "he who believes in Me, though he may die [physically], he shall live [spiritually]. And whoever lives and believes in Me shall never die [spiritually]." But did you notice that the Lord started with one of His famous "I am" statements? He said, "I am the resurrection and the life." What did He mean by "I am the resurrection"? What did He mean by "I am the life"? That is what the next two sentences explain.

As *the resurrection* He guarantees to resurrect physically all who believe in Him: "he who believes in Me, though he may die [physically], he shall live [physically]." All believers will have glorified bodies in the kingdom because He who is the resurrection will raise them from the dead and glorify them.

As *the life* He guarantees that the one who believes in Him is eternally secure: "whoever lives and believes in Me shall never die [spiritually]." That is another way of saying, "he who believes in Me has everlasting life" (John 6:47), or "he who comes to Me shall never hunger, and he who believes in Me shall never thirst" (John 6:35).

The question Jesus asks Martha in John 11:26 is the closest we get anywhere in the New Testament to what we might call *an evangelistic appeal.* Jesus' question to Martha—"Do you believe this?"—cuts to the heart of evangelism. While Jesus promised many things in the course of His ministry, this one promise is the key to gaining eternal salvation. Jesus is claiming to be "the resurrection and the life." Anyone who believes that He is the resurrection and the life, in the sense He explains it, has eternal life and will never die.

Believing in Jesus for Eternal Life Is Enough

When Jesus died on the cross, He took away the sins of the world (John 1:29; 1 John 2:2). When He rose from the dead, He showed both that His substitutionary death removed the sin barrier and that He indeed will one day raise from the dead all who believe in Him. That is obviously good news. Calvary means that no one will be eternally condemned because of his sins. Condemnation is only for those who do not believe in Jesus for everlasting life and hence who are not found in the Book of Life (John 3:16-18, 36; Rev 20:15). The reason why Jesus can fulfill His promise of everlasting life to the believer is because of who He is. He is the Savior, the Son of God, the Messiah.

Some people think they aren't good enough to be born again. They don't understand the point of the cross. Jesus has taken away our sins. They are no longer a barrier to us being born again. And they do not yet believe His promise that "he who believes in Me has everlasting life" (John 6:47). That just seems too easy. You must clean up your life first, they think. But that is man-made religion. Jesus gives everlasting life as a gift (John 4:10; Eph 2:8-9). If people have never believed that all who simply believe in Jesus have everlasting life, then they have not yet been born again.

Saving faith means believing in the Lord Jesus Christ for everlasting life (cf. 1 Tim 1:16). Nothing else is saving faith. Not only is believing in Him for everlasting life enough, it is the only way to have everlasting life. Jesus guarantees everlasting life to all who simply believe in Him for it—with no strings attached.

Do you believe this?

Chapter 2
Everlasting

Through most of college I was in a cult group and was led to believe that Bible reading was important to go to heaven. So I read the Bible a lot. I still have that Bible. It is heavily marked up.

The highlighting and underlining shows that I had read about everlasting life. Yet I don't remember ever being told about everlasting life. In our group it was *salvation* that we dreamed of. I imagine we equated everlasting life with salvation, but I can't recall. That was definitely not our emphasis.

I had the view that salvation was what we were striving for. In my mind salvation could be lost. If we sufficiently followed Christ and repented, then at some point God would save us. I understood that to mean that we would make it to heaven as long as we didn't sin again. In the teaching of the group I was in, one sin committed after achieving salvation would result in the loss of salvation, with no way to get it back.

If, however, we were fortunate enough to achieve salvation in the first place and then persevere in sinless perfection until death, then we would gain a final salvation that could never be lost.

While most people misunderstand what everlasting life is, the reason is because of tradition, not because the New Testament teachings about everlasting life are particularly hard to follow.

Most Prefer the Word *Salvation* and Rarely Even Speak of Everlasting Life

Church people miss the meaning of everlasting life by relating it to a low level of importance. What is important, most think, is *salvation*. The concept of everlasting life is understood in light of salvation, rather than the other way around.

Sadly many regular church attenders can go weeks or months or even years without speaking of *everlasting life*. Even most pastors rarely speak of everlasting life.

If people have little or no awareness of a Biblical expression like *everlasting life*, then they don't know what it means.

Yet the Lord Jesus spoke of everlasting life a lot and He rarely spoke of salvation. The Gospel of John is often called *The Gospel of Life* since everlasting life is mentioned so often by the Lord Jesus.

Sixty-four times in John's Gospel the words *life* (46 times) and *live* (18 times) occur, often with the adjective everlasting (17 times). Repeatedly the Lord made it clear that the person who simply believes in Him has, present tense, everlasting life that can never be lost. See, for example, John 3:16; 4:10-14; 5:24; 6:35, 37, 39, 47; 11:25-27.

If we are to do what Jesus did, then everlasting life would be a regular part of our language. He regularly talked about everlasting life. Do we?

Another reason why *everlasting life* is an expression we should use a lot is because it conveys the message of life clearly and succinctly. As Dr. Charles Ryrie, one of my seminary professors and the man who preached at my ordination service, likes to say, "If everlasting life could be lost, then it has the wrong name."

There is nothing wrong *per se* with speaking about *salvation*. But if we do, we should speak of *everlasting* salvation[1] or salvation that can never be lost. If our Lord emphasized that the life He gives is *everlasting*, then why not do what He did and follow His example?

Most Miss Its Eternality

If you brought up the expression *everlasting life* with a typical church-goer today, most would tell you that you can lose *everlasting* life. They might call it *salvation*, but when you point them to John 3:16 and ask about everlasting life, they'll say, "Oh, that's the same thing. Everlasting life is salvation and it can be lost prior to death."

Yet even the most superficial reading of John's Gospel shows that this is simply impossible. Jesus said that the one who drinks the water of life "shall never thirst" (John 6:35, cf. 4:10-14). In Greek the words translated "shall never thirst" mean *shall never thirst*. You don't have to be a Greek scholar to understand what the Lord is saying here. That means that the one who believes in Him will never lack everlasting life (see John 4:13-14).

Similarly the Lord Jesus said that the one who eats the bread of life "shall never hunger" (John 6:35). Again, the believer will never lack everlasting life. In John 5:24 Jesus directly said that the believer "has

---

[1] Even this could create some confusion since the expression *eternal salvation* only occurs once in the Bible and there it refers to ruling with Christ forever: "He became the author of eternal salvation to all who obey Him" (Heb 5:9). The condition is obedience and the consequence is being Christ's partner forever (Heb 1:9, 13).

[present tense] everlasting life, and shall not [future tense] come into judgment [regarding his eternal destiny], but has passed [past tense] from death into life." That is crystal clear. Jesus promises that the one who believes in Him has everlasting life that can never be lost.

The same truth is found in John 11:26 in which the Lord told Martha that "whoever lives and believes in Me shall never die [spiritually]." "Never die" means precisely what it says. Since we know from experience and indeed from the previous verse ("though he may die") that believers do indeed die physically, it is clear that the Lord is speaking of spiritual death. He is affirming *once saved, always saved* here. Once a person has everlasting life, he will never lose that life.

So if anyone who believed in Jesus later lost everlasting life, for any reason, the Lord Jesus would be proved a liar. *That* He is not and never will be.

Lest you think I am being too dramatic here, that is precisely what the Apostle John said in his first epistle: "He who believes in the Son of God has the witness in himself; he who does not believe God has made Him a liar, because he has not believed the testimony that God has given of His Son" (1 John 5:10). And what testimony did the Father give? John continues, "And this is the testimony: that God has given us eternal [or everlasting] life, and this life is in His Son" (1 John 5:11).

To reject the idea that God gives everlasting life that can never be lost to all who simply believe in the Lord Jesus is to call God a liar. It is to reject what the Lord clearly said. No matter how well intentioned, it is bad business to call God a liar.

The first thing we can say about everlasting life is that it is life that will never end. It will never be taken away. It can't be given back. Even if the believer later decided he would prefer to return the life and to spend eternity in the lake of fire, he can't do it. Jesus guarantees that.

A person can no more lose everlasting life now than he would be able to lose everlasting life once he is in the kingdom.

If a person has *never* believed this truth, then he is not yet born again, for this is the testimony of God that must be believed in order to have everlasting life.

Don't get me wrong. A person can be born again without ever hearing the words *everlasting life, once saved, always saved,* or *eternal security.* However, a person must believe that concept in order to believe in Jesus for that life which He promises. A person might believe that by faith in Jesus he is saved once and forever. He might believe he is justified and can never be unjustified. A guaranteed everlasting home with God in heaven for the one who simply believes in Jesus would be another way of believing the same concept.

While John Piper certainly does not agree with everything I am writing in this book, he agrees that everlasting life is everlasting life and that we must believe in Jesus for that life.[2] In a book responding to the writings of British theologian N.T. Wright, Piper said,

> But there is a misleading ambiguity in Wright's statement that we are saved not by believing in justification by faith but by believing in Jesus' death and resurrection. The ambiguity is that it leaves undefined what we believe in Jesus' death and resurrection *for* [emphasis his]. It is not saving faith to believe in Jesus merely for prosperity or health or a better marriage.[3]

But if a person has never believed that simply by faith in Jesus his eternal destiny is secure and cannot be lost or revoked or returned for any reason, then he clearly has not yet believed the truth of John 3:16.

Most Miss Its Variability

Everlasting life is more than unending life. It is more than a quantitative truth. It is also a qualitative idea.

Just as physical life here on earth is experienced in varying degrees of fullness, so is everlasting life now. In fact, everlasting life will be experienced in varying degrees of fullness in the life to come as well.

Let me explain. Let's start with the experience of life here and now. I was born of God nearly forty years ago. My experience of that life is much fuller now than when I first believed. At the start I didn't know anything about the doctrine of eternal rewards. Most of the Bible was a mystery to me. I didn't understand that growth in the Christian life came by the Word of God renewing my mind. I was struggling with legalism as a means of sanctification.

---

[2] Unfortunately, Piper comes from the Calvinist tradition and hence he isn't sure who has *really* believed in Jesus and who has not. Piper links assurance of having everlasting life to the works we do. The result is, by his own admission, that people in his own congregation struggle with doubts about their eternal destiny. See Phil Congdon, "John Piper's Diminished Doctrine of Justification and Assurance," *Journal of the Grace Evangelical Society* (Spring 2010): 59-73, esp. 68-70.

[3] John Piper, *The Future of Justification: A Response to N. T. Wright* (Wheaton, IL: Crossway Books, 2007), 85-86. He went on to indicate, by citing Acts 13:39, that what we must believe Jesus for is being justified by God (p. 86).

I have grown much in nearly four decades. But I have not arrived. Having come from an alcoholic family, I've had much to overcome. My wife, Sharon, can tell you that I'm better than I used to be, but I still have plenty of room to grow. I once was a horrible perfectionist. Now I'm a recovering perfectionist. I once struggled with lots of anger within me that I denied and tried to overlook. Now I struggle with anger within me that I accept and turn over to the Lord.

On a scale of 1 to 100 I'd say my experience of everlasting life was a 10 or so when I first believed the message of life and maybe it is a 50 today. It's hard, of course, to make a good estimate of our own spirituality. However, I clearly see that I've made progress—and that I have lots more growing yet to do as well.

Maybe some people start the Christian life with an experience of everlasting life that is 40 or even 50. I know as I look at some new believers I am impressed and challenged to see how beautifully everlasting life is manifesting itself in them right at the start of their everlasting experience. Their lives are already full and a joy to observe.

There will also be variation in people's experience of everlasting life in eternity, though most miss this truth. Remember that Jesus said that many who are first now will be last in the kingdom and that many who are last now will be first in the kingdom (e.g., Matt 19:30). Clearly this means that there will be gradations in the kingdom. At the least this concerns authority and honor and power (cf. 2 Tim 2:12; Rev 2:26). But it surely also concerns fullness of life.

While all believers in the kingdom will be in the kingdom forever, the quality of each one's life will vary depending on what he did with his life on earth. Paul makes that clear in 2 Cor 5:1-11. We will be recompensed for the deeds done *in the body*. That is, our future recompense at the Judgment Seat of Christ (2 Cor 5:10) will be based on what we did in these fallen, dying bodies.

It is a truly sobering truth that our fullness of life *forever* will be determined by what we do with the few decades that He gives us in this life. That is why it is so important that we endure to the end of our Christian lives (1 Cor 9:27; 2 Tim 2:12; 4:6-8; Rev 2:26).

Many, if not most, churchgoers today are just trying to be good enough to make it to heaven. Of course, that is a futile quest since no one can ever be good enough to make it to heaven. In order to have everlasting life and be guaranteed to spend eternity with the Lord and His people, we must believe in Him for that. If we try to work for it, we will miss it (cf. Matt 7:21-23). But in addition, most people in churches today don't know anything about fullness of everlasting life now or forever. That is not a concern for them. They just hope they make it to the streets of gold.

And of those who know for sure that they have everlasting life that can never be lost—the durative aspect of everlasting life—many of those don't realize that the quality of their everlasting life will depend on what they do in this life.

Wake up and get to work, believers (Rev 3:14-21). It's later than you think. The Judge is at the door (Jas 5:9).

Most Are Confused by Passages That Speak of Everlasting Life as a Possible Future Reward

One of the reasons why people miss both the quantity and the quality of everlasting life is that there are a handful of passages in the New Testament that speak of everlasting life not as a present possession, but as a possible eternal reward. Those passages clearly indicate that to gain this future possession one must endure in good works.

The solution is to realize that when we read of the present possession of everlasting life the emphasis is most often on its eternality, its permanent duration. Though the idea of its potential fullness is surely in the background, it often is not in the spotlight.

However, whenever we read of the possible future gaining of everlasting life by works done in this life, the emphasis is always on its potential fullness. The idea of its eternality is of course in the background. But its potential fullness is right in front of you in these passages.

Consider, for example, Gal 6:7-9. Here Paul uses a farming analogy, sowing and reaping. No one who has ever worked on a farm thinks that reaping a harvest is a free gift. It is very hard work both to sow and reap.

Paul says that the believer "who sows to his flesh will of the flesh reap corruption [or loss]." And he says that the believer "who sows to the Spirit will of the Spirit reap everlasting life." He then says, "And let us not grow weary while doing good, for in due season we shall reap if we do not lose heart" (Gal 6:9). This is unmistakable rewards language, not free gift language.

We see everlasting life as a potential future reward also in Matt 19:29 and 1 Tim 6:12, 19. In passages in which everlasting life is a possible future reward, its potential fullness is in view.

And what is everlasting life when it is a potential future reward? It is greater abundance of life caused by greater ministry for Jesus.

The more faithful we are in our service for Christ now, the greater our ministry for Jesus will be in the life to come (cf. Luke 19:17, 19). The more we will glorify Him in the kingdom, the more joy that will bring to us. Thus the one who reaps a fuller experience of everlasting life will glorify Christ more and reap more joy as a result.

But all believers, even ones who fail to persevere in faith and good works, will spend eternity with the Lord and will have joy forever. But the believer who squanders this life will not have the fullness of everlasting life he could have had forever (cf. Luke 19:20-26; 2 Tim 4:6-10).

The Bible is consistent. Whenever it speaks of the free gift of everlasting life that everyone who simply believes has right now and can never lose (by far the most common references to everlasting life), the Bible always uses a present tense verb (e.g., John 3:16; 5:24; 6:47). And the few times when the Bible speaks of everlasting life as a potential future reward for work done, the future tense is used. There should be no confusion on this point.

Must One Believe in the Promise of Everlasting Life to Have It?

Many people who personally believe in eternal security (also called *once saved, always saved*) nonetheless believe that such belief is advanced belief, like belief in the Pre-Tribulation Rapture. In the minds of many pastors, missionaries, and evangelists, one need not believe that Jesus gives *everlasting* life to the one who believes in Him.

There are many people who believe that the condition of everlasting life is believing that at the moment of faith in Christ a person is *temporarily secure*. Many think it is expecting too much of people to think they will accept that everlasting life is ever-lasting life.

I received an email from a pastor a few years back who indicated that he came to our annual conference and that he enjoyed hearing Zane Hodges speak. But, he said, he was bothered by and did not agree with Zane's suggestion that if a person has *never*[4] been sure that he had everlasting life by faith in Christ, then he had not yet been born again.

---

[4] Zane did not say, nor do I, that if a person once knew he had everlasting life by faith in Christ and now no longer believes that, then he is not born again. On the contrary, we both agree that once a person believes in Jesus for everlasting life he is eternally secure, even if he later stops believing that (or even if he can never remember believing that). Such people would be confused believers who once believed in the promise of everlasting life, but later were convinced that is not true. But if a person *never* believed that he had everlasting life by faith in Christ, then he has not yet been born again at all, for he has not yet believed the promise of everlasting life,

There are many pastors and laypeople like that. They think that a person is born again if he believes that Jesus has saved him *for the time being*. Many people believe that if they died at the moment of faith they'd go to heaven, but that if they live even for a few hours after coming to faith, then they must do good works to keep the life that Jesus gave them. They do not yet believe that Jesus has saved them *once and for all*. They do not yet believe that *everlasting* life is "not of works" (Eph 2:8-9). They believe they must avoid major sins and persevere in good works in order to stay "saved."

But is everlasting life really an *advanced* truth? Is this some deep truth that one needs years of instruction to understand? The Lord shared it with the woman at the well within minutes of meeting her, and she was hardly either a theologian or a person of high moral character (see John 4:1-26). This was basic truth the Lord shared with unbelievers. This was not some advanced truth He only shared with His inner circle.[5]

And what is this *temporary security* view but a direct contradiction of John 3:16; 5:24; 6:35; Rom 4:4-5; and Eph 2:8-9? If a person believes that the one who believes in Jesus will never die spiritually (John 11:26), then he obviously believes that a believer can never die spiritually no matter what he does or does not do in the future. If a person believes he must work to keep everlasting life, then he does not believe Jesus' beautiful promise of life everlasting for all who simply believe in Him.

We should tell people that everlasting life is ever-lasting life. We should tell them that Jesus promises not *temporary security*, but *eternal security*. If they initially reject that idea as too good to be true or as too "easy," then it should open the door to fruitful discussion. We can encourage them to pray about this issue and search the Scriptures to see if it might be true (Acts 17:11). If they do, at some point they will come to faith in Jesus *for everlasting life* (cf. 1 Tim 1:16).

I should mention that many people come to understand the concept of everlasting life or eternal security before they actually hear the expression. For example, someone who was taught *once saved, always saved*

---

the message Jesus and His apostles taught (cf. John 3:16; 5:24; 6:35; 11:26; Rom 4:4-5; Gal 3:6-14; Eph 2:8-9).

[5] Of course, as John 6:68 shows, the disciples, though they knew they had everlasting life, wanted to hear "words of eternal life" from the Lord Jesus. What Peter meant there is that the Lord taught them about this everlasting life which He had given them. The disciples learned how to have this life more abundantly (John 10:10) through Jesus' teachings. So while there might be discipleship aspects of fullness of life which are advanced, the promise of everlasting life to all who believe in Jesus is as basic as it gets.

believes in the concept of everlasting life even if he doesn't know that expression. Someone who believes that he is guaranteed to spend eternity with Jesus because of his faith in Him grasps the concept of eternal security, even if he hasn't heard about everlasting life *per se.*

The key is the word *everlasting.* As mentioned above, John Piper makes the outstanding point that one must clearly understand what he is believing in Jesus for. He says, "It is not saving faith to believe in Jesus merely for prosperity or health or a better marriage."[6] We must believe Jesus for our eternal destiny.[7]

Get to Know This Word Well

I consider it a tragedy that it is so rare for believers to use the word *everlasting* when evangelizing. Why not use the word the Lord Jesus regularly used? This word is so clear and powerful.

I realize that many of us were not evangelized with this word. So what? If you were evangelized in a way that wasn't crystal clear, do you really want to repeat that flawed method? Why not change and use the words of our Lord Jesus?

I also am grieved that those who disciple others rarely use the word *everlasting* to discuss the potential fullness of life we can have now and forever. This should be a regular part of the mentor's vocabulary.

Isn't it cool to talk about everlasting life? That's what we as believers in Jesus have. That's what the world doesn't have, but needs. And once we have it, we can grow in that life. We are storing up now the capacity to glorify Christ forever. How full our ability to serve Him will be then will be decided by how much we grow now.

I love the gift that the Lord Jesus has given me, everlasting life. That is the best gift anyone has ever given me. That gift means everything to me. Thank you, Lord Jesus, for giving me everlasting life and for challenging me to experience it fully.

Won't you join me in thanking Him? You can if you know what everlasting life is and who it is that has it.

---

[6] Piper, *The Future of Justification*, 86.

[7] Sadly Piper is not quite clear that what we believe Jesus for is everlasting. While he speaks of believing in Him for justification, he does not point out that justification is everlasting. Because he believes in a coming future judgment of works to determine who spends eternity with God, Piper believes it is not possible to be sure of one's eternal destiny.

Chapter 3
Saved

The Many Faces of Salvation

I was saved years ago. What do I mean by that?

I was saved from an early death in 1971 when I was in college. I easily could have been killed when a car travelling over 40 miles per hour hit the passenger door of my car as I was making a left in an intersection. Glass was everywhere. Fortunately my Ford Maverick (yes, there really was once such a car) did not flip or catch on fire.

A year later, in the Fall of 1972, I was saved from eternal condemnation. A staff member with Campus Crusade for Christ, Warren Wilke, led me to faith in the Lord Jesus Christ for eternal life.

On December 31, 1985 Woodcrest College, my first teaching job, folded. I was saved from the ranks of the unemployed when six months later I was hired by Multnomah Bible College in Portland to teach Greek and Bible.

In 1987 Sharon and I nearly lost the equity from the home we had sold when the Savings and Loan which held the equity went bankrupt. The S & L was government insured so we were saved from financial ruin.

I was saved in all of those senses—and more. And depending on the point I'm trying to make, "I was saved years ago" might refer to any of those events, or others. The words which follow would make clear what type of salvation I meant.

The words *save* and *salvation* in everyday life refer to a wide range of deliverances. The same is true in the Bible. In both the Old Testament (written in Hebrew) and in the New Testament (written in Greek), the words *save* and *salvation* refer to many types of deliverance and not just to deliverance from eternal condemnation.

Did you realize that there are no uses of the words *save* or *salvation* in the Old Testament that refer specifically to deliverance from hell and the gaining of eternal life? None.

And did you realize that in the New Testament only three in ten uses of *salvation (sōtēria) and save (sōzō) refer to salvation from eternal condemnation and to obtaining eternal life?* That means that 70% of the time in the New Testament the words *save* or *salvation* do not mean what most people think they mean, leading to misunderstandings that would be funny if they were not so calamitous.

It is no wonder that people become wildly confused about the condition of the new birth since they take most uses of *save* and *salvation* in Scripture as referring to the new birth.

Here are a few examples in which a failure to observe the context leads to a quite confusing view of the condition of eternal life.

Paul said, "Work out your own salvation with fear and trembling" (Phil 2:12). If that is talking about how we gain everlasting life, then we are required to put in a lifetime of effort during which we are concerned ("with fear and trembling") that we might not obtain it.

The author of Proverbs wrote, "Whoever walks blamelessly will be saved" (Prov 28:18). Here the condition for salvation is not faith in the Messiah, but *walking blamelessly*. Obviously many preachers use verses like this to teach either that faith must be joined with works to keep everlasting life, or, that faith must be joined with works to prove that we have *really* believed (which in their understanding of belief means that we have really committed and surrendered to the Lord).

In his first letter to Timothy the Apostle Paul wrote, "Nevertheless she [singular, a woman] will be saved in childbearing if they [plural, her children] continue in faith, love, and holiness, with self-control" (1 Tim 2:15). Now if this refers to how a woman is saved from eternal condemnation, it is teaching that to spend eternity with God she must train her children well and her children must then persevere in faith and good works. Even if she trains them well, if they nonetheless do not persevere, then she will end up in the lake of fire.

Later in that same epistle Paul warned Timothy directly: "Take heed to yourself and to the doctrine. Continue in them, for in doing this you will save both yourself and those who hear you" (1 Tim 4:16). Timothy was already a born-again man. Paul called him earlier in this same book "a true son in the faith" (1 Tim 1:2). Timothy was guiding the church in Ephesus as a representative of the Apostle Paul. Yet if this verse is talking about escaping eternal condemnation, then the eternal destiny of Timothy and of the believers in Ephesus depended on him continuing to teach sound doctrine, as well as on him being morally steadfast (note "take heed *to yourself* and..."). If this is an evangelistic verse, then Paul is warning Timothy that if he departed into false teaching or into moral failure, he'd end up being eternally condemned and so would the people in his church. Of course, that is ridiculous (cf. Eph 2:8-9).

In Second Samuel we read, "You [the LORD] will save the humble people" (2 Sam 22:28). There, and in Job 22:29 as well, the condition of *salvation* is humility, not faith in Christ.

The author of Hebrews said, "He became the author of eternal salvation to all who obey Him" (Heb 5:9). In context this obedience includes suffering for Christ (compare 5:8). Thus if this refers to how one gets eternal life, it is by obeying Christ throughout our lives, enduring in our confession of Christ even in the midst of persecution for our faith.

What did the Apostle Paul mean when he wrote, "Whoever calls on the name of the Lord shall be saved" (Rom 10:13)? This verse is often used for evangelism. But is that Paul's point in context? The verse comes from Joel 2 and refers to Jewish *believers* at the end of the Tribulation who will call out to Jesus to save them *from the Gentile armies* that have surrounded Jerusalem to destroy them. If it refers to how we get eternal life now, then it is saying that we must cry out in prayer to Jesus in order to gain eternal life. Thus believing in Him, by itself, would not give anyone eternal life. Calling upon Him must be added to believing in Him in order to be born again. And, by the way, that is precisely what many evangelists actually say.

In Ps 119:146 the Psalmist is bargaining with God for his salvation: "I cry out to You [the Lord]; save me, and I will keep Your testimonies." If this is salvation from eternal condemnation, then it was obtained by crying out to and promising to serve God.

However, if we realize that *save* and *salvation* refer to deliverance of many kinds (primarily from enemies in the Old Testament), then we will not become hopelessly confused about what we must do to have everlasting life.

The doctrine of salvation, called soteriology (after the Greek word for salvation, *sōtēria*), is not exclusively *or even primarily* the doctrine of what we must do to have everlasting life.[1] It is the Biblical teach-

---

[1] I realize, of course, that in Bible colleges and seminaries soteriology is typically taught as exclusively dealing with salvation from eternal condemnation. That is, however, a mistake. I recall one of my theology professors at Dallas Theological Seminary, Craig Glickman, pointing out that the Biblical doctrine of soteriology rightly covers all types of salvation found in the Bible. He is obviously correct since one cannot properly understand the Bible's teaching of salvation from eternal condemnation if he understands most Biblical references to *salvation* as referring to salvation from eternal condemnation. Even if a professor is simply teaching a class on salvation from eternal condemnation, he must teach the students that most references to salvation in the Old and New Testaments do not concern salvation from eternal condemnation. If he fails to do so, the students will almost assuredly fail to understand that the sole condition of everlasting life is faith in Christ, apart from any works before or after the new birth.

ing about various deliverances, plural. While deliverance from eternal condemnation is a small part of that, it is far from the entire doctrine of salvation.

Let's now look at some representative examples of the uses of the words *save* and *salvation*, beginning in the Old Testament.

Old Testament Salvation

Since the Old Testament is huge, I will illustrate the various ways in which it uses the words *save* and *salvation* by focusing on uses within the Psalms. These same types of salvation occur all through the Old Testament. The reader would be well advised to do a concordance study of every use of the words *save* and *salvation* in the Old Testament. I have done that myself and I've found it to be a very edifying study.

Deliverance from Enemies

Far and away the most common type of salvation in the Old Testament is deliverance from enemies. The Psalms are filled with these types of uses.

Most often this concerns the deliverance of the nation of Israel from her enemies. On occasion it refers to deliverance of the individual from his enemies.

For example, in Ps 18:2-3 David says, "The LORD is my rock and my fortress and my deliverer; my God, my strength, in whom I will trust; my shield and the horn *of my salvation*, my stronghold. I will call upon the LORD, who is worthy to be praised; *so shall I be saved from my enemies*" (emphasis added). This is a popular chorus sung in many churches. And it illustrates the most common use of *salvation* in the Psalms: deliverance *from enemies*.

Similarly David wrote, "The One who gives *salvation* to kings, who delivers David His servant *from the deadly sword*" (Ps 144:10, emphasis added). God delivered David, and many of the kings of Israel and Judah, from the deadly sword of Israel's enemies. And again David wrote, "O God the LORD, the strength of my *salvation, You have covered my head in the day of battle*" (Ps 140:7, emphasis added).

The nations that were Israel's enemies were notoriously wicked. Thus deliverance *from the wicked* is a closely related and often synonymous idea to deliverance *from enemies*. David lamented, "Do not take me away with the wicked and with the workers of iniquity, who speak peace to their neighbors, but evil in their hearts. Give them according to their deeds, and according to the wickedness of their endeavors; give them according to the work of their hands; render to them what they deserve"

(Ps 28:3-4). It is in this context that David then says of God, "He is the *saving refuge* of His anointed. *Save Your people*, and bless Your inheritance" (Ps 28:8-9, emphasis added; see also Ps 9:14, compare verses 15-16; Pss 37:40; 62:1, 7; 145:19).

If we do not grasp this, then a verse like Ps 7:10 would confuse us greatly. There David says, "My defense is of God, who saves the upright in heart." Salvation is for *the upright in heart*, not for the believer. Of course, the previous verse asks, "Oh, let the wickedness of the wicked come to an end, but establish the just." Ultimately David longs for the time when Messiah will rule and Israel will be delivered from all her enemies. In the short term he longs for deliverance from wicked enemies. He made this clear at the start of the Psalm with these words, "Save me from all those who persecute me" (Ps 7:1).

Deliverance from Trouble

The second most frequent type of salvation in the Psalms is deliverance from troubles in this life. For example, in Ps 50:22-23 we read, "Now consider this, you who forget God, lest I tear you in pieces, and there be none to deliver: Whoever offers praise glorifies Me; and to him who orders his conduct aright I will show the salvation of God." The *salvation* or *deliverance* is spelled out earlier in the context: "Call upon Me in the day of trouble; I will deliver you, and you shall glorify Me" (v 15). God provides salvation *in the day of the trouble*.

Similar wording is found in Ps 91:15-16, "He shall call upon Me, and I will answer him; I will be with him in trouble; I will deliver him and honor him. With long life I will satisfy him, and show him My salvation." God saves from troubles in this life those who call upon Him.

"May the LORD answer you in the day of trouble...May He grant you according to your heart's desire, and fulfill all your purpose. We will rejoice in your salvation, and in the name of our God we will set up our banners! May the LORD fulfill all your petitions" (Ps 20:1, 4-5). Salvation from troubles is a common theme in the Psalms.

Deliverance of the Poor and Needy from Their Afflictions

This is a special type of salvation from troubles. Specifically, on some occasions, the psalmist speaks of the salvation of the poor and needy from their afflictions.

"'For the oppression of the poor, for the sighing of the needy, now I will arise,' says the LORD; 'I will set him in the safety [salvation] for which he yearns'" (Ps 12:5).

"Let all those who seek You rejoice and be glad in You; let such as love Your salvation say continually, 'The LORD be magnified!' But I am poor and needy; Yet the LORD thinks upon me. You are my help and my deliverer; do not delay, O my God" (Ps 40:16-17). Of course, if David, the author of Psalm 40, can call himself "poor and needy," then surely we all are poor and needy. We all need deliverance from our afflictions. This is a principle we see elsewhere in Scripture. God resists the proud, but gives grace to the humble (Prov 3:34; Jas 4:6).

Deliverance of Israel from Captivity

God not only sent Israel into captivity for its disobedience, He also returned Israel from that captivity. That returning of Israel from captivity is called *salvation*: "Oh, that the salvation of Israel would come out of Zion! When the LORD brings back the captivity of His people, let Jacob rejoice and Israel be glad" (Ps 14:7; cf. 53:6).

David was writing prophetically here. When he wrote, Israel was not in captivity and hadn't been since leaving Egypt four hundred years before. Was he speaking of the return which took place starting in 538 BC? Or was he speaking about the *ultimate* salvation of Israel from captivity, when the Messiah returns Israel once and for all to the Promised Land after the Tribulation?

Actually the Hebrew which is translated "bring back the captivity" can also be rendered "turn the fortunes"[2] or "restore the fortunes."[3] Thus it may not refer specifically to restoration from captivity. However, regardless of the translation, it seems likely that David is thinking here of Israel's ultimate restoration when at the end of the Tribulation the Messiah returns and delivers Israel from all of her enemies.

No Old Testament References to Salvation from Eternal Condemnation

Most people in Christianity recognize that the Old Testament doesn't have near as much discussion of justification, regeneration, or salvation from eternal condemnation as the New Testament. But most do not realize that while the Old Testament does discuss justification and regeneration, it never calls that *salvation*. The words *save* and *salvation* are never used in the Old Testament to refer to salvation from eternal condemnation.

One verse that seems to be an exception is David's plea, "Restore to me the joy of Your salvation" (Ps 51:12). People think David is thinking

---

[2] A. F. Kirkpatrick, *The Book of Psalms* (Grand Rapids: Baker Book House, 1982), 304.

[3] A. A. Anderson, *Psalms 1-72* (Grand Rapids: Wm. B. Eerdmans Publ. Co., 1981), 135.

back to when he was first born again and the joy he experienced then. But that is not at all what he means. If we read Psalm 51, we see there is nothing here about the new birth. Indeed the second half of verse 12 goes on to say, "And uphold me by Your generous Spirit." David is remembering times when the Lord has saved him from his troubles in the past. He wants that joy again.

The superscription and the Psalm itself show that Psalm 51 concerns David's repentance after he was confronted by Nathan the prophet concerning his sin with Bathsheba. David was depressed and in pain after committing adultery and murder: "Make me hear joy and gladness, that the bones You have broken may rejoice" (Ps 51:8).

One other Old Testament reference to salvation that seems to refer to salvation from eternal condemnation is Zechariah's prophecy about Jesus Christ: "Rejoice greatly, O daughter of Zion! Shout, O daughter of Jerusalem! Behold, your King is coming to you; He is just *and having salvation*, lowly and riding on a donkey, a colt, the foal of a donkey" (Zech 9:9, emphasis added). The prophet is referring to the Messiah's triumphal entry at the start of Passion Week (cf. Matt 21:5).

Obviously Jesus is the Savior in the sense that He gives eternal life to all who believe in Him because he took away the sins of the world (John 1:29) when He died on the cross for our sins (cf. 1 John 2:2). However, that is not the only sense in which He is Savior, or in which He *has salvation* as Zechariah said.

Zechariah was writing to the nation of Israel. He was talking about Israel's salvation. The salvation Israel longed for was deliverance from all the Gentile nations that threatened and oppressed her. That is why when Jesus did enter Jerusalem on a donkey, the people of Jerusalem were shouting, thinking He was the conquering Messiah who would overthrow Roman rule and establish the kingdom.

Yet in His first coming He came to die for Israel and for all of mankind. He came first as the suffering servant of Isaiah 53. Only in His Second Coming would He establish His kingdom.

Actually the salvation spoken of in Zech 9:9 is explained in the very next verse: "I will cut off the chariot from Ephraim and the horse from Jerusalem; the battle bow shall be cut off. He shall speak peace to the nations; His dominion shall be 'from sea to sea, and from the River to the ends of the earth.'" Scholars point out that there is a great prophetic valley of thousands of years between verses 9 and 10. Verse 9 discusses Messiah's triumphal entry, which was during His first coming. Verse 10 discusses Messiah's Second Coming when He sets up His righteous kingdom.

The salvation of verse 9 is not individual regeneration or even the regeneration of Israel *per se*. Rather, the salvation spoken of is the deliverance of Israel from "the battle bow" and "the nations." It is the promise of worldwide peace: "peace to the nations."

I urge you to put in the time to do this study yourself. You will learn much about the Old Testament as you study all uses of *save* and *salvation* in it. And I'm convinced you will see that not one use of those words in the Old Testament refers to salvation from eternal condemnation.

If that is so, then one objection would be, *then why does the New Testament use those same words almost exclusively to refer to salvation from eternal condemnation?* The answer is, as we shall now see, that while the New Testament does *occasionally* use those words to refer to salvation from eternal condemnation,[4] such uses are the exception, not the rule.

New Testament Salvation

Deliverance from Death and Illness (Most Common)

The first few examples cited below admittedly do not confuse many people. However, many mistakenly think that these are the exceptions. They are not. This nuance of meaning is typical in that most of the New Testament uses of *save* and *salvation* do not refer to deliverance from eternal condemnation. And all the uses of save and salvation in both Romans and James fall under this category, resulting in tremendous confusion.

Matthew 8:24-25. "And suddenly a great tempest arose on the sea, so that the boat was covered with the waves. But He was asleep. Then His disciples came to Him and awoke Him, saying, 'Lord, save us! We are perishing!'"

---

[4] The Bible does not tell us why *save* and *salvation* never refer to salvation from eternal condemnation in the Old Testament, but do a significant amount of the time in the New Testament. The main reason is because there is so little in the Old Testament about justification or the new birth. The Old Testament was written not to small groups of individuals (house churches) and to individuals (e.g., Timothy, Titus, Philemon, Gaius) like the New Testament was, but to a nation. And in the Old Testament, unlike the New Testament, the oral evangelistic ministry (the prophets evangelized people) was not reported in Scripture. In the New Testament we have one entire book on the message of life which the Lord Jesus preached (i.e., The Gospel of John). There is no such book in the Old Testament. In John's Gospel everlasting life *is* once identified with *being saved* (John 3:17; 5:34; 10:9). Thus it is not surprising that we find *some* similar uses of *save* and *salvation* in the epistles. However, even there that meaning is rare, and if we do not realize that, we become confused.

Clearly this refers to saving them from the deadly storm. They feared for their lives. No spiritual salvation is going on here, although a miracle does follow.

Matthew 9:21. "If only I may touch His garment, I shall be made well [literally, shall be saved]." The woman with the issue of blood touched Jesus and was healed. This is a typical New Testament example of the word *sōzein*, the verb, to save. Unfortunately most translations interpret it for you rather than just leaving it as "I shall be saved" or "I shall be delivered."

Matthew 14:30. "But when he [Peter] saw that the wind was boisterous, he was afraid; and beginning to sink he cried out, saying, 'Lord, save me!'" Peter took his eyes off Jesus while walking on water. Thus he began to sink. He asked Jesus to save him from drowning.

Acts 27:31. "Paul said to the centurion and the soldiers, 'Unless these men stay in the ship, you cannot be saved.'" During a violent storm the ship was liable to sink at any time. Some of the crew let down a small skiff and were planning on escaping in that way. Paul had been told by God they all had to stay on the ship. The salvation here is surviving the shipwreck.

Acts 27:42-43. "And the soldiers' plan was to kill the prisoners, lest any of them should swim away and escape. But the centurion, wanting to save Paul, kept them from their purpose..." Clearly the salvation here is from physical death, from being killed by the soldiers.

Lots of New Testament texts are like this. This is what all five uses of the word *sōzein* mean in Jas 1:21; 2:14; 4:12; 5:15; and 5:20. It is also the most common use by far in the four Gospels and in Acts. Salvation in Romans is deliverance from God's wrath here and now, and hence it too falls in this category.

When in doubt, assume this type of salvation is in view.

Deliverance from God's Wrath Here and Now (Romans)

A failure to recognize that salvation in Romans is from God's temporal wrath, not from eternal condemnation, has led to a lot of confusion. Paul is talking in Romans about the salvation of believers, not of unbelievers (cf. Rom 1:16).

In Romans Paul uses the noun, salvation (*sōtēria*), five times (Rom 1:16; 10:1, 10; 11:11; and 13:11). He also uses the verb, to save (*sōzein*), eight times (Rom 5:9, 10; 8:24; 9:27; 10:9, 13; 11:14, 26). All of these refer to deliverance from God's wrath as Rom 1:16-17 shows. That section is immediately followed by a discussion of God's wrath in Rom 1:18-32.

Romans 10:13-14 also shows that the salvation is from God's wrath. After quoting Joel 2:32, "Whoever calls on the name of the Lord shall be saved," in Rom 10:13 Paul then says the following:

> How then shall they call on Him in whom they have not [first] believed? And how shall they believe in Him of whom they have not [first] heard? And how shall they hear without [there first being] a preacher?

Note the progression. First there is a Christian preacher who comes. Then people hear the preacher. Then they believe in Him whom the preacher preached about. Then the believers call on Him in whom they have already believed.

The believers are calling on Him for salvation from temporal wrath. This is easily seen in Joel 2, where the quote in Rom 10:13 originated. Joel 2 speaks of the Tribulation period when believing Jews will be in Israel and will be surrounded by Gentile armies about to destroy them. They will cry out to the Lord Jesus, in whom they will have already believed, to save them from annihilation by the Gentile armies.

This can also readily be seen in Rom 5:9-10. There Paul makes this amazing statement,

> Much more then, having now been justified by His blood, we shall be saved from wrath through Him. For if when we were enemies we were reconciled to God through the death of His Son, much more, having been reconciled, we shall be saved by His life.

Note that Paul specifically says, "we shall be saved *from wrath* through Him" (emphasis added). He uses a future tense there. Though we already "have...been justified by His blood," in the future "we shall be saved from wrath through Him." When he restates the idea in verse 10 Paul says that having in the past been "reconciled to God *through the death* of His Son...we shall be saved *by His life*" (emphasis added).

Since what follows is part of the sanctification section of the book (Romans 5–8), Paul's point is that we shall be saved from God's wrath in this life by means of the resurrection power of Jesus living though us. Compare Rom 8:13: "For if you live according to the flesh you will die," Paul says. That is premature physical death as a result of God's wrath. He continues, "but if by the Spirit you put to death the deeds of the body, you will live." That is deliverance from God's wrath by means of the Spirit applying the life of Jesus to our experience.

Here is part of what Zane Hodges says about salvation in Romans from his soon to be published commentary on Romans:

In the translation [of Rom 1:16-17] we give here, the word *deliverance* replaces the more familiar word *salvation* that is found in the English versions. The word *salvation* prejudices interpreters right from the start since it is traditionally understood as "salvation from hell." But this is a presupposition which ought not to be made here on the basis of traditional understanding alone. The word *deliverance* properly leaves the issue open and almost automatically elicits the question, "deliverance from *what?*" No expositor ought to fail to address this question.

An examination of the epistle to the Romans turns up the surprising fact that after Rom 1:16 the Greek word for deliverance or salvation (*sōtēria*) does not occur again until Rom 11:11 and the verbal form of this word (*sōzō*) occurs next at Rom 5:9-10. Thus the noun and verb are totally absent from Paul's discussion of justification in Chapters 2–4, where, in the traditional view of this word, it would be most natural for it to appear.

In addition, in Rom 5:9-10, the experience from which we are saved is specified as "wrath" (5:9). Although this word, too, has a traditional meaning (wrath = hell), Paul's epistle does not support this. In Romans *wrath* is a manifestation of God's *temporal* displeasure. This is clear from 1:18ff. and 2:5-9. Given the close proximity of 1:16 to 1:18, and in the light of 5:9-10, we may conclude that in Rom 1:16 *deliverance* refers to being rescued, or "saved," from the divine temporal anger that is so vividly described in Rom 1:18-32.

Of course, the final verification of this interpretation will depend on the degree to which it illuminates and clarifies the epistle as a whole. One purpose of this commentary is to show that this approach reveals the cohesiveness of Paul's argument in this epistle. For now, therefore, we shall assume this meaning. Thus verse 16 states that the gospel Paul preaches is the vehicle for *the power of God* by which men can be delivered from His *temporal* wrath.[5]

---

[5] Hodges, *Commentary on Romans*, s.v. Rom 1:16-17. This has not been published yet. We expect publication in mid to late 2012.

Deliverance from the Coming Tribulation Wrath (First and Second Thessalonians)

The words *save* and *salvation* are used in the Thessalonian epistles to refer to deliverance from the coming Tribulation wrath. For example, in the first chapter Paul says that the readers are "wait[ing] for His Son from heaven, whom He raised from the dead, even Jesus who delivers us from the wrath to come" (1 Thess 1:10). Though a different Greek verb (*rhuomai*) is used here, Paul conveys the same idea using *sōtēria* and *sōzō*.

Consider 1 Thess 5:9. There Paul says, "For God did not appoint us to wrath, but to obtain salvation through our Lord Jesus Christ." The wrath he is talking about there he began discussing in 1 Thess 4:13-18 when he discussed the Rapture. Then starting in 1 Thess 5:1, Paul discusses the Tribulation which is coming. But God did not appoint us for the Tribulation but to obtain deliverance from it via the Rapture. Note the very next verse, "who died for us, that whether we wake [literally, watch] or sleep, we should live together with Him" (1 Thess 5:10). The point is, whether we are watchful or spiritually indolent at the time of the Rapture, we will go to be with the Lord.

(The only use of the verb *sōzō* in First Thessalonians is in 2:16. There Paul refers to unbelieving Jews "forbidding us to speak to the Gentiles that they may be saved." *Saved* there might refer to regeneration. But in light of the use of the related noun in First Thessalonians, Paul more likely has the more specific deliverance from the Tribulation in view. While that includes regeneration, Paul seems to have more in mind. The same is probably true in the only use of *sōzō* in Second Thessalonians [2:10]. See also 2 Thess 2:13, the only use of *sōtēria* in the second epistle.)

Successfully Handling Persecution in a God-Honoring Way (Philippians)

In Philippians only the noun form, *sōtēria*, is used. Three times Paul speaks of deliverance or salvation.

That Paul uses the term *salvation* (*sōtēria*) in Philippians in a figurative sense is seen in his first of three uses. In Phil 1:19 he says, "I know that this [his imprisonment and various people preaching Christ from good and bad motives] will turn out for my deliverance [*sōtēria*] through your prayer and the supply of the Spirit of Jesus Christ..." Clearly Paul was already born again. He did not need the Philippians to pray so that he might have eternal life. He needed them to pray, and the Spirit to empower him, so that he might glorify Christ in his afflictions. In the very next verse Paul defines the salvation of which he is speaking: "That in nothing I shall be ashamed, but with all boldness, as always, so now also Christ will be magnified in my body, whether by life or by death."

Salvation in Phil 1:19 is enduring persecution for Christ with the result that Christ is glorified and that he will have boldness and not shame at the Bema.

The salvation of the Philippians in 1:28 and 2:12 is quite similar. In Phil 1:28 Paul said to the believers in Philippi "[Do not be] in any way terrified by your adversaries, which is to them a proof of perdition [literally, destruction], but to you of salvation, and that from God." Then he adds, "For to you it has been granted on behalf of Christ, not only to believe in Him, but also to suffer for His sake, having the same conflict which you saw in me and now hear is in me" (Phil 1:29-30). Salvation in 1:28 is again the successful handling of persecution for Christ's sake.

This helps explain Phil 2:12, "Work out your own salvation with fear and trembling." Paul means that the Philippian believers needed to work out their own successful handling of the persecutions they were undergoing with fear and trembling in light of the soon return of Christ.

Paul explains what that salvation is in Phil 2:15-16, "That you may become blameless and harmless, children of God without fault in the midst of a crooked and perverse generation, among whom you shine as lights in the world, holding fast the word of life, *so that I may rejoice in the day of Christ* that I have not run in vain or labored in vain" (emphasis added). Clearly Paul's focus is on the Judgment Seat of Christ, here called *the day of Christ*. If the Philippians handled their persecution in a way that glorified the Lord, this would mean reward both for them and for Paul at the Bema.

Becoming Christ's Partners in the Life to Come (Hebrews)

Salvation in Hebrews is being one of Christ's partners (Greek *metochoi*) in the life to come (compare 1:9 and 1:14). It is being a co-ruler with Christ in His coming kingdom. This is seen in all uses of the word in the book, especially 5:9. Eternal salvation, that is, eternal partnership with Christ, requires that we obey Him by enduring persecution for Him.

Deliverance from False Teachers and False Teaching (First Timothy 4:16)

The salvation in First Timothy is primarily from false teachers and their false doctrine. That is what 4:16 is talking about. Timothy would save himself and his hearers from the false teachers (and the shame that results from following them) by paying attention to Paul and his teaching.

The use in 2:15 is a bit different. In that context a woman is not permitted to teach or even ask questions in the meeting of the church, but she is to receive instruction in silence. This could be a very frustrating experience. A woman is "saved" from that frustration by pouring her life into her children. A mother is able to teach and disciple the next generation of Christian men and women and she is "saved" from frustration if her children go on to walk with the Lord. If her children do not go on, then her purpose in life will have not reached the fulfillment she wants, and she will not be saved in that sense.

It is possible that all uses of *salvation* in First Timothy refer to fullness of life here and now, a life well lived, a life to be proud of. That would fit both 2:15 and 4:16.

Deliverance from Eternal Condemnation

John 3:17. By comparing the reference to salvation in verse 17 with the preceding verse, it is clear that salvation here refers to having eternal life on the one hand, and to not being condemned on the other.

Ephesians 2:5, 8. Verses 1-5 deal with the fact that the readers who were once dead have now been made alive by God. That is clearly a reference to regeneration. And this being made alive is defined in verse 5 as "by grace you have been saved." Thus the salvation in verses 5 and 8 refers to being made alive in Christ, the new birth.

Titus 3:5. In light of verse 7, which speaks of "having been justified by His grace" and of "the hope of eternal life," it is clear that "He saved us" in verse 5 refers to regeneration, the new birth.

Other texts. The words *save* and *salvation* also refer to everlasting life or salvation from eternal condemnation in a number of other New Testament texts. But that number is surprisingly small. See also John 5:34; 10:9; Acts 11:14; 13:26; 15:1; 16:17, 30, 31; 1 Tim 2:4; and 2 Tim 1:9.

There are other texts that most likely refer to salvation from eternal condemnation, but it is not crystal clear that is the case. More study is needed in my opinion. Such texts include Matt 19:25; Mark 10:26; Luke 13:23; 18:26; John 4:22; Acts 4:12 (but compare Acts 2:40) and Titus 2:11.

Even if all these texts refer specifically to salvation from eternal condemnation, and even if there are a few others I have missed, the total is less than one in three New Testament uses of *save* and *salvation* that refer to everlasting life. That makes it the exceptional use, not the norm.

What Did the Angel Mean When He Said That Jesus "Will Save His People from Their Sins"?

This verse is a good test case. You know the account. An angel of the Lord appeared to Joseph and told him "that which is conceived in her [Mary] is of the Holy Spirit." Then the angel went on, "And she will bring forth a Son, and you shall call His name Jesus, for He will save His people from their sins." Matthew then goes on to say that this fulfills the prophecy of Isa 7:14.

So what type of salvation is in view here? Well, let me ask a few interpretive questions.

Who were "His people"? If you were Joseph, who would you understand "His people" to be? If you were a first century reader, especially in light of the reference to Isa 7:14, who would you understand "His people" to be?

What are "the sins" of "His people" that the angel is talking about here? Are these the sins of all of mankind? If so, does "His people" refer to all of mankind?

Here is my understanding of Matt 1:21. The baby to be born of a virgin is the promised Messiah who will deliver Israel from Gentile domination which had resulted from Israel's repeated rebellion against the Lord. This is a promise that Jesus will ultimately establish His kingdom in Israel over the whole world, and thus Israel will be the dominant world power it was intended to be. This is the same salvation spoken of in Zech 9:9-10.

Many people use this very verse to say that Jesus doesn't save us *in our sins*, but "from our sins." But this verse has nothing to say about whether a regenerate person in the Church Age sins or not. Hypothetically the new birth could result in an experience free from sin in this life. We know that isn't true (cf. Rom 3:23; 1 John 1:8, 10). But people prop up faulty theology, saying that God guarantees that born again people won't sin more than a little, by misusing a verse like this.

And in so doing, they miss the promise that Israel will indeed be a redeemed nation one day in the future. Jesus will return and rule from Jerusalem. This is a beautiful salvation. But it is not salvation from eternal condemnation.

The Three Tenses of *Sōzō* Do
Not Refer to Justification,
Sanctification, and Glorification

A popular saying is that the past tense of the verb *save* refers in the New Testament to deliverance from the penalty of sin. Similarly the present tense of *sōzō* in the New Testament is said to deal with deliverance from the power of sin. And the future use of the verb *save* thus refers to deliverance from the presence of sin.

The idea that the New Testament speaks of all three of those deliverances is clearly true. Believers have indeed been delivered from the penalty of sin, which is death. This truth is found in many texts. In the famous resurrection chapter the Apostle Paul says, "'Death is swallowed up in victory.' 'O Death, where is your sting? O Hades, where is your victory?'...Thanks be to God, who gives us the victory through our Lord Jesus Christ" (1 Cor 15:54d-55, 57).

God presently delivers believers from the power of sin. In John 8:30-32 Jesus said that if believers abide in His word, then they will know the truth "and the truth shall make [them] free [from slavery to sin]." While that is a future tense freedom from sin, the Lord is clearly referring to experiential freedom from sin *in this life.* In Rom 6:18 Paul said, "Having been set free from sin, you became [past tense] slaves of righteousness." Putting those two texts together, we see that once a person comes to faith, he has been, past tense, *positionally* set free from sin's power. And the believer who abides in Christ's word *experiences* freedom from sin in his daily life.

And it is true that in the future God will set believers free from the very presence of sin. That will not be true in the Millennium, of course, for people in natural bodies with fleshly inclinations (also called *the old sin nature)* will be alive on earth and will sin. However, after the Millennium, when the kingdom moves to the New Earth, believers will be free from the very presence of sin (Rev 21:4, 8, 27; 22:15).

But while all three of those concepts are sound, we do not find that the Biblical uses of the verb *to save* (*sōzein*) teach this. Notice that in none of the verses I cited in the previous three paragraphs is the word *save* even used. While the idea is taught, it is not taught using the verb *to save* (*sōzein*).

The past tense of *sōzein* is used in the New Testament to refer to past deliverance *from anything*, most often temporal problems. Only in Eph 2:5 and 2:8 does the past tense of *sōzein* refer to the new birth, but even there it doesn't refer specifically to deliverance from the penalty of sin.

It refers there to having been made alive spiritually as verse 5 makes clear.

In the New Testament the present tense of *sōzein* refers to present deliverance *from anything*, normally from temporal difficulties. While it sometimes refers to sanctification and spiritual well-being, as in 1 Cor 15:2, that is not the same as saying it refers to deliverance from the power of sin. In 1 Cor 15:2, for example, it refers to those who are *spiritually healthy* right now, not to those who are being delivered from the power of sin.

The future tense of *sōzein* is used in the New Testament to refer to *any type of future deliverance*, again normally concerning difficulties in this life. See, for example, Matt 9:21; 10:22; 24:13; 27:49; Rom 5:9-10; 10:9, 13; 11:26; Jas 5:15, 20. In none of its uses does it refer to deliverance from the presence of sin, that is, to glorification. (A few uses refer to fullness of life in the life to come. See Luke 9:24 and parallels; 1 Cor 3:15; 5:5.)

Understanding that this popular teaching is established by words other than the verb *save* is crucial in discipleship, for if we train people in the standard view of the three tenses of the verb *save*, they will become quite confused about the actual meaning of many passages when they look at the past, present, and future tenses of the verb *save*.

What a Difference a Little Confusion Makes

We make it harder for a person to believe the promise of eternal life to all who simply believe in Him. If a person thinks that most uses of salvation refer to the new birth, he will end up believing in some form of works salvation since much of the salvation in the New Testament is dependent on works.

For example, the following are some of the conditions of *salvation* which we find in the New Testament:

- the prayers of others (Phil 1:19; Jas 5:15),
- persevering in persecution for the salvation of others (2 Cor 1:6),
- adding works to our faith (Phil 2:12; Jas 2:14),
- confessing Christ (Rom 10:9-10),
- holding fast to the gospel (1 Cor 15:2),
- calling on the name of the Lord Jesus (Rom 10:13),
- touching the hem of Jesus' garment (Matt 9:21; 14:36),
- having children who go on to walk with the Lord (1 Tim 2:15),
- abiding in sound teaching (1 Tim 4:16),

- enduring to the end of the Tribulation (Matt 24:13),
- and believing in the Lord Jesus (Acts 16:31).

If a person doesn't realize that the words *save* and *salvation* normally do not refer to the new birth, he will become very confused about what a person must do to have eternal life.

Both justification and sanctification are derailed if we misunderstand the meaning of *save* and *salvation* in the Bible.

Salvation means *deliverance*. It would be easier if the words *deliver* and *deliverance* had been used and not *save* and *salvation*. But if the KJV had used those words, then probably today people would ask, "Are you delivered?" instead of "Are you saved?" Then we'd have people speaking of their deliverance. Since we have the words *save* and *salvation* in our English translations, we need to ask what they mean in each context. Ask yourself what type of salvation or deliverance the context is talking about.

Salvation from What?

Back to the five passages we began with. After our brief study you should be able to explain each.

"Work out your own salvation with fear and trembling" (Phil 2:12). What type of salvation is in view in this verse?

Paul is talking about successfully handling persecution in a God-honoring manner resulting in future rulership with Christ. Compare Phil 1:19.

"Nevertheless she [singular, a woman] will be saved in childbearing if they [plural, her children] continue in faith, love, and holiness, with self-control" (1 Tim 2:15). What type of salvation is in view here?

Paul is discussing deliverance from the frustration a woman might experience from not being able to teach in the church (that is, teach the whole congregation as a teaching elder/senior pastor) with a view toward ruling with Christ in the life to come.

"Take heed to yourself and to the doctrine. Continue in them, for in doing this you will save both yourself and those who hear you" (1 Tim 4:16). What type of salvation is in view in 1 Tim 4:16?

Paul is referring here to deliverance from false teachers with a view to ruling with Christ in the life to come.

"He became the author of eternal salvation to all who obey Him" (Heb 5:9). What type of salvation is in view here?

Salvation here is being Christ's partners (*metochoi*) and ruling with Him eternally in the life to come (cf. Heb 1:9, 14; 3:1, 14).

"Whoever calls on the name of the Lord shall be saved" (Rom 10:13). What type of salvation is in view in this verse?

This refers to deliverance from God's wrath here and now with a view toward ruling with Christ in the life to come. The very next verse makes it crystal clear that it is *believers*, not *unbelievers*, who are calling on the Lord for this salvation: "How then shall they call on Him in whom they have not [first] believed?" Then Paul continues, "And how shall they believe in Him of whom they have not [first] heard?" And then he concludes with two final rhetorical questions, "And how shall they hear without a preacher? And how shall they preach unless they are [first] sent?"

Romans 10:14 makes clear that the people calling on the Lord in Rom 10:13 are believers and that the salvation is the salvation of believers from calamities in this life, not the salvation of unbelievers from eternal condemnation.

That will mess up many evangelistic tracts and presentations. But shouldn't our evangelism use the Bible accurately? It surely can't be a good thing to mislead people, no matter how well intentioned we are.

What is the doctrine of salvation? It is not the doctrine of how we are born again. It is the doctrine of how we are delivered from death, from disease, from enemies, from persecution, and from a life of less significance to one of more significance (both now and in the life to come). And, by the way, about 30% of the time it does refer to being born again, being delivered from eternal condemnation (e.g., John 3:17; Eph 2:5, 8). But that is a relatively rare use and you should not expect to see it very often in the New Testament, and not at all in the Old Testament.[6]

---

[6] The New Testament words most often used to refer to regeneration are *born again*, *everlasting life*, *life*, or the opposites, such as *shall never die* or *shall never perish*. The word *to justify* is related to regeneration in that all born again people are also justified. But they are not identical truths. Regeneration is a work of the Holy Spirit whereby He gives the believer everlasting life. Justification is a work of God the Father whereby He declares the believer righteous in His sight. And there is both justification before God, which is by faith alone, and justification—or vindication—before men, which is by works (cf. Rom 4:1-2; Jas 2:21-25).

Chapter 4
Lost

Introduction

I first believed in Christ for the free gift of everlasting life at the start of my senior year in college. Though I had been very active in a cult group, I don't recall thinking in terms of saved *or lost* until after I was born again. During my cult years I thought in terms of saved *or not saved*. In the cult we were taught that there was a moment in time which God had ordained when each person could be born again. That time occurred, our leader, Mr. H., told us, between the ages of five and twenty. Mr. H. said that normally a person only had one chance. If you weren't ready (by having repented and followed Christ until then) when your day came, then most likely you'd never have another opportunity to be saved.

According to Mr. H. he was given his chance at age five and he blew it. He didn't go forward at the church service when he felt the Spirit calling him to go. About eight years later he was given a rare second chance and he took it, sort of. He told us that when the altar call was given, he was struggling to get up, but didn't find any strength to do so. A person sitting next to him saw his struggle, helped him up, and went forward with him. Mr. H. said he came that close to eternal condemnation. He told us if he had not gone forward that day, he would never have had a third opportunity. He urged us to be ready and to give our lives to Christ when that moment came. (Of course, we often asked how we would know when our time came. He would always say, "Oh, you will know." I personally did not find that answer helpful or comforting.)

I never recall Mr. H. or any of the other leaders speak of people being *lost*. But once I believed in Christ, I heard that all the time. In Campus Crusade for Christ everyone would talk about people either being saved or lost. Campus Crusaders were seeking to win the lost to Christ.

Soon I picked up this way of speaking. By the time I got to seminary, I was thoroughly ingrained in referring to unbelievers as *the lost*. And I don't recall being challenged in that view by my seminary professors.

I graduated from seminary in 1982 with my Master's degree in New Testament studies. Then in 1985 I received my Ph.D. in New Testament studies. And I still used the term *lost* to refer to those who lacked everlasting life.

It wasn't until somewhere around 2000 that I began to shift my thinking. At first I began to think that the New Testament only rarely uses the term *lost* to refer to the unregenerate. Later I came to doubt that the New Testament *ever* uses the term *lost* to refer specifically to unbelievers.

Of course, if that is true—and you must decide based on the evidence—then that will cause a major adjustment in the way you read the New Testament. Indeed, it may even cause an adjustment in the way you refer to those who lack everlasting life. (For example, I no longer refer to the unregenerate as *the lost*.)

Perish the Thought

Years ago there was a campy television show called *Lost in Space*. More recently there was a famous American television show simply called *Lost*. Neither show was about unbelievers who were bound for the lake of fire. Both were about people who were literally lost. They did not know where they were. One group was lost in space and another group was lost on a deserted island.

In everyday conversation the word *lost* means *to lose one's way* or *the destruction of a person or thing*. Here are some examples:

> *We lost four men today at the hands of a sniper in Afghanistan.*

> *Farmer Jones lost his entire crop of corn due to the flooding in the Midwest.*

> *I'm sorry I'm late. I got lost and went south instead of north on I-5. When I saw the international border crossing sign, I knew what I'd done.*

> *Steve was lost in Organic Chemistry. He didn't have a clue what was going on.*

The Greek word translated *lost* is *apollumi*. That same Greek word is sometimes instead translated as *perished* or *destroyed*. While *lost* and *perish* look totally unrelated in English, we should realize that the same Greek word translates each and that the two English words have related meanings too.

Look how we use *perish* in everyday conversation to refer to something which has decayed or died:

He perished in the fire trying to save his daughter.

Thousands of people perish daily around the world due to malnutrition.

Milk is perishable. Don't leave it out of the refrigerator for more than a few minutes.

Perish the thought. That is, let that idea die here and now.

But when people trained in Christianese see the words *lost* or *perish* in the Bible, most automatically think that eternal condemnation is in view. That is a terrible mistake as I hope to prove in this chapter. It leads to major misunderstandings as to what God is saying in His Word.

Apollumi occurs 92 times in the New Testament, with over 75 percent of the uses found in the four Gospels, mostly from the teachings of the Lord Jesus.[1]

Before we see how the word is used throughout the entire New Testament, let's start with a look at just one place in which it occurs. This is the most famous usage of the word *perish* in the Bible since this is arguably the most well-known verse in the entire Bible: John 3:16.

John 3:16 Is Not a Typical Use of the Word *Perish*

I'm really not speaking facetiously. John 3:16 misleads people about the meaning of *perish* (*apollumi*) in the New Testament. Many think that since *perish* means *eternal condemnation* in John 3:16, then it means that everywhere in the New Testament.

It is true that the word *perish* in John 3:16 refers to *eternal condemnation*. This is clear both in verse 16, where it is contrasted with having everlasting life, and in verses 17 and 18, where it is identified as being condemned.

It is an exegetical error, a mistake in interpretation, to assume that the meaning of a word in one context is the meaning, or the primary meaning, it has in the entire Bible (or New Testament). Just because a

---

[1] Seventy of the 92 uses occur in the four Gospels: Matthew, twenty times; Mark, ten times; Luke, 28 times; and John, twelve times. The other 22 break down as follows: Paul's epistles, twelve uses; Peter, three uses; James and Jude, two uses each; Acts, Hebrews, and Second John, one use each.

word is used one way in one place in Scripture doesn't mean it always means that, or even that it mostly means that.

In fact, the meaning that *apollumi* has in John 3:16 is actually quite rare.

Apollumi in the New Testament most often refers to physical death or to temporal destruction or loss.

Physical Death Is a Very Common Meaning

Part of the problem is that so few people, even among Bible scholars, actually take the time to study the uses of words like *lost* or *perish* in the New Testament. Most people assume that we all know what words like this mean. After all, everyone knows what they mean, right?

Wrong.

By my study 32 of the 92 uses of *apollumi* in the New Testament refer to physical death, making it the single most common meaning. We can easily see that this word often refers to physical death by looking at some of the passages in which it occurs.

Second Peter 3:6. Referring to the flood Peter says,

> The world that then existed [at the time of the flood] *perished* [emphasis added], being flooded with water.

Clearly this refers to the destruction of all life, human and animal, on the face of the earth during the Noahic flood. It doesn't mean that 100% of the people who died in the flood were unregenerate. Almost certainly there were believers who did not heed Noah's call to repentance and righteousness. In addition, as John Whitcomb has speculated, it is quite reasonable to assume that when the flood began, people went to higher ground to avoid drowning. Whitcomb estimates they could have lived for about a week by climbing to higher and higher ground. Whitcomb suggests that during that week surely some came to faith in the coming Messiah for eternal life as they reflected on what Noah had preached.

So there were likely people who died in the flood who had been believers for years before it and others who came to faith after it started. But they all *perished*, that is, they all *died*, in the flood. Compare this with 1 Pet 3:20 in which Peter indicates that eight souls (Noah and his three sons and all their spouses) *were saved through water.* The rest died/perished.

Second Peter 3:9 uses the same word in the same way. However, since this verse is so widely understood as referring to eternal condemnation, I have reserved an entire section below to discuss this verse.

Matthew 8:25. "Lord, save us! We are perishing." The context is that the disciples were in a "boat that was covered with the waves" during "a great tempest." The disciples feared physical death, not hell. Without the Lord's intervention they would have soon died.

Acts 5:37. Judas of Galilee "also perished." The word *also* points the reader back to the previous verse in which Gamaliel is reported to have said that Theudas "was slain." Clearly the perishing in verse 37 is parallel to being killed or slain in verse 36. Gamaliel wasn't making any comment on the eternal destiny of either man.

First Corinthians 10:9-10. During the forty years in the wilderness some "were destroyed [*apollumi*] by serpents" (10:9) and "some of them also complained, and were destroyed [*apollumi*] by the destroyer" (10:10). Here are two uses of the Greek word *apollumi* in which the destruction in view is clearly physical death. A comparison with Exodus shows that physical death is in view here.

Jude 11. Here the Lord's half-brother speaks of those who "*perished* in the rebellion of Korah." He is alluding to Num 16:1-35 and the death of a group of 250 who were descendants of Korah. Again, physical death is in view.

John 11:50. Here Caiaphas makes an unwitting prophecy about the death of Jesus for the nation. He said,

> "It is expedient for us that one man [= Jesus] should die for the people, and not that the whole nation *should perish* [emphasis added]."

Clearly the options are one person dying versus the whole nation dying. Caiaphas feared that Rome would kill the nation, or at least most of it, if Jesus was allowed to live. The ironic truth is that by killing Jesus, Caiaphas and the others brought on the death of over a million Jews and the destruction of Jerusalem and the temple in the Jewish War three decades after Calvary.

John 18:14. John here reminds the readers of the Fourth Gospel that Caiaphas had said "that it was expedient that one man *should die* for the people." It is a bit misleading to translate *apollumi* as *should die* here and yet *perish* in the parallel context in John 11:50, using the same word.

Matthew 2:13. Joseph was warned in a dream to take Mary and Jesus to Egypt "for Herod will seek the young child *to destroy* Him." Again, the word is *apollumi* and it refers to physical death. Herod wished to destroy Jesus in the sense that he wanted to kill Him.

Luke 11:51. The Lord Jesus spoke of the blood of the prophets which was shed "from the blood of Abel to the blood of Zechariah *who perished* between the altar and the temple" (emphasis added). Zechariah was stoned with stones in the court of the house of God (2 Chron 24:20-21). The next verse makes it clear that he was killed: "Thus Joash the king did not remember the kindness which Jehoiada his father had done to him, but killed his son [Zechariah]; and as he died, he said, 'The LORD look on it, and repay!'" (2 Chron 24:22). The Lord Jesus was speaking of the death of Zechariah and the death of Abel. Their eternal destiny was not being considered.

Luke 13:3, 5. Here is another widely misunderstood passage. Some men came to Jesus and "told Him about the Galileans whose blood Pilate had mingled with their sacrifices" (Luke 13:1). In other words, they were asking Jesus about people from Galilee whom Pilate had killed. It is important to remember the question that leads to Jesus' response. The question concerns physical death, not eternal condemnation.

Jesus then asked if they thought "that these Galileans were worse sinners than all other Galileans, because they suffered such things?" (verse 2). Not waiting for their reply, Jesus answers His own question: "I tell you no" (verse 3a). Then He goes on to say, "But unless you repent *you will all likewise perish*" (emphasis added).

The word *likewise* here is crucial. The Galileans were killed. Thus Jesus is saying that if the Jews hearing His words did not repent, they would be killed as well. It is crystal clear that *perish* here refers to physical death.

The Lord then tells of 18 people who died when a tower in Siloam fell on them. Again, physical death, not eternal condemnation is in view. This is followed by repeating the words of verse 3. Unless the listeners repented, they would perish, meaning, they too would be killed.

This statement was fulfilled in AD 66-70 when over a million Jews were killed during the Jewish War.[2]

---

[2] We should not press Jesus' words to mean that 100% of those listening to Him would die prematurely if they didn't repent. He was speaking to the group before Him as representatives of the nation. He was saying that they had a chance to repent. If they did, and, of course, if this was combined with national faith in Jesus, then the kingdom would have come for that generation. However, since that generation rejected His offer of the kingdom and the reoffers of the kingdom by the apostles, then the nation was going to be destroyed and there would be widespread death. Of course, the destruction was not total since a remnant had to remain so that when Jesus returns there will be a nation of Israel which indeed will repent and believe in Him.

Luke 15:17. In the Parable of the Prodigal Son, the prodigal, when he realized how bad off he had it in the far country away from his father said to himself, "How many of my father's hired servants have bread enough and to spare, and *I perish* with hunger!" (emphasis added). He is referring to being exceedingly hungry. Possibly his condition was so bad that eventually he would have literally died if he did not have relief. But clearly in view is that he is in much worse shape here than he would be if he were back with his father.

Luke 17:27, 29. Concerning the deadly effects of the flood in Noah's day the Lord Jesus said, "The day that Noah entered the ark...the flood came and *destroyed* them all" (emphasis added). Similarly, concerning the deaths that God brought upon the sin-laden cities of Sodom and Gomorrah He said, "On the day that Lot went out of Sodom it rained fire and brimstone from heaven *and destroyed* them all" (emphasis added). These two uses clearly refer to physical death.

Luke 20:16. Jesus told a parable about a group of wicked men who were tending a man's vineyard for him. When the time of harvest came, the man sent a servant to get some of the grapes, but the wicked men beat the servant and sent him away with nothing. After this scene was repeated with several servants in succession, the owner sent his beloved son, a clear allusion to Jesus Himself. The wicked men then killed him. Jesus then said, "He will come and *destroy* those vinedressers and give the vineyard to others" (emphasis added). The destruction here could refer to temporal destruction less than death (the next category), but it is more likely that physical death is in view. Verse 16 likely refers to the Jewish war and the death of over a million Jews (as well as the destruction of the temple and much of Jerusalem). Of course it also alludes to the birth of the church, the new group to whom the vineyard would be given.

We could consider all of the remaining places in which *apollumi* refers to physical death,[3] but since they follow the same pattern we've already seen, let's consider the second leading category, temporal loss or temporal destruction.

---

[3] See also Matt 12:14; 21:41; 22:7; 26:52; 27:20; Mark 3:6; 4:38; 9:22; 11:18; 12:9; Luke 6:9; 8:24; 13:33; 19:47; Jas 4:12; and Jude 5.

Temporal Loss or Destruction Is
Another Very Common Meaning

Of the 92 uses of *apollumi* in the New Testament, 21 refer to temporal loss or destruction by my count. Now there is some overlap between this category and the category I call *losing the life* or *being lost in a temporal sense*. If we were to combine both of those categories, then those two would be the single biggest category.

John 6:12. After feeding 5,000 men plus their families with a few fish and loaves, the Lord Jesus said to His disciples, "Gather up the fragments that remain, so that nothing *is lost*" (emphasis added). This too is the word *apollumi*. It doesn't refer to life after death, but to destruction or loss here and now.

Matthew 9:17 (and Mark 2:22 and Luke 5:37). If new wine is put in old wineskins, the wineskins break and *"are ruined"* (emphasis added). That is, the wineskins are destroyed. The opposite which the Lord states in this same verse is that if you put new wine in new wineskins, "both are preserved."

Luke 21:18. "But not a hair of your head *shall be lost*" (emphasis added). The Lord is promising the disciples and all who suffer for Him that He will protect them, not in the sense that they wouldn't be put to death, for they would, but in the sense that they would have ultimate restoration of all for which they suffer. Not one hair would be lost in service for Christ for which there would be no reward in the life to come. Clearly Jesus is not speaking of the condemnation of hairs here.

Romans 14:15. In this weaker brother/stronger brother discussion Paul warns the stronger brother, *"Do not destroy* with your food the one for whom Christ died" (emphasis added). The sense of *apollumi* here is *ruin, injure, hurt,* or *damage.*

First Corinthians 15:18. Here is an unusual usage. Paul says that if Christ is not risen from the dead, "Then also those who have fallen asleep [died] in Christ *have perished*" (emphasis added). Here *apollumi* refers not to physical death, but to a loss of physical existence.[4] With no resurrection, believers who have died have permanently lost their bodies, never to regain them again. If there is no resurrection from the

---

[4] Hypothetically this could refer to eternal condemnation. However, in New Testament thought eternal condemnation is physical. Besides, following Paul's argument, if Jesus was not raised physically, then there will be no literal kingdom, no rewards, no Bema. It is thus unreasonable to conclude that Paul has eternal condemnation in mind here.

dead, then believers who have died will not take part physically in Jesus' coming kingdom. Of course, that's because He won't either, since there won't be a coming kingdom if Jesus is not risen. The entire Christian faith is overthrown if Jesus is not raised and if He doesn't raise those who believe in Him.

It is interesting to see how commentators explain this verse. Several think that Paul is speaking of eternal condemnation, which wouldn't make sense, for if Christ is not risen then there is no physical existence beyond the grave. Remember that eternal condemnation is a physical existence too. See Rev 20:11-15. The unsaved dead will be raised before they are judged at the Great White Throne Judgment and then cast into the lake of fire.

First Peter 1:7. This is the only use of *apollumi* in Peter's first epistle (along with two in Second Peter). Peter says that our faith is "much more precious than gold *that perishes*" (emphasis added). Peter means that gold is temporary. Gold will ultimately be destroyed. In the final meltdown after the Millennium, gold and everything in the universe will be burned up (2 Pet 3:10-11).

Second John 8. The Apostle John urges his readers to abide in the doctrine of Christ (verse 9) so that the apostles *do not lose* those things that they worked for, but that they may receive a full reward (at the Bema). *Apollumi* here refers to loss of potential rewards at the Judgment Seat of Christ. If people who are discipled continue with the Lord, then the one who trained them will have a greater reward at the Bema than if those people do not continue with the Lord. In a sense disciplers get a cut of the rewards of their disciples.

Matthew 5:29-30. Jesus here says that if something we see causes us to sin, then we should stop looking at it, "for it is more profitable for you that one of your members [e.g., an eye] *perish*, than for your whole body to be cast into hell [Gehenna]" (emphasis added). Leaving aside for a moment the reference to Gehenna,[5] it is clear that *perish* refers to the

---

[5] Clearly the Lord isn't contradicting what He said in John 3:16, 5:24, 6:35, etc. He likely means one of two things. First, if eternal torment in the lake of fire is meant, then He is saying, if there is something which is keeping you from believing in Him for eternal life, then abandon it. Some people cling to drugs and never go to church to hear the saving message and never listen if a person tries to evangelize them. Others are so addicted to video games or pornography or television or the internet that they never go to church or listen to people trying to witness to them. Better to lose those things than go to hell. Second, the word used here is not Hades, but Gehenna. Hades is the normal New Testament word for hell. Gehenna refers to a dump outside of Jerusalem where trash was continually burned. This is understood by some, such as

loss of something precious to us, an eye. Similarly in the next verse the Lord says that if something we do causes us to sin, then we should stop doing it, "for it is more profitable for you that one of your members [e.g., an eye] *perish*, than for your whole body to be cast into hell [Gehenna]" (emphasis added). Again, *perish* refers to temporal loss, in this case of a hand.

Loss of Life And *Lost* People

A fairly common and yet terribly misunderstood use of *apollumi* in the New Testament is when it is translated as *lost* or as *losing*.

Don't we often speak of *lost people* as unregenerate people, as people who do not have eternal life? Yet in the New Testament lost people are often born-again people who are not in fellowship with God.

We err seriously if we equate lostness with eternal condemnation. As we shall see in the section on eternal condemnation, there are a few places in which *lost* is a viable translation and in which it refers to eternal lostness. However, those are exceptions. They are not the rule.

Losing One's Life/Soul

The Lord Jesus on a number of occasions taught about *the saving of the psychē* [the Greek word for *soul, life, the inner person*, or even *living being*], often translated as *saving the life* or *saving the soul*. Jesus laid out two options: saving your life or losing your life. The word translated *losing* is our word, *apollumi*.

Matthew 16:25. Here, in a passage about discipleship, about following Christ, the Lord Jesus makes this puzzling statement, "Whoever desires to save his life [*psychē*] *will lose it*, but whoever *loses* his life [*psychē*] for My sake will find it" (emphasis added). This isn't referring to who spends eternity with Jesus and who goes to the lake of fire. Only believers are in view. Jesus is telling Peter and the other born-again apostles that in order to save their fullness of life forever, they must deny themselves, take up their crosses, and follow Him on a path that ultimately means they *lose* their lives in some sense (in their cases, ultimately resulting in martyrdom) here and now.

The Lord makes it clear in verse 27 that He is speaking about His return and about how much believers will share in His glory at that time. He is alluding to the Bema when He says, "then He will reward

Jody Dillow, to be a reference to *temporal judgment*. Thus the Lord might be warning that if something we see or do causes us to sin, it is better to lose that thing than to fall under God's temporal judgment.

each according to his works." Regeneration is not a reward for work done. However, fullness of life and ruling with Christ is.

The same concept appears a number of times in the New Testament.

Matthew 10:39, 42. Here is the same teaching as in Matt 16:24-28, though with less explanation given. "He who finds his life *will lose it*, and *he who loses* his life for My sake will find it" (Matt 10:39, emphasis added). This is immediately followed in the next few verses (Matt 10:40-42) with a discussion of eternal rewards, showing that the issue here is primarily fullness or lack of fullness of life in the life to come. In fact, in verse 42 the Lord uses the word *apollumi* to say that the one who gives even just a cup of cold water in His name "shall by no means lose his reward."

Luke 17:33. Here the Lord is teaching about the seven-year Tribulation period. At the midpoint the world ruler will defile the temple, an event Daniel called *the abomination of desolation.*

When that event occurs believing Jews during the Tribulation are to flee immediately from their homes to the mountains:

> "In that day, he who is on the housetop, and his goods are in the house, let him not come down to take them away. And likewise the one who is in the field, let him not turn back.
>
> "Remember Lot's wife.
>
> "Whoever seeks to save his life will lose it, and whoever loses his life will preserve it" (Luke 17:31-33).

Lot's wife turned back and died. She tried to save the old life and instead she lost her life.

If Jewish believers in the Tribulation turn back to their homes to get some prized possessions, then they will die. Whether this will be at the hands of the unbelievers, or whether God will simply take that believer's life as He did with Lot's wife, physical death will occur.

Verse 33 has broader application than simply to Tribulation saints. The same applies to believers today. If we cling to our goods and possessions, that is, if we lay up treasure on earth, then we will forfeit treasure in heaven (Matt 6:1-18). The only way to gain treasure in heaven is by having our hearts set on heavenly treasure (Matt 6:19-21).

If we longingly cling to the old life, the life that God has told us to leave behind, then we too will be destroyed. Our lives will be forfeited. The Lord's point here certainly applies to our present lives, both in terms of quality and quantity. And it also has application to our fullness of life in the life to come.

This same teaching is found in Mark 8:35; Luke 9:24-25; and John 12:25.

Lost People

Luke 15:4, 6. In the Parable of the Lost Sheep, the Lord told of a shepherd with 100 sheep who "loses one of them." The shepherd then will "go after the one which is lost until he finds it." According to the next verse, when he finds it alive, he puts it on his shoulders rejoicing and brings it back to the fold. A sheep which has literally become lost is in view in these two uses of *apollumi* in this verse, as well as the one use in verse 6, "Rejoice with me, for I have found my sheep which was lost!"

Of course this parable applies to born again people who leave the fold and become lost in the world. When they are found by the Lord (the shepherd) and brought back, all believers should rejoice.

Luke 15:8, 9. In the Parable of the Lost Coin, a woman "loses one coin." The coin was likely one of many coins on a bracelet passed down from mother to daughter. To lose one of the coins would greatly diminish the beauty and value of the heirloom.

Then after the woman finds the lost coin she says, "Rejoice with me, for I have found the piece which I lost!" These two uses also refer literally to something which was misplaced or lost.

Once again the application concerns believers who have become lost from the congregation and then found again. We all should rejoice in such cases, though sadly many wonder why we are letting the fallen return to fellowship without a long time out.

Luke 15:24, 32. The father of the prodigal twice speaks of rejoicing because his younger son has returned. Both times the father says, "[he/your brother] was dead and is alive again" (Luke 15:24, 32). The second time he adds, "and was lost and is found" (Luke 15:32). To be out of fellowship is to be *dead* and *lost*. To be in fellowship is to be *alive* and *found*. There is no doubt that the Lord Jesus in this parable is speaking of the same kind of lostness as in the first two parables of Luke 15. The lost sheep was no longer in the fold. The lost coin was no longer on the bracelet with the other coins. So too the lost son was no longer in his father's house or even country. He was lost to his father in the sense that his father no longer saw him each day and no longer experienced fellowship with him each day.

The three parables of Luke 15 all speak of God as seeking and bringing back believers who've strayed. Of course, God always knows where everyone is. The Lord is using a figure of speech called *anthropomorphism,* describing God in human terms. Jesus pictures God as a shepherd, a woman, and a loving father. The main point is that God loves believers and desires their fellowship. If we stray, God takes the initiative to restore us to fellowship.

Many think that *lost* and *found* in these three parables concern the eternal destiny of people who are represented by the sheep, the coin, and the son. Actually the issue is fellowship with God. Lost believers are out of fellowship with God. When they repent, they return to fellowship with Him.

The sheep that are not lost clearly represent believers in fellowship with God. The one who strays was originally with the ninety-nine, and hence he was once in fellowship with God. He must represent a believer who strays and is brought back by the Lord. The same is true with the lost coin, which was with the other coins on the bracelet before becoming lost, and with the lost son, who was with his father and brother at home until he went to the far country.

The son did not become a son by returning. Nor did the sheep become part of the fold by returning. Nor did the coin become part of the bracelet by returning. They all had that status before they left and when they returned they regained the place, the fellowship, they had before.

There Are Actually Only a Handful of Uses That Refer to Eternal Condemnation

Six of the uses of *apollumi* that refer to eternal condemnation appear in John's Gospel. We've already discussed 3:16. The verse before John 3:16, that is, John 3:15, applies as well. So does John 6:39 in which Jesus indicates that it is the will of the Father that He *lose* nothing. In that context losing is the opposite of having eternal life. So also in John 10:28, none of Jesus' sheep *will perish*.

In John 17:12 and 18:9, the Lord Jesus reminds the Father that none of His disciples *is lost*, except for Judas the betrayer. These uses of *lost* might refer to eternal condemnation. Assuming they do, then six out of twelve uses in John's Gospel, or half, refer to eternal condemnation. But the other half, even in the book that most heavily uses the word in reference to eternal condemnation, refer to physical death or loss (John 6:12, 27; 10:10; 11:50; 12:25; 18:14).

There are approximately 80 other uses of *apollumi* in the New Testament outside of the twelve in John, and only a few of the remaining 80 likely refer to eternal condemnation. For example, in both First and Second Corinthians Paul refers to *those who are being saved* and to *those who are perishing.* While it is possible that *those who are perishing* refers to those who are dying under God's judgment and that *those who are being saved* refers not to believers generally but to overcoming believers specifically, it appears that at least some of the time *those who are perishing* refers to those who are condemned and on their way to eternal condemnation unless they come to faith. For example, in 2 Cor 4:3 Paul says, "Our gospel is veiled...to those who are perishing." The next verse says that they've been blinded by Satan and that they "do not believe." (See also 1 Cor 1:18; 2 Cor 2:15; and 2 Thess 2:10.)

There are only two places in English Bible translations in which the word *lost* may be used to refer to the unregenerate, John 17:12 and 18:9.[6] Both of these refer to the same saying by the Lord. In a handful of other places *apollumi* refers to the unregenerate, but the English translation is always *the perishing* or *those who are perishing*, not *the lost*.

What about Second Peter 3:9?

Probably the most famous single verse on perishing and repentance in the New Testament is 2 Pet 3:9. There Peter says, "The Lord is...not willing that any should perish but that all should come to repentance." Many people understand Peter to be saying, *God doesn't want anyone to be eternally condemned but He instead wants all to come to repentance and hence spend eternity in Jesus' kingdom.*

But that isn't at all what is being said. In fact, that not only totally misses the point of this verse, but it also changes justification by faith alone into justification by repentance alone.

A simple rule of hermeneutics is that you determine the meaning of a word by its use in context. Well, here it is obvious what *apollumi* means in context if we just read the words before and after verse 9. In verse 6 the same word is used to refer to those who died in the Noahic flood (see discussion above). That's the only other use of this word in Second Peter and it is in the immediate context. (There is also one use of the word in First Peter and it also carries this meaning.)

In addition verse 9 is culminating a discussion begun in verses 3 and following about the delay in the Lord's promised return. Peter is saying in verse 9 that the Lord will fulfill His promise, but He is delaying since He is longsuffering toward us. He doesn't want to kill billions of people on earth. He would rather people repent and live full lives here and now prior to the kingdom. But when the sins of mankind are filled up, then

---

[6] See my article "Who is the Lost Person According to Scripture?" (*Grace in Focus*, January-February 2011) in which I discussed these verses.

the Tribulation will begin and billions will die. Even then, however, God will show that He would prefer men repent and avoid premature death (Rev 9:20-21; 16:9, 11).

The verses which follow discuss not hell, but the destruction of the current earth and heavens by fire. Temporal destruction is what is being discussed.

Thus we might paraphrase 2 Pet 3:9 in this way: *God wishes that none should die prematurely under His hand of temporal judgment (especially during the calamitous judgments of the Tribulation) but that all should come to repentance and extend their lives and their experience of His blessings.*

But Didn't Jesus Come to Seek and to Save the Lost?

After publishing a short portion of this chapter in the January-February 2011 *Grace in Focus* newsletter (now magazine), several readers asked me to explain Matt 18:11 and Luke 19:10.

Luke includes the fuller statement, "For the Son of Man has come to seek and to save that which was lost" (Luke 19:10). Matthew has the shorter form, "For the Son of Man has come to save that which was lost."

The reader of Luke's Gospel would surely hearken back to the three parables of Luke 15 when he read Luke 19:10 about the Son of Man coming to seek and *to save that which is lost*. As explained above, the lost sheep, the lost coin, and the lost son all represent believers who were once in fellowship with God but who strayed. Then the Lord came and sought for the lost and found it and brought it back (i.e., delivered it from its position as a stray).

What follows Luke 19:10 is the Parable of the Minas, which seems to be a new, but related, subject and not an explanation of Luke 19:10. The third servant buried his mina and ended up being rebuked at the Judgment Seat of Christ, though he does not go to the lake of fire. This is in contrast to the unbelieving Jews, Jesus' enemies who did not want Him as their king, who were "slain" (Luke 19:27).

What follows Matt 18:11, however, *does* appear to be an explanation of that verse. Matthew 18:12-14 is a brief form of the Parable of the Lost Sheep (cf. Luke 15:3-7). The Lord says that "if a man has a hundred sheep, and one of them goes astray, does he not leave the ninety-nine and go to the mountains to seek the one that is straying? And if he should find it, assuredly, I say to you, he rejoices more over that sheep than over the ninety-nine that did not go astray" (Matt 18:12-13).

Straying in verses 12-13 explains being *lost* in verse 11. A lost person in these contexts is one who has strayed away from the Lord.

When the Lord says He came *to save* the lost, He might be talking about salvation from eternal condemnation. But in the illustration, the saving is restoring the lost sheep back to the fold, not giving eternal life to the sheep.

Since most of the nation was unregenerate (cf. John 1:11), it is hard to see how the ninety-nine could refer to the unbelieving nation of Israel in Jesus' day. The ninety-nine sheep more naturally refer to believing Jews in that day, a very small minority. If that is the case, then the one who strayed was once in the flock. Thus before falling, he was a believer and he was regenerate. Since everlasting life cannot be lost, the straying sheep was still regenerate during his time away from the flock. When the Lord brought him back He restored the sheep to fellowship.

But what of verse 14: "Even so it is not the will of your Father who is in heaven that one of these little ones should perish"? The word translated *perish* is the same Greek word as *lost* in verse 11.

The answer is that Matt 18:11-14 is not *starting* a discussion about *these little ones*, it is *concluding* one. The discussion started in verse 2 when Jesus placed "a little child" in their midst. The word *these* in verse 14 is directed to the child in the midst of the disciples and others like the child. In verses 3-4 Jesus indicates that kingdom entrance requires being like a child, that is, believing. Then in verse 6 He says, "Whoever causes one of these little ones *who believe in Me* to sin, it would be better for him if a millstone were hung around his neck, and he were drowned in the depth of the sea" (emphasis added). Note the words in italics. The little ones of verse 6, surely the same little ones of verse 14, *believe in Jesus*. We know from John 3:16 that whoever believes in Him has everlasting life. Thus the little children of verses 6 and 14 have everlasting life and the sinning in verse 6 is what leads to the potential perishing in verse 14. The perishing there is temporal judgment, possibly culminating in premature death.

I think we need more study on this important topic. For too long our Christian language has been dictated not by the meaning of terms or phrases in Scripture, but by popular usage. Words like *saved, lost, perishing, gospel, judgment* and many others have taken on popular meanings that are not backed up by the Scriptures. I welcome further study on what it means to be *lost*, as well as studies on all important Biblical words and phrases. I am not seeking to end the discussion. I am seeking to start it.

Don't Assume That Eternal Condemnation Is Meant

It is your job to decide how a word should be translated in the New Testament. I realize you may not know Greek and you may feel this is the translator's responsibility. Well, the truth is that you are responsible to study the Word for yourself. You need not know Greek to follow what I'm saying about the word *perish* (*apollumi*). You simply need to be willing to question the translation you are reading.

The reason why many serious students of the Bible have multiple translations of the Bible is for this very reason. By comparing translations people can get a feel for the translation options in a given verse. The problem comes when all of the major translations mistranslate a word. A book like this can help you even in cases like that.

If you see the word *perish*, ask yourself what this is referring to, death, temporal loss, loss of eternal reward, or, in rare cases, eternal condemnation. Don't just assume that eternal condemnation is in view. In fact, assume it is not unless and until the evidence persuades you it is.

If you don't see the word *perish*, but you see words like *lost, destroy*, or *lose*, ask yourself what type of loss or destruction is in view. Often these words will be translating *apollumi*.

If you don't understand this key word, it can rob you of assurance of your eternal destiny. How can you know for sure that you are eternally secure if those who cling to their lives will lose their eternal lives? How can you know for sure that you are saved once and forever if you think that repentance is necessary to avoid eternal condemnation?

What about evangelism? How can you share the saving message with people clearly if you are confused by this word *perish*? You will end up mixing in works and repentance and self-denial as conditions of eternal life.

Perish the thought that the word *perish* should confuse you. If you've taken the effort and time to read this book, then this concept is one that you will take to like a grizzly to salmon. It is quite liberating to see what *apollumi* actually means. It opens up the meaning of so many passages which are potentially quite confusing.

Chapter 5
Heaven

The Popular Misunderstanding:
Heaven Is the Eternal Home of Believers

We sing many songs about heaven, including:

- When We All Get to Heaven;
- Heaven Is a Wonderful Place;
- Beulah Land;
- Shall We Gather at the River?
- When the Roll Is Called Up Yonder;
- City of Gold.

But what are we thinking about when we sing such songs? Are we thinking about where we will be if we die before the Rapture? That is not what these songs are about. These songs are about where we will spend *eternity*.

The reason we sing about heaven as our eternal home is because most pastors and theologians believe it *will be* our eternal home. As a result, most churchgoers believe that as well.[1]

Many people evangelize not by talking about eternal life that can never be lost, but instead about the future experience of heaven. I did that for years. Most of us have done that, and many of us are still doing that. But is that the best way to evangelize?

Jesus said, "He who believes in Me *has everlasting life*" (John 6:47, emphasis added). He used a present tense. Everlasting life is not only permanent, but it is also a present possession.

---

[1] Of course, there is widespread disagreement about what one must do to make it to that eternal home. Most in Christianity say that it takes faith plus perseverance in good works and avoidance of major sins. Others say that it only takes faith, but that if the faith is real, then the person will indeed avoid major sins and will persevere in good works. Very few believe that the sole condition of reaching heaven is believing in Jesus, apart from any works. However, the issue in this chapter is not what one must do to spend eternity with the Lord Jesus, but whether heaven is that place or not.

Not once did the Lord Jesus say, "He who believes in Me will spend eternity in heaven." In fact, Jesus said that at the end of the age (i.e., after the Millennium), "Heaven and earth will pass away" (Matt 24:35; Mark 13:31; Luke 21:33).

Of course, as we shall soon see, by "heaven" in that saying the Lord did not mean what most people think of as *heaven*. But that saying should surely cause us to question the wisdom of calling heaven our eternal home, don't you think?

Jesus promises the one who believes in Him a present reality that will last forever: everlasting life. We tell people that He promises something else.

I realize that some people present both concepts: "If you believe in Jesus then you have eternal life right now, and you will spend eternity with Him in heaven." Well, that first part is right. And many people are born again hearing a message like that.

But what if the second part is not true? What if Jesus and His people aren't going to be living in heaven in eternity?

Shouldn't we start people out right in the Christian life? If heaven is not the eternal home of believers, then why tell people that?

If God has something *better* in store for us than heaven, then wouldn't that be a real encouragement to us as well as to people we evangelize?

Let's first consider the three heavens the Bible talks about, starting with *the first heaven.*

Good Heavens: There Are Three Heavens

The First Heaven: The Air in Which Birds Fly

The word which is most often translated *heaven* is *ouranos* in Greek. It is sometimes used to refer to the atmosphere around the earth. This is where birds and planes fly.

The expression "the birds of the [first] heaven" occurs ten times in the New Testament (Matt 6:26; 8:20; 13:32; Mark 4:4, 32; Luke 8:5; 9:58; 13:19; Acts 10:12; 11:6). However, Bible translators typically translate this as "the birds *of the air*," even though there is a separate Greek word for *air*. This helps confuse the English reader into thinking that heaven always refers to where God dwells (obviously God is omnipresent, but the third heaven refers to the place His glory is especially localized).

Sometimes *ouranos* is translated as *sky*, as in "the sky is red" (Matt 16:2, 3) or "you can discern the face of the sky" (Luke 12:56). Other times it is translated *heaven* and appears to refer to the atmosphere around the earth. For example, "He [Elijah] prayed again, and the heaven gave rain" (Jas 5:18), and "Then, looking up to heaven, He [Jesus] sighed, and said to him..." (Mark 7:34). (See also Rev 13:13: "He even makes fire come down from heaven on the earth in the sight of men.")

While the expression *the first heaven* does occur once (Rev 21:1, see below), there the word *first* refers not to the atmosphere around the earth, but to the stars and planets, that is, to what scholars call *the second heaven*. This is because the word *first* there means something like *former*. One day the current heavens and the current earth will pass away, just as the Lord Jesus had said in the references we cited earlier.

Bible scholars have adopted this designation, *the first heaven*, for the air and atmosphere around the earth because, as we shall see, the Bible does speak of the *third* heaven. Thus there must be a first and second heaven.

We now turn to consider the *second* heaven.

The Second Heaven: Outer Space

The second heaven is what we typically call *outer space*. It is where the stars and the planets are. Once we travel beyond the earth's atmosphere, we have moved into the second heaven. Thus the astronauts who went to the moon saw a little bit of the second heaven. They even lived in the second heaven for a time.

There are lots of New Testament references to the second heaven, though, of course the term *second* is not specifically given. (See under "the third heaven" for the only time in the New Testament when we learn there are three heavens.)

Peter, amplifying on the Lord's saying that "heaven and earth will pass away," says "the heavens will pass away" (2 Pet 3:10, cf. vv 7, 12). We find the same thing in Rev 21:1, "the first heaven and the first earth had passed away." The author of Hebrews, citing Ps 102:25, says, "The heavens are the work of Your hands" (Heb 1:10), going on to say, "They will perish, but You remain" (Heb 1:11).

While there are many clear examples in which *ouranos* refers to where the stars and planets are, it must be admitted that there are also many times *ouranos* is used that could conceivably refer to any of the three heavens.

Let's now consider the third heaven.

The Third Heaven: Where God's Glory Dwells, and Where Believers Go Till the Rapture

There is only one place in the New Testament in which the expression *the third heaven* occurs: 2 Cor 12:2. There Paul says, speaking of himself, "I know a man in Christ who fourteen years ago—whether in the body I do not know, or whether out of the body I do not know, God knows—such a one was caught up to the third heaven."

Paul goes on to say that this man was "caught up into Paradise and heard inexpressible words, which it is not lawful for a man to utter" (2 Cor 12:4). Clearly the third heaven is where God's localized presence is. This is where Jesus stays until His Second Coming.

The term *ouranos* is used 54 times in the Book of Revelation, with most referring to the third heaven (though see the following which all refer to the first or second heaven: Rev 6:13; 8:10; 11:6; 12:1, 3, 4; 16:21).

The third heaven is, of course, what most people think heaven is. While it is often used this way in the New Testament, it is far from the only use of *ouranos*, and it is never presented as the eternal home of believers.

That the third heaven is where believers currently are is shown by several texts. In Luke 16:19-31 the Lord says that the rich man and Lazarus both went to Hades. Yet Lazarus was separated from the rich man and was with Abraham. Clearly before Jesus' ascension all believers were in *the air conditioned portion of Hades*. This is supported by the fact that the Lord told the thief on the cross, "Today you will be with Me in Paradise" (Luke 23:43). Jesus went to Hades until He rose from the dead. The good part of Hades was Paradise.

After Jesus ascended to the third heaven (1 Pet 3:22), He took all of the believers out of Hades and took them with Him to the third heaven. Ephesians 4:8 is a citation of Ps 66:18, "When He ascended on high, He led captivity captive, and gave gifts to men." Paul went on saying, "Now this, 'He ascended'—what does it mean but that He also first descended into the lower parts of the earth?" (Eph 4:9).

Remember that Paul said, "to be absent from the body" is "to be present with the Lord" (2 Cor 5:8). In Philippians Paul similarly said that he had "a desire to depart and be with Christ" (Phil 1:23). Since He is in the third heaven, that is where departed believers are.

But that is not where departed believers will remain.

The *Eternal* Dwelling Place for Believers Is Not Heaven—Humans Were Made to Live on Earth with Physical Bodies

When I was on staff with Campus Crusade for Christ, we used to sing a song at our weekly on-campus meetings. It was a chorus called, "Heaven Is a Wonderful Place." We'd sing about how wonderful heaven is. Heaven, we'd sing, is filled with glory and grace. "I want to see my Savior's face! Heaven is a wonderful place. I want to go there." Students and staff alike loved the song. But, unfortunately that song presents a flawed view of heaven.

Yes, heaven is a wonderful place, filled with glory and grace. And yes, my Savior is there right now. However, the song gives the distinct impression that we will spend eternity in heaven in the presence of Jesus. But neither the Lord Jesus nor believers will spend eternity in the third heaven. Jesus and believers will spend eternity on the new earth. The third heaven wasn't made for humans. And humans weren't made for the third heaven.

We know this simply by reading the opening chapters of Genesis. If Adam and Eve had not sinned, then there is no question but Adam and Eve and all their descendants would have lived on earth at least until they filled it. Think about that for a moment. God's design for human beings was not that they live in the third heaven forever. He didn't design us for the third heaven. He gave us bodies and a planet on which to use those bodies. While angels arguably were designed to spend at least some of their time in the third heaven, humans were not.

What would have happened if Adam and Eve had not fallen and had fulfilled God's command to fill the earth? At that point either God would have cut off reproduction (remember, no one would have ever died), or else He would have allowed humans to go out and colonize the planets, the second heavens.

Quite possibly before the fall of Adam and Eve, all of the planets would have been not only capable of sustaining human life, but would have been Edenic. But even if the situation before the Fall was as it is now in terms of the percentage of inhabitable planets, there would have been millions of planets that could sustain human life. And the universe is ever expanding, so that new planets are coming into existence all the time.

Adam and Eve and their offspring, which includes you and me, were not made for the third heaven. Of course, God knew that one day we would fly in the first and even the second heaven. But He did not create us to live in the third heaven. We were created to be earthly beings.

"Ah," some would say, "but after they sinned, that meant that humans were no longer destined to live on earth, but in heaven, that is, in the third heaven." While God certainly could have changed His plans for humans, the Bible does not support this notion. Indeed, the last two chapters of the Bible are very clear that the place believers will live is not the new heavens, but the new earth.

The Apostle John "saw the holy city, New Jerusalem, *coming down out of heaven from God*, prepared as a bride adorned for her husband" (Rev 21:2, emphasis added). Clearly the holy city, which is where the streets of gold will be (Rev 21:9-27), will be on the new earth, not in the third heaven where God the Father dwells.[2] This is reinforced in the very next verse in which John says "I heard a loud voice from heaven saying, 'Behold, the tabernacle of God is with men, and He will dwell with them, and they shall be His people'" (Rev 21:3). Note that *He will dwell with them.* John doesn't say, *Men will dwell with Him.* Rather, He will dwell with us. He is coming to our place. That is one of the reasons He took a body, so that He could live among us. (Of course, another reason is that He had to be fully human to die on the cross to take away our sins and make it possible for us to have eternal life by faith.)

The first and last chapters of the Bible make it clear that God has come to earth to dwell with us on earth. If your aim has been to spend eternity in heaven, I hope you will give up on that ambition. That isn't for you.

I Hope Heaven Is Never My Home

A pastor friend of mine, Bob Bryant of Cypress Valley Bible Church in Marshall, Texas, told me that he tells his congregation that he hopes heaven is never his home. When he says that, he gets the attention of the congregation. Unfortunately, there aren't many pastors who say that or who teach about the new earth and the new heavens.

I agree with my friend. I too hope that heaven is never my home. I would love to be alive at the time of Christ's return. To be caught up alive in the Rapture would be great.

Don't get me wrong. I'd love to *visit* heaven. It would be great to see the glory of God and the host of angels around the throne of God the Father.

But I don't want heaven as my home. Humans weren't made for that environment. That is a temporary location for believers who have died. Since a thousand years with the Lord is as a day, then even for someone like Abraham who has been in heaven for 2,000 years (remember, his first 2,000 years after his death were in *the air-conditioned part of Sheol*

---

[2] Of course, God is omnipresent. That means that He is everywhere present at once. That is true not only of God the Father and of God the Holy Spirit, but of the second member of the Trinity, the Son of God, the Lord Jesus. Though in His body He is localized in one place, in His spirit He is omnipresent. But the Bible does teach that in some sense which we cannot fully grasp—or at least *I* cannot fully grasp—God's presence (and His glory) is manifested in some special way in the third heaven.

as Luke 16:19-31 clearly shows), his stay in heaven will only seem to him to have lasted a few days.

I would prefer to go up to meet the Lord in the air, in the first heaven, in the Rapture. While I would be happy to leave this world via death and go to the third heaven for a time, that isn't my preference. I'd like to be alive at the time of the Rapture. I long for Christ to return in my lifetime, as I'm confident you do as well if you know about the Rapture. When Jesus comes, those believers who are alive (as well as all "the dead in Christ," 1 Thess 4:16) will meet Him in the air (1 Thess 4:17), that is, in the first heaven. Seven years later we will go with Him and His angelic army to overpower the enemies of Israel that have surrounded Jerusalem. After that we will spend 1,000 years on the millennial earth and then the rest of eternity on the new earth (or on the new earth and on various planets in the new universe).

But believers will never have the third heaven as their permanent address. We weren't made to live in heaven. And heaven wasn't made for us.

What Will the New Earth Be Like?

Okay, you might ask, then what will the new earth be like? If this chapter has led you to ask that question, then I've accomplished my goal.

It is much easier to find out for yourself what the new earth will be like, rather than what the third heaven is like. Both the Old and New Testaments tell us a fair amount about the new earth.

We know the following about the new earth:

1. It will be a literal planet (Rev 21:1).
2. If the new earth has similar topography to the Millennial Earth, then the mountains will be much lower than today (Isa 40:4; Rev 16:20) and the New Jerusalem will be the highest city on the highest mountain on earth (Isa 2:2).
3. The New Jerusalem will be a city larger than any country on earth today. It will be 1,500 miles long and wide and high too (Rev 21:16). Most likely—I'm speculating here since we are not specifically told why the New Jerusalem is so large— every single believer from the Church Age will have a condo there, though we likely will have our primary residence in whatever our "home country" was (which could be an adopted country in the cases of immigrants and missionaries). That Church Age believers will live all over the new earth is

suggested by the fact that there will be nations and that the nations will annually bring their gifts to Jesus at the New Jerusalem (Rev 21:24). If overcoming Church Age believers will rule (2 Tim 2:12; Rev 2:26), then surely they will rule over the nations.

4. The New Jerusalem will have streets and buildings of gold (Rev 21:18, 21).

5. Since the New Jerusalem will have streets, homes, and walls, it is evident that the entire new earth will be made up of beautiful cities, countries, and roadways. The designs will certainly exceed even the most beautiful designs today.

6. The New Jerusalem will be like the Garden of Eden (see Ezek 36:35, referring to the Millennial Jerusalem, which certainly will be no better than the New Jerusalem to follow).

7. There will be twelve gates. Each gate will be made of pearl (Rev 21:21).

8. Though the new earth will have a new sun and moon,[3] there will be no night in the New Jerusalem (Rev 21:25). As on the first three days of creation, the Lord Jesus will Himself light up the New Jerusalem, which will not need the sun or moon (Rev 21:23).

9. Jesus' throne will be in the New Jerusalem (Rev 22:1).

10. From His throne will flow a river of living water (Rev 22:1).

11. On both sides of the river will be the tree of life (Rev 22:2). The tree of life will yield a different fruit each month (Rev 22:2). The fruit will only be for believers who were overcomers in this life (Rev 22:14). The leaves of the tree of life will be for the healing of the nations (Rev 22:2).

12. There will be nations all over the new earth (Rev 21:24).

13. The kings of the nations will annually bring their glory (precious gifts) to the New Jerusalem to present to the King of kings (Rev 21:24).

---

[3] Many people misread Rev 21:23, 25 to say that there will be no sun or moon. I did that for years until one day I mentioned that to my friend and mentor, Zane Hodges. He pointed out that John does not say that there will be no sun or moon. Instead he says, "The city *has no need of* the sun or of the moon to shine in it, for the glory of God illuminated it. The Lamb is its light" (Rev 21:23). Zane pointed out that "has not need of" actually suggests that there will be the sun and moon, but that the city won't need their light. He also pointed out that John did not say that this was true of the whole new earth. Most likely the rest of the new earth will have day and night and will need the light of the sun and of the moon.

14. There will be no more sea (Rev 21:1). That might mean that there will be no oceans of any kind. Or it could be that there will be fresh water oceans. In any case, we know there will be water in the New Jerusalem and likely all over the planet for vegetation, such as the tree of life, to grow (see Rev 22:1-2 and the river of the water of life).

15. Overcomers will have special white garments (Rev 3:4-5) and likely will have faces that shine, much like Moses' did when he met with Jesus at Mount Sinai, and as Jesus' face did when He was transfigured at the Mount of Transfiguration (Matt 17:2).

16. Overcomers will have unique white stones which will have nicknames engraved on them (Rev 2:17). That nickname will be a special name that Jesus has for each overcomer. This will be a prized piece of jewelry.

17. The manna which was hidden in the Ark of the Covenant will be available for all overcomers to eat (Rev 2:17). The hidden manna will be tasty and will enhance one's life.

18. We will serve Christ on the new earth (Rev 22:3). Certainly humans will have the same wide range of occupations we have today (sculptors, painters, playwrights, novelists, teachers, farmers, ranchers, engineers, architects, politicians = rulers, carpenters, etc.), except that certain jobs that were related to the Fall and the sinfulness of man will no longer be needed (e.g., jailers, police, wardens, prison guards, morticians, psychiatrists, psychologists, surgeons, doctors, lawyers, thieves, hit men, and so on). The greatest of everything will be produced then: books, plays, movies, buildings, cities, spacecraft, aircraft, cars, paintings, sculptures, music, etc.

19. Most likely we will have a much different sense of time then. Surely we will never be bored. We will never worry about how the kingdom can forever be expanding and improving. It will be an amazing adventure that will never end. And we will love it. We will finally experience what God has created us to be and to do. Until now our experiences have been very far below what God intended for us.

20. We may even travel through worm holes and go throughout the universe. Exactly how all that will play out is certainly not discussed in Scripture. But unless God put all the planets and stars out there purely as an art gallery, those planets and stars will play a role in God's eternal kingdom.

21. No one on the new earth[4] will ever die (Rev 21:4).[5] Nor will there ever be tears of grief or sorrow (Rev 21:4). There will be no more pain, physical or emotional (Rev 21:4). While there will be injuries for people in the nations, these will be pain-free injuries and once the leaves of the tree of life are brought to the injured person, his injuries will be healed (Rev 22:2). Probably every person on the new earth will have a supply of those leaves on hand.

22. There will banquets in which the Lord Jesus will preside. He promised this at the Last Supper (e.g., Matt 26:29). Most likely celebratory meals will be a big part of our eternal experience.

23. There will likely be a library of all of human history (cf. the books mentioned in Rev 20:12-13). Possibly that will include being able to actually go back in time and watch history as it unfolded. Much if not all of human history will likely be open for our edification.

24. There will be three groups of people on the new earth: Israel, the Church, and the nations (cf. 1 Cor 10:32). Israel will be made up of Jewish believers from Abraham until Pentecost, from the Tribulation, and from the Millennium. The nations will be made up of Gentile believers from those same time periods. The Church will be made up of believers from Pentecost until the Rapture.

25. It is possible, though highly speculative, that there will be children born forever. If so, the Church, fixed in number, would become more and more of a minority in the kingdom as Israel and the nations would expand forever. The way in which this could happen would be if people from Israel and the nations in natural bodies will go from the Millennium on to the new earth, but without sin natures and without the ability to pass on a sin nature to their children. Evidence that children will be born in eternity includes: 1) there is no

---

[4] Of course, people will die on the Millennial Earth. See, for example, Rev 20:9, as well as Matt 5:22. While some think that the Millennial Earth is the New Earth, Rev 21:1-3 shows that it is not. The New Earth does not come into our universe until after the destruction of the current heavens and earth described in 2 Pet 3:10-13.

[5] Possibly not even animals will die. It seems that before the Fall man was designed to eat the fruits of the Garden and not to eat animals at all. It wasn't until after the Flood that God gives men specific freedom to eat animals (Gen 9:3). Possibly animals would have died even if Adam and Eve had not sinned. But it is certainly conceivable that God intended animals to live forever as well.

Scripture that says otherwise (in Matt 22:30 when the Lord spoke of people in the next age not being given in marriage, and thus not having children, He was speaking of people *in resurrected bodies*; we know children will be born at least during the Millennium [cf. Isa 65:20-23]); 2) Isaiah 9:7 says of the increase of the Messiah's government there shall be no end; 3) if Adam and Eve had never sinned, there would have been children forever unless God eventually cut off reproduction, which seems unlikely; 4) God loves children and will want to see children forever (but there would be no babies, toddlers, and small children on the new earth if everyone was a glorified person); 5) Jesus said that the kingdom is for children (Mark 10:10); 6) studies show the universe is ever expanding, suggesting it would forever accommodate an ever increasing population.

26. If children are born in eternity future, eventually Christians would be extremely rare people in the kingdom. (Imagine a day, for example, when there might be one Christian for every million people.) Since Christians will be assigned to rule over Israel and the nations, this makes a lot of sense. Christians, in glorified bodies, would thus rule over people in natural bodies, not primarily over other glorified saints.

27. The bottom line is that the new earth will be a literal, physical, tangible place. We will not float on clouds and live as disembodied spirits. We will live on terra firma with glorified bodies. We will then experience life as God originally intended Adam and Eve to experience it.

We Need to Change the Way We Think about Heaven

What we sing reflects what we believe. There are lots of songs about heaven and nearly all of them are misleading. Consider the song entitled, "This World Is Not My Home":

This world is not my home;
I'm just a passing through.
My treasures are laid up
Somewhere beyond the blue.
The angels beckon me
From heaven's open door.

And I can't feel at home
In the world anymore.

Now if by *this world* the hymn writer had meant the cursed post-fall *earth*, he is right. But if he means earth, then he is greatly mistaken. And it is clear that he does mean that when he goes on to say, "If heaven's not my home, then Lord what will I do." Even if we ignore the lack of assurance evident in that line, we are still left with a song that mistakenly sees heaven and not the new earth as our eternal home.

In reality we go from this earth to the cleaned up and improved Millennial earth and then to the new earth. Actually the song would better read just the opposite:

Heaven is not my home;
I'm just a passing through.
My treasures are laid up
Somewhere beyond the blue.
One day soon I'll meet Him
In the air above.
Then He will take me with Him,
To earth's open door.

How about the song entitled, "When We All Get to Heaven"? Consider its words:

When we all get to heaven,
What a day of rejoicing that will be!
When we all see Jesus,
We'll sing and shout the victory!

The song goes on to say:

Soon the pearly gates will open;
We shall tread the streets of gold.

The song gives the impression that the pearly gates and the streets of gold will be in the third heaven, rather than on the new earth. But Revelation 21–22 makes it clear that the pearly gates and the streets of gold are in the New Jerusalem on the new earth.

And when we all see Jesus, we will not be in heaven—if by that we mean the third heaven—but in the air, the first heaven.

Another famous song about heaven is called "I Can Only Imagine." The song never actually specifies that it is talking about heaven. But note what the author says that believers will do forever:

I can only imagine,
When all I will do

Is forever,
Forever worship You.
I can only imagine.

Clearly the author envisions a situation such as is described in Revelation 4 where the four living creatures, angels, are forever crying out "Holy, holy, holy, Lord God Almighty, who was and is and is to come!" (Rev 4:8). And whenever they do that the 24 elders, another group of angels (see Rev 7:11-12), cast their crowns before the Lord Jesus in worship (Rev 4:10), and say, "You are worthy, O Lord, to receive glory and honor and power; for You created all things, and by Your will they exist and were created" (Rev 4:11). But that scene takes place in the third heaven. The third heaven is not the eternal home of believers.

While we will surely spend time on the new earth worshipping the Lord Jesus, that is not all we will do. Surely Adam and Eve prior to the Fall didn't spend most of their day in worship. And neither did believers prior to the birth of Israel. And neither did believing Jews in the Old Testament. And neither do believers today in the Church Age. And neither will believers during the Tribulation or the Millennium.

We were made to work, to use our creativity to the glory of the Lord Jesus. To suggest that we will be floating on some cloud singing praise hymns forever is a near complete misreading of where God has called us to live and what He has called for us to do.

The greatest paintings have not yet been painted. They will be painted on the new earth. Architecture, transportation, technology, the arts, sports, science, recreation, literature, worship—all of that pales in comparison to what will be on the new earth and in the new universe.

And imagine, things will continue to improve forever and ever. We will never run out of creativity, resources, or manpower to do what the Lord wants us to do. And we likely won't be limited simply to the new earth. The entire new universe will be a canvas on which we can glorify our Lord. Possibly all of the planets will then be inhabitable and inhabited.

The way we think about heaven is wrong and we need to be transformed by the renewing of our minds (Rom 12:2; 2 Cor 3:18). Our eternity is more glorious than we can imagine. But we should be imagining living in the right place to start with. And we should imagine *serving* the Lord Jesus Christ forever (Rev 22:3).

Most likely believers who are now in heaven are longing for the Rapture. They want to be reunited with living believers. Earth is calling them home. They long to see Israel restored to her glorious position as God's chosen nation. The thought of seeing the Lord Jesus sitting on the throne of David and ruling from Jerusalem thrills them. The Millennium is such a glorious time to anticipate. And the New Jerusalem (with the twelve gates of pearl, and the streets of gold), the nations, and the glorious sinless new earth in which righteousness dwells, are future realities to capture our imaginations, as well as the imaginations of those now in heaven.

Of course, no one in heaven is upset or disappointed. But they know that heaven is not their home. They realize that they are just passing through heaven on their way back to earth.

I've found that longing for the millennial and new earth is very motivating to me. Until seminary I longed for heaven. Frankly, I wasn't too excited about it. But then one day Sharon and I were walking with our friends Will and Sue Nece. I said something about how I longed to spend eternity in heaven. Will looked over and asked, "Why would you long for that? Our eternal home is the new earth, not heaven. Revelation 21–22 shows that."

That was a eureka experience for me. I saw right away he was right. And I began to study more. And my enthusiasm grew for the life to come. I believe your enthusiasm will grow as well if you get your eternal focus on the new earth, where it should be.

Chapter 6
Hell

"I Know Hell Is a Bad Place"

Toward the end of a Bible study on hell I was teaching recently, I received a comment that summed up the thoughts of most in the group: "I don't know much about hell, but I know hell is a bad place and heaven is a good place."

Before I had given the lesson, I don't think the group realized that they didn't know much about hell. Most Evangelicals I've met give the impression that they have a good idea of what hell is like. However, despite what many preachers say, the Bible doesn't have much to say about hell. Thus no one can have a detailed picture of what hell is like. God hasn't told us. We can make some guesses. That is what I will do in this chapter. But we have very little in the way of a detailed picture.

I found my friend's comment to be very insightful. It seems childlike to say that we know that hell is a bad place, but the truth is, that is the picture we get of hell. We know it is a place of torment. But we don't know much more.

In this chapter I will share what we know about hell from Scripture and I will speculate on what I think it is like. I will be careful to separate what we know from my speculations. I believe that my speculations are reasonable inferences from what we know. But I readily admit that some of what I suggest in this chapter about hell and the lake of fire is speculation.

Let's start with looking at a few of the leading passages in Scripture about hell.

Key Biblical Passages on Hell

Maybe you've heard this saying, "Jesus said far more about hell than He did about heaven." That saying is misleading, because it suggests that Jesus told us a lot about hell. In reality, He didn't tell us much about what it is like.

There is only one passage in the Gospels in which the Lord Jesus told us what hell is like. There is also one passage in the Old Testament and another in the Book of Revelation that gives us some insight into what hell is like.

After we look at these three passages, then we will look at the various Greek and Hebrew words that are translated as *hell*, engage in some speculation on what the evidence *might* point to, and finally we will consider what practical difference our view on hell makes.

The Rich Man, Lazarus, and Abraham

The first thing to note is that the unnamed man in Luke 16:19-31, the rich man, is in Hades, not in the lake of fire. So whatever this man is experiencing is not necessarily the same as he will suffer in the lake of fire.[1] It is reasonable to assume that his suffering will be the same in the lake of fire. But that is an assumption and is not stated in this text (or any other).

The second observation is that born-again people are in his vicinity. They are close enough that he can see Abraham and Lazarus and that he can carry on a conversation with Abraham. This place is Hades, which before Christ's ascension contained both the regenerate and the unregenerate (the former in an air conditioned part of it).

Thus we could accurately say that before Jesus' ascension everyone who died, believers and unbelievers, went to hell. Indeed, we would even be correct to say that Jesus spent three days in hell between His death and resurrection, provided we understand that He was in the good part of Hades.

The third note to be made is that we really don't know the level of the rich man's torment. Since he is able to carry on an intelligent conversation, it is highly unlikely his suffering is at the very top end of the scale. When most people are suffering in the 8-9 range on a 1 to 10 scale, they only talk briefly, and then only to get some help. Here the man continues talking after Abraham says Lazarus can't bring him any water. He then asks for Abraham to send someone back from the dead to speak to his brothers.

Fourth we should observe that the man's torment is conscious and that the flames in his environment are real flames.

---

[1] Walter Briscombe in a book entitled *Hades, Heaven, and Gehenna (or Hell)* (London: J. Haddon & Co., 1890) argues that the suffering in Sheol/Hades is relatively minor and that the suffering of unbelievers will increase dramatically when they reach the lake of fire (see pp. 17-23). I think that is unlikely. But this is a matter of speculation and not specific revelation.

Fifth, there is no hint here that the man is on fire. He is in a fiery environment,[2] like being near a roaring fire or a lava flow with fire shooting out of the lava.

Sixth, we do not know how this man's sufferings compare to others in Hades. Is this the worst type of suffering there? Is this average? Is this the least?

Seventh, this is but a snapshot of the man's experience in Hades. Is his experience like this all the time? Or might his experience be worse than this at times and better than this at times? The Lord does not reveal that information.

The bottom line is that while this text gives us some ideas about what hell is like, it doesn't tell us much.

The Smoke of Their Torment Ascends Forever

An angel reports that all who take the mark of the beast during the Tribulation will be tormented forever: "And the smoke of their torment ascends forever and ever; and they have no rest day or night, who worship the beast and his image, and whoever receives the mark of his name" (Rev 14:11).

This verse strongly suggests that the torment in the lake of fire for unbelievers from the Tribulation will be eternal. That they have no rest day or night (cf. Rev 4:8; this is a figure of speech called a merism) probably is not saying one way or the other about whether the torment varies in intensity throughout each day, but about an inability to escape the torment. Walvoord comments, "To emphasize the idea of continuing suffering, they are declared to have no rest day or night."[3] Torment will be a daily experience forever for those in the lake of fire.

The reason I say *strongly suggests* rather than *proves* in the last paragraph is because verse 11 does not specifically mention the lake of fire. However, when we compare Rev 20:10 and Rev 20:15, the linkage is evident. The former reads, "The devil...was cast into the lake of fire and brimstone where the beast and the false prophet are. And they [the devil, the beast, and the false prophet] will be tormented night and day forever and ever."

---

[2] The words *in this flame* mean he is living in a fiery place. It is hot there, hence his thirst. If he had been literally on fire as some might think, then he would not have been concerned about being thirty. People who are literally on fire have pain much more intense than the pain of being thirsty. And he wouldn't express himself in this way if he were on fire. He would use much more direct language, like, "I'm on fire," or "My flesh is burning."

[3] John F. Walvoord, *Revelation*, edited by Philip E. Rawley & Mark Hitchcock (Chicago: Moody Press, 2011), 226.

Notice that Rev 20:10 has the same language as Rev 14:11. Both speak of day and (or) night, torment, and forever and ever.[4] And in the section immediately following Rev 20:10, the passage on the Great White Throne Judgment (Rev 20:11-15), we learn that "anyone not found in the Book of Life was cast into the lake of fire" (Rev 20:15). While the lake of fire was evidently designed for the devil and fallen angels, the two world rulers of the Tribulation are not the only humans who will be tormented there forever. So will all humans who are not found in the Book of Life.

While we get some general idea here of what torment in the lake of fire will be like, there is no specificity.

Mocking New Arrivals in Hell

Isaiah 14:9-11 is little known, but adds some information about Sheol that we do not find in other texts.

The passage speaks of the king of Babylon going to Sheol (vv 9-11) as well as the fall of Lucifer when he led an angelic rebellion against God (vv 12-15).[5]

Motyer's comments are helpful here:

> In verses 9-15, Isaiah takes us on an imaginative trip to Sheol, the abode of the dead. We hear how Sheol reacts to the arrival of the king (9-10), and what a contrast this is (11-15) to his ambitions and self-estimation. Imaginative though this is, great Old Testament truths are accurately expressed. First, the dead are alive. In the Bible "death" is never "termination" but always change of place (from earth to Sheol), change of state (from body-soul unity to the separate life of the soul) and continuity of person. Thus, in Sheol, there is personal recognition: the king is recognized as he arrives (10); the existing residents rise from their thrones—not because there are thrones in Sheol but because they are

---

[4] G. H. Lang says that "this same expression [*forever and ever*] comes eleven times in the Revelation. In Rev 1:6; 4:9; 4:10; 5:13; 7:12; 10:6; 11:15; 15:7 it refers to the life, glory, sovereignty, worship of God and the Lamb and cannot mean aught [anything else] but unlimited duration," *The Revelation of Jesus Christ*, Selected Studies (Miami Springs, FL: Convey & Schoettle Publishing Co., 1985) 357. Lang goes on to discuss the other three uses as well, Rev 14:11; 19:3; and 22:5, showing they too refer to everlasting experiences (pp. 357-58).

[5] It should be noted that many commentators (including Motyer, cited in the next note) suggest that verses 12-15 also refer to the king of Babylon. In this view the designations Lucifer (NKJV) should be translated as *day star* or *morning star* and is being used figuratively of an earthly king, not of Lucifer himself. However, there is good reason to believe that verses 12-15 do refer to Lucifer. Compare Ezek 28:12-15.

the same people as once they were on earth. But the dead are "shades/shadowy ones" (9), weak (10) because death has sundered body and soul; the soul by itself is but a half-life. The Old Testament awaits the Lord Jesus to meet its implied need of the resurrection of the body. This is an illustration of the progressive, cumulative revelation which runs through the Bible.[6]

Verse 9 speaks not of Lucifer, but of a Babylonian king who, though he was alive at the time, is pictured as having already died: "Hell from beneath is excited about you, to meet you at your coming; it stirs up the dead for you, all the chief ones of the earth; it has raised up from their thrones all the kings of the nations."

Thrones in Sheol? Probably not. Most likely this is merely poetic language. But the thrones do symbolize the former status of these men, which in some sense they have carried with them even to Sheol.

Verse 10 continues: "They all shall speak and say to you: 'Have you also become as weak as we? Have you become like us?'"

When new people enter Sheol (at least important people, but likely all), those who are already there gather to mock the person. The impression is given that the people doing the mocking actually get some perverse pleasure out of taunting the new arrivals ("hell is excited").

The weakness mentioned here is probably more than simply loss of the body (which is Motyer's suggestion above).[7] Likely it refers to loss of power and majesty and ambition. On earth these kings had strength in that sense. Here, they are weak in comparison. Even if there are literal thrones, their comparative power and majesty is so low that they admit their own fall and weakness.

Verse 11 concludes the discussion about the king of Babylon, saying: "Your pomp is brought down to Sheol [*the grave* in the KJV], and the sound of your stringed instruments; the maggot is spread under you, and worms cover you." The king no longer will have musicians with instruments to entertain him. Currently his body is rotting in the grave and they mock him for that as well. (One day all unbelievers will be resurrected, brought before Christ at the Great White Throne Judgment, and then cast into the lake of fire. See Rev 20:5, 11-15.)

---

[6] J. Alec Motyer, *Isaiah: An Introduction and Commentary*, Tyndale Series (Downers Grove, IL: Inter-Varsity Press, 1999), 119.

[7] Besides, the people in both the good and bad parts of Sheol/Hades have some sort of intermediate body, as Luke 16:19-31 shows. The rich man wants Lazarus to dip his finger in water and place the water on his tongue. These are real bodies, though they are not the resurrected bodies to come.

Of course, there will be no new arrivals in the lake of fire after all of unsaved humanity gets there at the same time. But if there is some measure of pleasure in mocking new arrivals in Sheol, it seems likely that people in Sheol also mock each other from day to day. And it seems likely that they will mock each other for eternity in the lake of fire. This will, of course, cause emotional pain to the ones being mocked. But it will also cause a measure of sadistic delight for the ones doing the mocking. That won't eliminate their torment. But it might well distract them from it to a degree.

Those Cast into the Lake of Fire Are First Resurrected

Revelation 20:13 speaks of the reuniting of body and soul of which Motyer spoke: "The sea gave up the dead who were in it, and Death and Hades delivered up the dead who were in them." But where are the unsaved dead now? Are they in Hades (Sheol) or in the sea? The Biblical answer is that they are in both places because their souls are in one place (Sheol) and their bodies in another (the sea).

Death and Hades have the souls of people. The sea (and land)[8] has their bodies. The bodies and souls, via resurrection of the bodies, are brought together again (cf. Rev 20:5; see also Dan 12:2). In the lake of fire, unlike Sheol today, unbelievers will have their bodies once again. But these will not be glorified bodies free from pain and suffering like believers will have (cf. Rev 21:4).

At the Great White Throne Judgment those sent to the lake of fire will be those not found written in the Book of Life (Rev 20:15). Though their works are judged by what is in the books (plural) to determine their degree of torment in the lake of fire,[9] they are not sent to the lake

---

[8] There are two possible reasons why the sea is mentioned and not the land and the sea. First, the sea in the Bible, and especially in Revelation, symbolizes that which is in rebellion against God. See Ps 89:9; Dan 7:2; and Rev 13:1, in which the beast rises up "out of the sea." See also the odd comment in Rev 21:1b: "And there was no more sea." Why mention that unless there is also some symbolic significance? Second, it may well be that more people are buried in the sea than on land, since it possible that more people died in Noah's flood than have died since then. A biologist friend calculated that there could have been 10 billion or more people who died in the flood.

[9] Many verses teach this. See, for example, Matt 16:27, which refers to all being judged according to their works, including unbelievers, Matt 11:21-24, which refers to degrees of torment based on how much Biblical revelation a person rejected in this life, and Gal 6:7, which, while being applied to believers in this context, is a general principle that applies to unbelievers as well: "whatever a man sows, that he will also reap." While no one gains or loses out on eternal life because of his works, all will be recompensed for their works, believers with degrees of reward on the new earth and unbelievers with degrees of torment in the lake of fire.

of fire on that basis. Their unbelief meant they didn't get in the Book of Life and that meant they would go to the lake of fire.

Whatever a Man Sows, That He Will Reap

While neither the word *hell* nor the expression *lake of fire* appears in Gal 6:7-8, these verses tell us an important truth about the torment there: what people sow in this life they will reap in the life to come (cf. Matt 16:27).

John tells us that at the Great White Throne Judgment, books, plural, will be opened, along with the singular Book of Life. The contents of that single book determine who avoids the lake of fire and who is sent there. Anyone not found in the Book of Life will be cast into the lake of fire.

So why even consult the books? And what is in these books?

The most natural conclusion is that the books contain all the deeds of all people of all time. Those books will be used to judge not the eternal destiny of those present—the Book of Life does that—but to determine what the person will reap in eternity. Not all unbelievers will have the same level of torment in the lake of fire. Each one will reap what he has sown in this life.

While this doesn't really tell us much about the lake of fire *per se*, it does reveal an important point. The torment in the lake of fire will not be uniform. It will vary from person to person depending on what that person did in this life.

Thus while the condition of everlasting life is simply believing in Jesus for it, the one who rejects Christ not only misses out on everlasting life, but he will reap what he sows. The same concept applies to the person who believes in Jesus and receives the free gift of everlasting life. While everlasting life is a gift, the quality of the believer's eternal experience is dependent on what he sows in this life.

Where Is Hell?

Hell (also called Hades, Sheol, Abbadon, and the Pit—and possibly the Abyss, Tartarus, and Gehenna) is not where Satan, fallen angels, demons, and unbelievers will spend eternity. That is called the lake of fire.

The location of hell is almost certainly the center of the current earth. Whenever people died prior to Jesus' ascension, they are said to have gone down. The only place down from the earth's surface is under the earth. The earth's core is molten, fitting the description of flames.

Of course, no human with a normal body could survive in the earth's core. The temperature is high enough to melt metal. The pressure is enormous. But the resurrection has not occurred yet, so anyone in hell does not have a regular human body. They evidently have some sort of intermediate body, but it is clearly one that can exist in the earth's core. Of course, we do not know how God modulates things there. Certainly the Lord made it so that Abraham and Lazarus were not even hot or thirsty there (cf. Luke 16:25-26). While the rich man was hot and thirsty (Luke 16:24), he was not a pool of liquid.

It seems likely that the Abyss, which is probably the same as Tartarus, is not hell *per se*, but is a part of it that is worse than the rest (cf. Luke 8:31; Rom 10:7; Rev 9:1ff.). No humans are in this place. Only a small group of fallen angels are being held there now (cf. 2 Pet 2:4). The torment there is presumably worse than that in Sheol/Hades.

The angels who intermarried with women are now being held in torment (cf. Gen 6:1-4; 2 Pet 2:4). Peter speaks of this place when he says, "God did not spare the angels who sinned, but cast them down to hell [*Tartarōsas*, that is, Tartarus] and delivered them into chains of darkness, to be reserved for judgment" (2 Pet 2:4).

The Scriptures specifically tell us that unbelievers will one day go from hell (i.e., Sheol/Hades) to a different place, the lake of fire: "The sea gave up the dead who were in it; and death and hell delivered up the dead which were in them: and they were judged every man according to their works. And death and hell were cast into the lake of fire. This is the second death" (Rev 20:13-14, KJV). Other translations (NKJV, NASB, NIV) of these verses speak of Death *and Hades*, choosing not to translate the Greek word, but instead merely bringing the Greek letters over into English. Yet the point is clear. Hell will one day give up the dead in it and deliver them to the Great White Throne Judgment. After judgment there, all who are not found written in the Book of Life (all unbelievers), will be cast into a different place, the lake of fire (Rev 20:15).

The Scriptures do not say or even hint where the lake of fire will be. Hypothetically it might end up being in the center of the new earth. However, since the new earth and indeed the new universe will be free from sin and from its remnants, it is extremely likely that the lake of fire will be in a completely different place than the new earth and the new universe. It may well be in a different universe. Or it might be in a different dimension.

Possibly it will be a planet on which land masses will be surrounded by molten lava. Wherever and whatever the lake of fire will be, it will be hot and it will be a place where eternal torment will occur.

The idea that anyone is on fire now or will be in eternity is unbiblical. There is not a single verse that even hints at that. To be in a hot place where there are flames is far different from being on fire.

Most likely Sheol/Hades and Tartarus/the Abyss will cease to exist after the Millennium and will be replaced by the lake of fire. Both unsaved humans and fallen angels, including Satan, will spend eternity there, in varying degrees of torment.

Sheol and Hades are the same place and can rightly be called *hell*.[10] Tartarus (the Abyss) is either a set apart place within Sheol/Hades, or it is a separate place altogether.

Gehenna might sometimes be a synonym for the lake of fire, and on other occasions, it might be a reference to temporal judgment. Gehenna only occurs twelve times in the New Testament. All but one, Jas 3:6, "the tongue...is set on fire by hell [Gehenna]," in the Synoptic Gospels.[11] Most of these tell us little about what Gehenna is other than it is a place of pain (i.e., Matt 5:22, 29, 30; 10:28; Luke 12:5), of fire (Matt 18:9), of unquenchable fire (Mark 9:43, 45, 47), or of judgment/condemnation (Matt 23:33). One verse speaks of being "a son of Gehenna" (Matt 23:15).

The eternal destiny of unbelievers is not hell, but the lake of fire. It would be helpful if we would change our language about hell (and about heaven). Hell is where the unsaved dead reside now, not where the unsaved dead will spend eternity.

Two Extreme and Unbiblical Views about the Nature of the Suffering in Hell

The View That Hell Is Intolerable

Most conservative Christians have a view of hell that is medieval in its origins. Their view of hell does not come from Bible passages on the subject.

---

[10] *Sheol* occurs 65 times in the Old Testament. *Hades* occurs eleven times in the New Testament, primarily in the synoptic gospels (Matt 11:23; 16:18; Luke 10:15; 16:23) and in Revelation (1:18; 6:8; 20:13, 14). See also Acts 2:27, 31; 1 Cor 15:55.

[11] For further discussion of Matt 5:22 see Bob Wilkin, "Whoever Says "You Fool!" Shall Be in Danger of Hell Fire (Matthew 5:22)," *Grace in Focus* (Sept-Oct 1997), 1, 4. For an explanation of Mark 9:43, 45, 47 see Barry Mershon, Jr., "The Warning of Stumbling Blocks" (Mark 9:42-48), *Grace in Focus* (2010), 2-3.

Henry Buis writes, "There is a noticeable increase in the crudeness of the description of hell" in the middle ages.[12] He goes on to tell of the descriptions of Venerable Bede (673-735) and of Dante Alighieri (1265-1321) in his famous poem *Inferno*. Bede speaks of flames coming out of people's ears, eyes, nostrils, and even every pore of their skin.[13]

Many conservative Christians listen to preachers who have a medieval view of hell. These preachers speak of hell as a place of *intolerable* pain, of pain *worse than* anything ever suffered here on earth.

In a booklet entitled *What Is Hell?* Morgan and Peterson write, "Being cast into hell is likened to being thrown into a fiery furnace and means *suffering unimaginable sorrow, remorse, and pain*" (emphasis added).[14] Using an adjective like *unimaginable* clearly implies that no pain on earth is as great as the pain unbelievers will experience forever. We know about the pain of kidney stones, childbirth, broken bones, migraines, back ache, and so forth. Unimaginable pain we do not know.

After supposedly spending forty nights in hell, Baxter says, "Hell was infinitely worse than anyone could think or imagine."[15] Thus not only is hell worse than any pain or suffering in this life; it is infinitely worse than any *conceivable* pain or suffering.

I must admit, however, that if God in His Word clearly said that torment in the lake of fire will be *intolerable*, then I'd accept it. If He said the torment will be worse than the worst pain ever experienced on earth, then I would believe it, even though I would not be able to reconcile that with my understanding of God as He is presented in the Bible. I would live with the confusion and know that when I go to be with the Lord, then it will make sense to me.

While this may get someone to join a church and get involved, it leaves him with two faulty views: his view of hell and his view of what one must do to avoid hell. Sadly the person remains an unbeliever and he now has a view of hell that is even worse than what the Bible presents. Both of these faulty views may be hard for him to shake. After all, if his new view of hell was instrumental in him giving his life to Christ so that he might avoid hell, he will have a hard time ever coming to the conclusion that his view of hell or of works salvation is unbiblical.

---

[12] Henry Buis, *The Doctrine of Eternal Punishment* (Philadelphia, PA: Presbyterian and Reformed Publishing Company, 1957).

[13] Ibid., 67.

[14] Christopher W. Morgan and Robert A. Peterson, *What Is Hell?* (Phillipsburg, NJ: P & R Publishing, 2010), 17-18.

[15] Mary K. Baxter, *A Divine Revelation of Hell: Time Is Running Out!* (Whitaker House: New Kensington, PA, 1993), 21.

Various Views That There Will Be No Everlasting Torment

The medieval view is so horrendous that it is no wonder that liberals have developed various ways of taking the sting out of hell. However, today it is not simply liberals who believe that unbelievers will not be tormented forever. Many conservative Evangelicals now adopt this unbiblical view.

Many cannot imagine that God would allow for eternal suffering. So they create an eternal future which makes more sense to them.

There are several different ways in which people speak of a future in which no one (or maybe just a small number of incorrigibles) suffers.

Annihilationism. Some teach that after the Great White Throne Judgment (Rev 20:11-15) all unbelieving humans will be annihilated. That is, they will cease to exist. This view is called *annihilationism, conditional immortality,* or simply *conditionalism.* This view has gained the support of some leading Evangelicals who are considered to be conservatives, not liberals. These include well known scholars such as John R. W. Stott, Philip Edgcumbe Hughes, F. F. Bruce, Clark Pinnock, John Wenham, and Graham Scroggie.

The beauty of this system is that those who long for nothingness after this life is over will eventually get their wish. They won't be forced to serve Jesus in His kingdom. Nor will they be required to suffer forever. This is a form of eternal euthanasia.

The problem with this view, as with the ones which follow, is that it does not do justice to the teachings of Scripture about eternal torment.

One solution is to suggest that the fires of the lake of fire are indeed eternal and unending, but the unbeliever is burned up in the first moments after being cast into the lake of fire (Rev 20:15). So the torment is *eternal* not in the sense the unbeliever experiences torment forever, but in the sense that the fire that caused the temporary torment is itself eternal. But that is not a normal understanding of language. It is the smoke "of their torment" that ascends forever (Rev 14:11). If their torment ever stopped, then the smoke would no longer be "of their torment." It would then simply be smoke.

A second solution is simply to ignore the teaching in the Bible and fall back on logic. Surely God would not allow anyone to suffer forever, the reasoning goes. How could the new earth and the new universe be truly glorious and righteous if there were in some corner of the universe a planet on which a huge number of people were suffering forever?

Neither of those "solutions" really solves anything. The Bible teaches that every unbeliever will be resurrected and will spend eternity in torment in the lake of fire (cf. Rev 20:10-15).

Others argue that the torment of unbelievers will be eternal, but that people have the opportunity to hear and believe the message of life after they die. Thus people die and go to a place of suffering in Sheol. While there they should become quite open to the promise of life.

But then one day they will appear before Jesus Himself at the Great White Throne Judgment. If a person has not come to faith in Jesus by that time, he certainly can, according to this unbiblical view, once he appears before Jesus. In this view the Lord Himself will share the message of life at that time, giving each person one last chance to be born again and to escape the lake of fire.

The idea here is that most people will come to faith in Jesus and escape the lake of fire. Thus while the lake of fire is indeed a place of eternal suffering, most people won't be there. Clark Pinnock argues for this view which he calls "the postmortem encounter."[16] He goes on to suggest that all who have heard of Jesus and who sought God in this life, but who do not quite come to faith in Jesus in this life, will meet Jesus, hear the message of life, and get a final opportunity to believe and be saved. In Pinnock's view, very few people will end up in the lake of fire since most people would prefer not to go there.

While this view is not universalism, it is close to it. Instead of few finding the way (Matt 7:13-14), most find the way, at least eventually.

Universalism. Still others indeed argue for universalism. In this view all of mankind enters the kingdom. No human being will have the lake of fire as his eternal abode.

In the past this view was widely rejected by conservative Evangelicals. The Bible clearly rejects this notion. However, over the past decade or two, an increasing number of Evangelicals hold this view.[17]

Once again, this view fails because it ignores or rejects the clear teaching of the Word of God.

Unconscious Torment. Another view is that the suffering will be unconscious. What is unconscious suffering? I don't know. I suppose it is

---

[16] Clark H. Pinnock, *A Wideness in God's Mercy: The Finality of Jesus Christ in a World of Religions* (Grand Rapids: Zondervan Publishing House, 1992), 168-80.

[17] Brennan Manning, an advocate of contemplative spirituality, has promoted this view for years and has won many Evangelicals to his view. Many in the contemplative spirituality movement believe in either universalism or annihilationism. In March of 2011 famed emerging church pastor, Rob Bell, pastor of a church of 10,000, released a book, *Love Wins*, in which he argued that unbelievers will not spend eternity in hell. Many others in the emerging church movement have rejected the idea of anyone being tormented forever.

pain which a person is unaware that he is experiencing. But is it really pain if a person doesn't feel it?

Back in the early nineties I remember discussing this issue with some pastor friends who had graduated from Dallas Theological Seminary with me in the early eighties. These men were both pastoring large Bible churches. They both shocked me by saying that they believed that the torment in hell, though eternal, will be unconscious.

David C. Pack, formerly a minister in Herbert W. Armstrong's Worldwide Church of God, is the founder and head of a new cult, the Restored Church of God.[18] In an article in *The Real Truth* (a takeoff of Armstrong's *The Plain Truth*) called "Does Hell Exist?" Pack selects a few passages from Psalms (Pss 6:5; 115:17) and Ecclesiastes (Eccl 3:19-20) to suggest that the dead experience nothing at all after death.[19]

Whatever those verses mean, they cannot and do not contradict the clear words of the Lord Jesus in Luke 16:19-31. Kidner's comments on Ps 6:5 are helpful. He says that David's poetic remarks about Sheol

> highlight the tragedy of death as that which silences a man's worship (as here [Ps 6:5]; cf. 30:9; 88:10f.; 115:17; Is. 38:18f.), shatters his plans (146:4), cuts him off from God and man (88:5; Ec. 2:16) and makes an end of him (39:13). These are cries from the heart, that life is all too short...They are not denials of God's sovereignty beyond the grave...[20]

Spiritual and Mental, But Not Physical, Torment. One final view is that the torment is spiritual but not physical. This view is a bit unique. In a book entitled *Sense and Nonsense about Heaven and Hell*, Boa and Bowman say: "We embrace the view that there will be endless torment in Hell, but it will be spiritual rather than physical in nature."[21] Here is how they define *spiritual torment*: "It will consist of spiritual or mental anguish, perhaps in the form of regret, an abiding sense of loss, and

---

[18] Actually the Worldwide Church of God underwent a dramatic change in soteriology, the doctrine of salvation. Those who took over after Armstrong died began teaching justification by faith alone, apart from works. However, Pack did not stay with the Worldwide Church of God and its new leadership. Instead, he started another works-salvation cult, albeit one that does not believe in conscious torment in hell.

[19] See http://www.realtruth.org/articles/070503-005-dhe.html. Accessed June 3, 2010.

[20] Derek Kidner, *Psalms 1-72*, Tyndale Old Testament Commentaries (Downers Grove, IL: Inter-Varsity Press, 1973), 61-62.

[21] Kenneth D. Boa and Robert M. Bowman, Jr., *Sense and Nonsense about Heaven and Hell* (Grand Rapids: Zondervan, 2007), 119.

the devastation of permanent exile from God, the world, and all that is good, beautiful, whole, and meaningful."[22] Thus in their view there will be eternal suffering that is conscious, but it will not be physical.

None of these views is supported by Scripture.[23]

In the first place, the Bible never compares pains in this life with pains the lost will experience in the life to come. Never. Thus it is impossible and indeed adding to Scripture to say that the pains people will suffer in hell are worse than the pains they suffered in this life. One might *speculate* that to be true, but one wonders what evidence that might be cited which could even infer such a view.

In the second place, the Bible calls the suffering that will be experienced *eternal torment*. The rich man of Luke 16 is clearly conscious of the torment he is suffering in Sheol. And Sheol is a precursor to the lake of fire. Eternal torment is conscious suffering. Thus, the second view is not Biblical either.

The truth lies somewhere in between. Hell will be a bad place in which to spend eternity. There will be no escape from the torment experienced there. However, and I am speculating here, the torment might well be less than some of the pains a person has experienced in this life. And, as we shall see, the Bible does not say whether the torment is steady or fluctuating in nature. It is conceivable that on a 1 to 10 scale a person might experience suffering all along that scale during the course of a single day. Of course, all this is speculation too. But these are Biblically-possible options.

Other Misconceptions about Hell

When a reader of the Bible wrongly assumes that a given expression always refers to the same thing, he is guilty of what is called *illegitimate identity transfer*. That is where someone transfers the meaning of an expression to another context in which that meaning does not fit.

---

[22] Ibid., 115.

[23] I would say that the view of Boa and Bowman is closest to the truth. Surely there will be plenty of regret, mental anguish, and a profound sense of loss. And we must not underestimate that pain. It will be torment. But will there not also be headaches, thirst, fatigue, overheating, muscle and joint pain, etc.? Why would people in the lake of fire have a complete elimination of physical pain when in this life they experienced physical pain daily? What is the point of resurrecting them (Rev 20:12-13) if they will not experience any torment in their raised bodies?

**Misconception: Weeping and Gnashing
of Teeth Always Refers to Hell**

A prime example of illegitimate totality transfer concerns this expression. Clearly it is sometimes used to refer to what unbelievers will be doing in the lake of fire (cf. Matt 13:42, 50; Luke 13:28).

However, this expression is not some formal expression that is only used of the suffering in the lake of fire. It is also used to refer to suffering that will be experienced by unfaithful believers at the Judgment Seat of Christ.

The expression only occurs seven times in the Bible, all in the Synoptic Gospels: Matt 8:12; 13:42, 50; 22:13; 24:51; 25:30; and Luke 13:28. In one of them, Matt 8:12, it is "the sons of the kingdom" who will be weeping and gnashing their teeth because they are "cast out into outer darkness." However, the only other use of the expression *the sons of the kingdom* in Matthew is definitely a reference to *regenerate people*. In the Parable of the Wheat and the Tares, "the good seeds are the sons of the kingdom, but the tares are the sons of the wicked one" (Matt 13:38).

Two of the other six uses of *weeping and gnashing of teeth* occur in the other two "outer darkness" passages. Since the outer darkness refers to missing out on ruling with Christ and not to hell (see discussion below), at least three of the seven uses of this expression refer to the grief some *believers* will experience at the Judgment Seat of Christ.

Matthew 24:51 also refers to the grief some believers will experience at our judgment. Thus, only three of the seven uses of this expression refer to the grief of those in hell (Matt 13:42, 50; Luke 13:28). Far from *always* referring to grief in hell, it does so less than half the time.

Misconception: Fire Typically Refers to Hell

Clearly fire is associated both with hell and with the lake of fire. However, the word *fire* actually most often in Scripture refers either to literal fire in this life or figuratively to God's fiery temporal judgment (of either unbelievers or believers).[24]

**Misconception: Destruction and
Perishing Typically Refer to Hell**

The expression *perishing* is so important that it made our top ten. See Chapter 4.

---

[24] See Robert N. Wilkin, *Confident in Christ* (Irving, TX: Grace Evangelical Society, 1999), 154-55.

Most people think that *perishing* in the Bible always refers to eternal condemnation. In reality, it does so only occasionally (cf. John 3:16). For example, the death of all animals and humans except for those in the ark is called *perishing* by Peter (2 Pet 3:6).

Misconception: The Outer Darkness Refers to Hell

This expression only occurs three times in the Bible and all in one book, Matthew. A comparison of the three uses shows that this expression never actually refers to the lake of fire or eternal condemnation.

In all three of its uses the Lord is talking about believers who will be excluded from the joy of ruling with Him in the life to come.[25]

Misconception: The Suffering in the Lake of Fire Will Be Worse Suffering Than Any Torment on Earth

Though we touched on this issue above, it deserves additional attention because of the seriousness of this charge. If it is true, then we surely should warn people. If it is not true, then we surely should not mislead people in this way.

Pastor, author, and theologian John Piper writes:

> I know of no one who has overstated the terror of Hell...We are meant to tremble and feel dread. We are meant to recoil from the reality. Not by denying it, but by fleeing from it into the arms of Jesus, who died to save us from it.[26]

Internationally known British evangelist John Blanchard similarly writes:

> "If all the pains, sorrows, miseries and calamities that have been inflicted upon the sons of men...should meet together and centre in one man they would not so much as amount to one of the least of the pains of hell." Those words by Thomas Brooks remain as true today as when they were originally written, nearly 400 years ago.[27]

Where is the Biblical support for this notion?

---

[25] See, for example, Michael Huber, "The 'Outer Darkness' in Matthew and Its Relationship to Grace," *Journal of the Grace Evangelical Society* (Autumn 1992): 11-25.

[26] John Piper. Quoted by Bill Wiese, *23 Minutes in Hell* (Lake Mary, FL: Charisma House, 2006), 3.

[27] John Blanchard, *Whatever Happened to Hell?* (Durham, England: Evangelical Press, 1993), 143.

It is one thing to say that the lake of fire will be the experience of torment forever. It is another to identify that torment in ways the Bible does not.

I fear adding to God's Word. God doesn't want us to represent our thoughts as what He says.

The article on *hell* in *The New International Dictionary of New Testament Theology* makes this important observation: "In contrast with later Christian writings and ideas, the torments of hell are not described in the New Testament."[28]

Let me repeat that: "In contrast with later Christian writings and ideas, the torments of hell are not described in the New Testament." While I critically evaluate all comments and reject much of what I read, I find, based on my study of Scripture, that this comment is right on the money. The closest we get to a description of the torments is the rich man who indicates he is thirsty and in torment in the fiery environment (Luke 16:19-31). But that is no description of his torments. That is just an acknowledgement that he is in torment. We have no indication if he experiences headaches, depression, guilt, muscle ache, joint pain, back pain, neck pain, itching, nausea, cramping, fatigue, and so on. We have no comparison between the pain he is suffering and say childbirth or dealing with a kidney stone or any other pain (other than being thirsty, and he doesn't tell us the level of his thirst or whether this is constant or variable).

In light of what happened in the Holocaust, in Stalin's Russia, in Mao's China, in Pol Pot's Cambodia, in Idi Amin's Nigeria, in all the wars ever fought, and all the terrible torturing that has been done, I find it unbelievable that the torments in hell equal or even surpass the torments some have had to endure for a time in this life. If that is the case, we certainly are not told that anywhere in the Bible. Indeed, as we shall soon see, the Lord actually tells us that the torment in the lake of fire will be tolerable.

In my opinion when an unbeliever who is undergoing torture dies, his experience immediately improves. He goes from an unbearable level of torment at the hands of a torturer, to a bearable level of torment in Hades.

The Lord made a remarkable statement to the residents of the Jewish cities of Chorazin and Bethsaida. Those people rejected the preaching of the Lord Jesus Christ. Jesus' remark to them has implications

---

[28] H. Bietenhard, *The New International Dictionary of New Testament Theology*, ed. by Colin Brown (Grand Rapids: Zondervan Publishing House, 1975), Vol 2, S.v., "Hell," 209.

regarding eternal torment in the lake of fire: "It will be more tolerable [*anektoteros*, the comparative of *anektos*] for Tyre and Sidon in the day of judgment than for you" (Matt 11:22). He then turned right around and addressed the Jewish citizens of Capernaum who also rejected Him: "It shall be more tolerable [*anektoteros* again] for the land of Sodom in the day of judgment than for you" (Matt 11:24). Tyre, Sidon, and Sodom were Gentile cities, and notoriously sinful ones as well. Yet the Lord says that their experience *in the day of judgment* would be *more tolerable* than it would be for the unbelieving Jews in Israel. The reason is because the Jews rejected more direct revelation from God and more proofs of that revelation than did the Gentiles mentioned.

The word which is translated *more tolerable* comes from a word which means "bearable, endurable" in its basic form (BDAG, p. 76D). This word only occurs six times in the New Testament and all in this very context (Matt 10:15; 11:22, 24; Mark 6:11; Luke 10:12, 14). It is clear that the contrast the Lord makes is between *bearable* and *more bearable* torment or between *endurable* and *more endurable* torment.

Why would the Lord compare *tolerable* and *more tolerable* if the torment in the lake of fire will be *intolerable*? That makes no sense out of His words.

The expression *the day of judgment* in this context concerns the Great White Throne Judgment (Rev 20:11-15). But the Lord is not merely saying that for one day in all of eternity the experience of those Gentiles would be more tolerable than that of these Jews. He was using *the day of judgment* as the starting point for their eternal experience. He meant that forever, starting with the Great White Throne Judgment, the Gentile unbelievers of Tyre and Sidon and Sodom and Gomorrah would have a more tolerable experience in the lake of fire than would the Jewish unbelievers of Chorazin, Bethsaida, Capernaum, or any city in Israel that rejected the miracle-attested preaching of Jesus and His disciples.

The Lord taught both degrees of joy in the kingdom and degrees of suffering in the lake of fire.

God is not going to give unbelievers an eternal experience that is unbearable. He could. He could set it up so people had level 10 suffering 24/7/365, with no breaks and no escape. But He will not do that. Such suffering could not be described as *tolerable* or *more tolerable*.

If that were the case, then He would have said, "It shall be not be tolerable for the land of Sodom in the day of judgment just as it shall not be tolerable for you."

It should surprise us which unbelievers get the more tolerable torment. Those of Sodom and Gomorrah and Tyre and Sidon were notorious sinners. Yet their torment will be more tolerable than law abiding, legalistic, self-righteous Jews of the first century who rejected the Messiah when they saw and heard Him directly. Degree of torment will be based in great part on how much revelation from God a person rejected.

Misconception: Hell Is a Vital Evangelistic Concept

Up until the middle of the twentieth century the preaching of hell and hell fire was a regular part of evangelistic meetings and personal evangelism. This can be traced back to the eighteenth century preaching of Jonathan Edwards who, as Davidson points out, often preached about hell in evangelistic messages "with the aim of shocking the complacently unrepentant."[29] For Edwards "hell enhances the meaning and urgency of salvation from that doom in Christ."[30]

In the last sixty years many have rejected this thinking as we will discuss in the next section. However, a more basic question should be asked. *Did the Apostle John use hell in his evangelistic efforts in the Fourth Gospel?*

The Gospel of John is the only book in Scripture written to unbelievers and it is only evangelistic book (John 20:30-31). Yet did you know that the words *hell* (or Hades or Tartarus or Gehenna) and *the lake of fire* were not used at all in John's Gospel? Not once do we find the Lord Jesus warning people that unless they believe in Him they will be tormented forever in hell and the lake of fire. If hell and the lake of fire were vital evangelistic concepts, they would be found in the only evangelistic book in Scripture.[31]

---

[29] Bruce W. Davidson, "Hell as an Essential Element in the Theology of Jonathan Edwards," *Journal of the Evangelical Theological Society* (December 2011): 813.

[30] Ibid., 822.

[31] Of course, the Lord did speak about hell (Matt 11:23; 16:18; Luke 10:15; 16:23) and Gehenna (Matt 5:22, 29, 30; 10:28; 18:9; 23:15, 33; Mark 9:43, 45, 47; Luke 12:5) as reported in the Synoptic Gospels. And some of these references do appear to be aimed at moving those who did not believe in Jesus to reconsider whether He really is the Messiah or not. However, even in the Synoptics it is not possible to argue that the preaching of hell was a *vital* evangelistic doctrine. At best one might say that the Lord sometimes used it pre-evangelistically.

It should be noted that teaching about hell is almost nonexistent in the epistles as well. Hell (Hades) is only found once in all of the epistles, and there it is typically translated as *grave*, not hell (1 Cor 15:55).[32]

In the Book of Acts hell is found only twice, both times referring to the fact that God the Father did not leave the Lord Jesus in Hades, but raised Him from the dead (Acts 2:27, 31).

While a proper understanding of hell and the lake of fire might well cause unbelievers to cry out to God for insight into what they must do to escape that destiny, that is far from saying that hell is something we must preach in order to be clear about the message of life. John's Gospel (and the New Testament epistles) explodes that myth.[33]

Practical Concerns about Hell

Even if we can't figure out what practical difference there is in our lives, it always makes a difference that we understand and believe what God says (2 Tim 3:16-17). It is never good for us to misunderstand and misapply the Word of God.

If our view of hell sees *more torment* than will actually exist, then this can actually hinder our efforts at evangelism. If an unbeliever is presented a view of hell that is far worse than the Bible portrays, he may be repelled from Christianity entirely. Many people under forty today are turned off by the medieval view of hell. They figure that nothing could be worse than what Hitler or Stalin or Mao did. They cannot conceive of God as doing something to people that is more painful that what these men did. Thus they reject hell, and sometimes with it heaven, the kingdom, life after death, and Christianity.

Certainly 50 to 100 years ago preaching hell as intolerable did draw many people toward Christianity. Of course, even then it repelled many more, possibly far more than it drew. But today the intolerable view of hell is drawing fewer and fewer people and it is repelling more and more. Possibly that is why we hear such little teaching on hell today.

A secondary problem is that this teaching of hell is normally not coupled with the message of justification by faith alone. Instead, it is routinely joined with a call to turn from one's sins, give one's life to Christ, follow Him, and serve Him. The message of an intolerable hell

---

[32] There is also one use of Gehenna in the epistles, Jas 3:6 (see p. 93).

[33] There are also four references to Hades in the Book of Revelation. All four refer to where the unbelieving dead are currently being held (Rev 1:18; 6:8 [figurative use]; 20:13, 14).

fits well within works salvation, but not so well with justification by faith alone.

What if our view of hell is *too lenient*? If a person is taught the view of annihilationism or no conscious torment, he would certainly be less concerned about his eternal destiny and the possibility that he may be wrong than he would be if he had a Biblical view of hell and the lake of fire. There are many people who are not too bothered by an eternal loss of consciousness or ceasing to exist.

And if the person who believes in no eternal suffering is born again, this view might make him much less concerned about the fate of unbelievers.

Conclusion

When an English reader of the Bible sees the word *hell*, he should realize it sometimes refers to a place in which both unsaved and saved dead were prior to Jesus' ascension, sometimes to where the unsaved dead currently are, and sometimes to where a notorious group of fallen angels are. But it never is used to refer to the future location of all fallen angels and all unsaved humans, which is instead the lake of fire.

What all these locations have in common, other than the saved part of Sheol prior to Jesus' ascension, is that those there are experiencing conscious torment that will go on forever.

The exact nature and level of the current torment in hell and the future torment in the lake of fire are unknown. There are clues in Scripture that it is and will be tolerable for all. It certainly is and will be more tolerable for some than for others.

Contrary to popular thought, we really have little information in the Bible about what hell is like or what the lake of fire will be like. Much of the current thinking about hell is based not on the Bible, but on speculation that has been passed down for centuries.

It is time that we move back to Scripture. The lake of fire will indeed be, as my friend pointed out in a recent Bible study, a bad place. It will be a place of eternal conscious torment. But that doesn't mean that the torment there will be unbearable or that it will be worse than any pains experienced in this life. We don't even know for sure if pain there will be steadily at one level, or whether there might be fluctuations throughout the day concerning the level of the pain.

If we are to have a Biblical view of the lake of fire, then we must avoid two popular yet unbiblical extremes: a place in which the torment is unbearable and where pain exceeds the most insidious torture of this world, on the one hand, and a pain-free place with no conscious suffering at all, on the other. The truth is clearly in between.

Chapter 7
Repentance

Introduction

Go to a church at random on Sunday morning and ask ten people what a person must do to be born again. Eight of them will say that you must repent of your sins. They may attach repentance to faith in Jesus, or to inviting Him into your life, or to receiving Him as your Lord and Savior, or to committing your life to Him. But well over half of all churchgoers will say that you must repent of your sins to be saved.

Ask those same people what it means to repent of your sins and most will say that it means that you must turn from your sins. Jesus saves us *from our sins*, they will say, not *in our sins*.

Some of these people, those from a Reformed background, will likely point out that repentance is not a human work. They will say it is a work of God in our lives. But most of these people haven't given much thought to whether turning from sins is a work or not. They just know that you must repent in order to be born again.

My personal experience was that I was taught and believed that one must repent of all his sins and follow Christ until the time came when God gave him his chance to give his life to Christ and be born again. However, that never gave me assurance of my eternal destiny. Was I *sincere enough*? Did I turn from *all* my sins? Was I following Christ *faithfully enough*? Was that day when I felt something *really* my chance? Did I *really* give my life to Christ?

Then in my senior year in college I was challenged. A friend, John Carlson, asked me if I was sure my view of the gospel was correct. He talked me into going to a Campus Crusade meeting. That led me to meeting with staff member Warren Wilke. He kept hammering away at Eph 2:8-9, which, of course, does not mention repentance. Warren stressed that if we simply believe in Jesus, then by God's grace we are saved once and forever and that this salvation was not of works lest anyone should boast.

Thus when I came to faith, I thought that the sole condition of eternal salvation was faith in Christ, not faith and repentance. However, I soon found that was not the normal position in Campus Crusade (or later at Dallas Theological Seminary, either).

What Is Repentance?

For the person who believes in justification by faith alone, this question is, in a sense, *the* question. If repentance in the New Testament, for example, is turning from sins, then it cannot be a condition for justification before God, since the sole condition of that justification is faith in Christ and turning from sins is not the same as believing in Jesus. (An atheist can turn from his sins. So can a person from any religion or philosophy.)

When I wrote my doctoral dissertation on the subject of repentance, I had to deal with this question. I came at it backwards, however. Instead of looking to see what the words *metanoeō* and *metanoia* mean in the New Testament, I assumed that they meant *a change of mind* and then I set about to prove it.

I held to what is called the change-of-mind view because it was the only view that I was aware of, or that I could conceive of, that would both affirm justification by faith alone and also handle texts that seemed to clearly show that repentance is a condition of eternal life. That I did not think carefully enough about other options led me to miss the clear teaching of Scripture.

Both in the Old Testament and in the New Testament repentance is turning from sins. It is never a change of mind about oneself (recognizing one is a sinner) or a change of mind about Christ (recognizing He alone is the Savior).

I cannot in a short book go through every passage proving my point. However, below I cover the eleven passages which are most often cited as teaching that repentance is a condition of everlasting life. None of them actually do teach that repentance is a condition of spending eternity with the Lord.

However, in this portion of this chapter my goal is simply to show what Biblical repentance is. For that let's turn to Jesus' teaching about the repentance of the Ninevites under the preaching of Jonah. Jesus used Old Testament repentance to teach what New Testament repentance is.

Jesus said, "'The men of Nineveh will rise up in the judgment with this generation and condemn it, because *they repented at the preaching of Jonah*; and indeed a greater than Jonah is here'" (Matt 12:41, emphasis added). The Lord is referring to Jonah 3:5. There we read, "So the people of Nineveh believed God, proclaimed a fast, and put on sackcloth, from the greatest to the least of them." Verse 10 concludes the chapter saying, "Then God saw their works, *that they turned from their evil way*; and God relented from the disaster that He had said He would bring upon them, and He did not do it."

Clearly the Ninevites repented when *they turned from their evil way*. Their repentance was not a change of mind about themselves and God. They believed God when through Jonah He said, "Yet forty days, and Nineveh shall be overthrown!" (Jonah 3:4).

What then was the repentance that Jesus was rebuking that generation of Jews for not doing? They, too, were not turning from their sins.

That same understanding fits every single New Testament use. During the Tribulation the unbelieving world "[will] not repent of the works of their hands, that they should not worship demons, and idols... And they did not repent of their murders or their sorceries or their sexual immorality or their thefts" (Rev 9:20-21; see also Rev 16:9, 11).

Repentance is turning from one's sins in order to escape temporal judgment. The issue in repentance is not who is born again and who is not. The issue is who is walking in open rebellion against God and who is not. The consequence of turning from one's sins is not the gaining of eternal life, but the improvement of and extension of one's life here on earth, whether for the believer or unbeliever.

Repentance and Regeneration in the Old Testament

The Old Testament never links repentance and salvation from eternal condemnation. Of course, the Old Testament rarely if ever even uses the term *salvation* to refer to the new birth, so the fact that the Old Testament doesn't link repentance and regeneration is no surprise.

Ezekiel 18 is a key chapter devoted to the Old Testament concept of repentance. There the prophet, speaking for God, says that "if a wicked man turns from all his sins which he has committed, keeps all My statutes, and does what is lawful and right, he shall surely live; he shall not die" (Ezek 18:21). However, if the wicked man does not turn from his wicked ways, then he will die. Physical life and physical death are in view. Ezekiel 18 ends with these powerful words that could be said at any twelve-step meeting: "'For I have no pleasure in the death of one who dies,' says the Lord GOD. 'Therefore turn and live!'" (Ezek 18:32).

In the Old Testament repentance is the medicine the nation of Israel needed in order to escape ongoing pain and suffering due to her sins. The Pentateuch, as well as Judges, 1-2 Samuel, 1-2 Kings, and 1-2 Chronicles, teaches this over and over again.

Since I've written in more detail elsewhere on repentance in the Old Testament, I urge the interested reader to check out my online journal articles on the subject.[1] We now turn to see what the New Testament says about the linkage between repentance and regeneration.

Repentance and Regeneration in the New Testament

The New Testament never conditions regeneration upon repentance. I realize that statement is in direct opposition to what most church people believe. However, we should not base our view of what God says on what the majority says. We should base it on our own personal study of the Word of God. We are each accountable to God for our own understanding of His Word. We are not allowed to pass that responsibility on to some church or denomination or pastor or priest. God holds each of us accountable for our own study of the Bible.

How do I know that the New Testament never indicates that repentance is a condition of regeneration? There are two ways I know this with certainty.

First, there are many crystal clear passages in the Gospel of John in which the Lord Jesus Christ, the authority on regeneration, says that the sole condition of the new birth/everlasting life is believing in Him (e.g., John 3:14-18; 4:1-14; 5:24; 6:35-40, 47; 11:25-27; 20:30-31). For example, Jesus said, "He who believes in Me has everlasting life" (John 6:47).

You may think, yes, but doesn't the Lord somewhere in John say that unless you repent you will perish? Actually, no. Those are words of Jesus found in Luke 13:3, 5. That is explained below (and in Chapter 4). But in John's Gospel, the words *repent* (*metanoeō*) and *repentance* (*metanoia*) do not occur even once. That is quite telling.

Here is a syllogism that makes the point that repentance is not a condition of regeneration:

Major premise: The Gospel of John tells us what we must do to be born again (John 20:30-31).

---

[1] Go to www.faithalone.org and click on Journals & Newsletters. Then go down and select *Our Semi-annual Journal*. Now go down to the search box and type in *repentance*. You will find one article by me from 1998 and six articles from 1988 through 1991. The one on repentance in the Old Testament is from Spring 1989 and was part two in a six-part series.

Minor premise: The Gospel of John never once mentions repentance.

Conclusion: The Gospel of John teaches that repentance is not a condition of the new birth.

Some might say that is an argument from silence. I agree with Zane Hodges who famously said that this is an argument *about silence*.[2]

Imagine a book about the leading generals of the Allied forces in WWII. Let's say it never mentioned General George Patton. If so, it would be clear that the author did not consider Patton to have been one of the leading generals in the Second World War. No other conclusion would be possible. That would be a legitimate argument about silence.

Similarly, the fact that John knew about repentance (witness his twelve uses of the term in the Book of Revelation) and likely was a disciple of John the Baptist—who preached repentance—before he became a disciple of Jesus (cf. John 1:35-42), yet didn't even mention repentance in his evangelistic book, is proof he did not consider it to be a condition of everlasting life.

Second, there is not a single verse anywhere in the New Testament that says that one who repents has everlasting life or even that one must repent in order to have life everlasting. Not one.

From 1983 to 1985 I wrote my doctoral dissertation on this very subject. The title of my dissertation is "Repentance as a Condition for Salvation in the New Testament." In my dissertation I argued—wrongly, I now realize—that there are eleven passages that indicate that repentance is a condition of eternal life. I later came to see that none of those actually say that repentance is a condition of the new birth.

Let's examine those eleven passages now.

Eleven New Testament Passages That Only Seem to Teach That Repentance Is a Condition for the New Birth

Matthew 3:2. John the Baptist was famous for proclaiming, "Repent, for the kingdom of heaven is at hand!" I once read that as though he were saying, *repent so that you can be born again.*

That is obviously not what he said or meant. The fact that the King of the coming kingdom was on the scene meant that the nation should repent in order for Him to establish His earthly reign. The issue here

---

[2] See Zane C. Hodges, "Arguments from Silence, And All of That: Repentance Reconsidered," *Grace in Focus* (May-June 1998): 1, 4.

is not individual regeneration. The issue is national deliverance from Gentile bondage. In order for the kingdom to come to that generation of Jews, the nation had to repent at the preaching of John and the Messiah, the Lord Jesus Christ.

John the Baptist did not say that the kingdom would have come if the nation had merely repented. He said that the nation should repent since the kingdom of God was at hand. In reality John also called for faith in the Messiah as a second condition for the kingdom to come for that generation (cf. John 1:7; Acts 19:4). In order for the Lord Jesus to give the kingdom to that first century generation of Jews, the nation had to both repent of her sins and believe in Him. In fact, those two conditions must still be met. During the Tribulation, they will be. At the end of the Tribulation every surviving Jew on earth will have repented and believed in the Lord Jesus (cf. Rom 11:26).

Matthew 4:17. Jesus began His ministry with exactly the same message, "Repent, for the kingdom of heaven is at hand." He too called for national repentance, and, of course, faith, in order for the kingdom to come (e.g., Matt 23:37).

Mark 1:14-15. Mark says that "Jesus came to Galilee, preaching the gospel of the kingdom of God, and saying, 'The time is fulfilled, and the kingdom of God is at hand. Repent, and believe in the gospel.'"

At first blush it might appear that the Lord is saying that to be born again one must both repent and believe in Him. However, a careful examination shows that is not at all what He means.

First, notice that He was preaching "the gospel of the kingdom of God." *The gospel of the kingdom* occurs only in the Synoptic Gospels and always refers to the good news that the kingdom has drawn near. That is why it is called "the gospel [or good news] of the kingdom of God."

Second, the Lord was not speaking about the new birth here. This text is nothing like John 3:16, for example. In light of the good news of the kingdom being offered to that generation, they were being called to repentance and faith *so that the kingdom might come*, not so that individual Jews might be born again. Jesus was offering that generation the kingdom.

Third, Jesus does not say, "repent, and believe *in Me*." Instead, He says, "repent, and believe *in the gospel.*" While many automatically assume that *gospel* means the saving message, that is not the case here or in any New Testament uses of the expression *the gospel of the kingdom*. Here the words *the gospel* in verse 15 refer to "the gospel of the kingdom" in verse 14. (See Chapter 9 for more details about the expression *the gospel*.)

Thus Jesus is calling for national repentance and national faith that the kingdom is at hand (which would, of course, include the fact that Jesus is the King/Messiah).

Of course, if an individual Jew did believe "the gospel of the kingdom," then he should believe as well that Jesus is the Messiah who guarantees eternal life to all who simply believe in Him (e.g., John 11:25-27). Of course a person might believe the gospel of the kingdom and not yet have understood the Old Testament teaching on justification by faith alone (e.g., Gen 15:6) or have heard the Lord Jesus say that all who believe in Him have everlasting life. However, once a person who believed that Jesus was the King of Israel, the Messiah, heard Him say that all who believe in Him have everlasting life (e.g., John 5:24), he certainly should believe Him, even if he had up to that point believed in the works salvation taught by the rabbis of the day.

It should have been obvious to me when I was working on my dissertation that the message, "Repent, and believe in the gospel," is not the message of life. That I tried to make it into that (I argued Jesus meant, "Change your mind; that is, believe the gospel") shows that I was not allowing the Scriptures to speak, but was instead imposing my Free Grace theology on the text. While Free Grace theology is true, not every text is evangelistic. Not every text explains what one must do to be born again.

Luke 13:3-5. What did Jesus mean when He said, "Unless you repent you will all likewise perish"? This text is discussed in greater detail in Chapter 4. As a recap, the context is clear that physical death is in view, both with the people "whose blood Pilate had mingled with their sacrifices" (Luke 13:1) and with the eighteen people "on whom the tower in Siloam fell" (Luke 13:4). They died *physically*. Whether they were born again is not discussed. Some might have been. All might have been. None might have been. That isn't the point. The point is that they all died physically.

Jesus was saying that unless that generation of Jews repented, they would all likewise perish, that is, die, at the hands of Rome. Of course, that is what happened in the Jewish War of AD 66-70 in which Jerusalem was destroyed and over a million Jews were killed.

Remember Nineveh? Though God didn't tell Jonah to preach repentance, the people did repent and were spared. God could have said, "Repent or you will all perish." They did repent, so they did not perish.

The Jews of the first century did not repent; hence, they perished in the Jewish War.

Luke 16:19-31. The Lord told a story about a rich man and a poor man who died. The rich man went to torment in Hades, whereas the poor man went to the good part of Hades where Abraham was.

The Lord reports a dialogue between the rich man and Abraham. In the course of the discussion the rich man asks Abraham to send Lazarus back from the dead to visit his brothers. Abraham says, "They have Moses and the prophets; let them hear them." Then the rich man responds, "No, father Abraham; but if one goes to them from the dead, they will repent."

The rich man did not say, "If one goes to them from the dead, *they will believe.*" He spoke of repentance. So what does that tell us?

Here I was led astray by the comments of an unregenerate man who is in Hades. That the man was an unbeliever should have given me pause before I interpreted him to be proclaiming the Free Grace message.

The story of the rich man and Lazarus is probably not a parable. There is not a single parable in which the Lord gives an actual name of a person. Here we have the actual name of one of the characters, Lazarus.

The rich man looks across a great gulf and sees Lazarus right next to Abraham. What ensues is a fascinating conversation between the rich man and Abraham.

What is clear is that Abraham grasps the Free Grace message. It is not clear that the rich man does.

The rich man wants Abraham to send someone back from the dead so that his brothers might repent. The rich man seems to think that the way to avoid his tormented fate is to repent. Yet Abraham keeps steering the rich man back to the truth that the issue is belief in Jesus, or persuasion about Him, not repentance: "They have Moses and the prophets; *let them hear them*...If they do not *hear Moses and the prophets*, neither will they *be persuaded* though one rise from the dead" (vv 29, 31, emphasis added). While Abraham does not explicitly say the name of Jesus, it is clear that Abraham means that the issue is what Moses and the prophets wrote about the Messiah, the Lord Jesus (cf. John 1:45).

The rich man says, "No, father Abraham; but if one goes to them from the dead, they will repent" (v 30). His statement does not follow from what Abraham had said.

It is possible that the rich man believes that if his brothers repented, then they would also come to faith in Jesus. But if so, why didn't he say that? It is more likely that the rich man still doesn't understand the saving message. Abraham is moving him to grasp the real reason why he is in torment.

Of course, even if the rich man got it, he would remain in torment. As the Lord Jesus taught, *"whoever lives* and believes in Me shall never die"* (John 11:26, emphasis added). Once a person dies, he is unable to escape his fate even if he eventually comes to believe the message of life (cf. Heb 9:27).

The Lord Jesus was not teaching in Luke 16:30 that repentance is a condition of eternal life.

Luke 24:47. This is Luke's version of the Great Commission. The Lord says, "Thus it is written, and thus it was necessary for the Christ to suffer and to rise from the dead the third day, *and that repentance and remission of sins should be preached in His name* to all nations, beginning at Jerusalem" (Luke 24:47, emphasis added). As should be obvious to anyone reading the Great Commission in Matthew (Matt 28:18-20), the Great Commission was primarily a charge to make disciples, not to evangelize.

If the Lucan account of the Great Commission is viewed narrowly as evangelistic, then one will likely conclude that repentance is a condition for everlasting life. However, that is not what the Lord says, nor is it what He means.

What the repentant person gets, according to the Lord in Luke 24:47, is not everlasting life, but "remission of sins." While many people equate these two, they are not at all the same. For example, as 1 John 1:9 shows, regenerate people need ongoing forgiveness.

If we compare this passage with Acts 2:38, discussed next, then there is reason to believe that the Lord wanted the disciples, "beginning at Jerusalem" (Luke 24:47), to call Jews and Gentiles to repent that they might have fellowship forgiveness.

This is part of a discipleship message, not an evangelistic one. This verse in no way contradicts John 3:16. They are not talking about the same subjects.

Acts 2:38. "Then Peter said to them, 'Repent, and let every one of you be baptized in the name of Jesus Christ for the remission of sins; and you shall receive the gift of the Holy Spirit.'" In Peter's great sermon on the Day of Pentecost, he preached Jesus. He preached that the Lord Jesus is Israel's long-awaited Messiah. But he responded to the question, "What shall we do?" (Acts 2:37) with a call to repent and be baptized. Why did Peter say that? Why didn't he call his audience to believe in the Lord Jesus Christ (cf. Acts 16:31)?

After giving the compelling evidence of Jesus' bodily resurrection, of which Peter and his brethren were eyewitnesses (Acts 2:32), Peter then said, "Let all the house of Israel know assuredly that God has made this Jesus, whom you crucified, both Lord and Christ" (Acts 2:36).

At this point Luke says, "Now when they heard this, they were cut to the heart, and said to Peter and the rest of the apostles, 'Men and brethren, what shall we do?'" That is far from a hostile response. That is not an unbelieving response. They were grieved at what they had done. The reason for their grief is obvious: they realized they indeed had a part in killing *the Messiah*. They had believed what Peter said. That is clear.

While Luke's report of Peter's sermon does not mention everlasting life, it is certainly possible that in what surely was a lengthy sermon Peter mentioned the promise of life. In any case, Peter's audience would have been very familiar with Jesus' claim not only to be the Messiah, but also to give eternal life to all who believe in Him (cf. John 20:31). Thus once they believed what Peter said, they also believed the promise of life and they knew they had eternal life. What they did not know was how they could escape the guilt of having killed the Messiah.

Note they do not ask what the Philippian jailer asked, "What must I do *to be saved*?" (emphasis added). Their concern is a fellowship concern, not an eternal life concern. They ask, "What shall we do?" (v 27). The implied conclusion to their question is, "What shall we do *to escape the guilt of having killed the Messiah*?"

The answer is that they should do two things, repent and be baptized. As in Luke 24:47, repentance is linked with the forgiveness of sins. Baptism is linked with the reception of the Holy Spirit.

Wait a minute, some will say. If they had not yet received the Spirit, then they were not yet regenerate.

A person might think that, but he would be wrong as the Book of Acts makes clear. In Acts 8, for example, Philip leads a group of Samaritans to faith in Christ. They are born again and baptized. Only later did Peter and John come and lay hands on them and they at that point received the Holy Spirit. In the early Church the reception of the Spirit often followed the new birth.

The Apostle Paul himself is another example in the Book of Acts. He was born again on the road to Damascus (Acts 9:4-9; Gal 1:11-12). Three days after his new birth he received the Spirit when Ananias laid hands on him (Acts 9:17). (He also was required to submit to baptism before he was forgiven, as Acts 22:16 shows.)

Even Jesus' own disciples did not receive the Spirit until nearly four years after they were born again. They came to faith at the start of Jesus' three and a half year ministry (cf. John 2:11). Yet they did not receive the Spirit until Pentecost after Jesus rose from the dead (Acts 1:8; 2:1-21).

Acts 2:38 is not teaching that repentance and baptism are conditions *of everlasting life*. It is teaching that for the new Jewish believers who had personally participated in the death of Jesus, they must repent and be baptized to have fellowship forgiveness and to receive the indwelling Holy Spirit.[3]

Acts 11:18. After hearing Peter's report about Cornelius and his household coming to faith, Jewish believers with him said, "Then God has also granted to the Gentiles repentance to life." What is *repentance to life*?

In my dissertation I assumed the expression referred to repentance *to everlasting life* because Peter was clearly saying that these Gentiles were born again and had received the Spirit and hence he was in no position to refuse to baptize them. However, while that is what Peter was saying, that doesn't mean that that is what his Jewish companions were saying. These Jewish believers might have been saying that God has granted to Gentiles that they might turn from their sins and have *fullness of life*, including equal footing in the church, that is, life every bit as full as Jewish believers.

Zane Hodges argues for that second possibility:

> It was thus evident that the Gentiles had entered into the same "life experience" that believing Jews enjoyed, that is, they were fully blessed by the God with whom they were now obviously in harmony. We might say, "They entered into the Christian life."[4]

Hodges viewed the statement of Peter's friends as meaning that God had granted Gentile believers every bit the same life as Jewish believers. They would not be second-class members of the Church. They too would have the Spirit and the forgiveness of sins.

A third possibility is that these men were saying that turning from sins *leads to* everlasting life. If they meant this they would not be

---

[3] For more detailed explanation of this passage, see Lanny Thomas Tanton, "The Gospel and Water Baptism: A Study of Acts 2:38," and "The Gospel and Water Baptism: A Study of Acts 22:16" in *Journal of the Grace Evangelical Society* (Spring 1990 and Spring 1991): 27-52 and 23-40, respectively. These articles are available online at http://www.faithalone.org/journal/index.html.

[4] Zane C. Hodges, *Harmony with God: A Fresh Look at Repentance* (Redencion Viva: Dallas, TX, 2001), 118. In an earlier 1998 newsletter article, cited above (fn 2), Hodges said, "No text in the NT (not even Acts 11:18) makes *any direct connection* between repentance and *eternal life*. No text does that. Not one" (emphasis his).

saying that it is a condition of eternal life. They would simply mean that repentant Gentiles are people to whom God would bring the message of eternal life so that they could simply believe in Jesus and be born again. In favor of this view is that Cornelius is evidently a man who has repented at some point in the past. His alms and prayers ascended to God (Acts 10:4, 31). Acts 10:35 may support this interpretation as well. Against this view, however, is the fact that repentance is not mentioned at all in Acts 10:1–11:17. While it is apparent that repentance occurred at some point in the past, it is not mentioned even once.

If this third view is correct, it would mean that repentance makes faith more likely, not that repentance is a condition of everlasting life or that all who repent come to faith.

Of course, as Hodges points out, if the first view accurately reflects what these men meant, then these Jewish believers were in major error.[5] Even the Old Testament is clear that Gentiles could know God and be guaranteed a place in the coming kingdom, as Paul shows by means of Old Testament quotations in Rom 15:8-13. And the Lord was clear that this message is for all, even to the ends of the earth (Matt 28:18-20). This interpretation is highly unlikely since 1) Peter does not correct them, 2) Luke does not correct them with some sort of editorial comment, and 3) there is no indication in the text that these Jewish brethren are in some way defective in their understanding of the saving message.

Zane Hodges argued for the second option, the equal life view. I believe he is correct, though the third view is possible as well. In any case, there is no reason here to see these Jewish brethren as contradicting the message of John 3:16 (or the later findings of the Jerusalem Council [Acts 15:1-29]). Surely if they had done so, Peter would have soundly corrected them (cf. Acts 15:7-11).

Acts 19:4. "Then Paul said, 'John indeed baptized with a baptism of repentance, saying to the people that they should believe on Him who would come after him, that is, on Christ Jesus.'" In my dissertation I argued that Paul was saying that the "baptism of repentance" of John the Baptist was designed to call an individual "to first give up self-righteous attitudes and recognize his sinfulness and need of forgiveness."[6] I argued that Paul saw this as a prerequisite to believing in Jesus for eternal life, which was clearly the ultimate aim of John the Baptist's ministry.

---

[5] Hodges, *Harmony with God*, 117-19.

[6] Robert N. Wilkin, "Repentance As a Condition for Salvation in the New Testament," Doctoral Dissertation (Dallas Theological Seminary, 1985), 88.

The problem with this view is that it has no support in the text. Even in my dissertation I said that in this verse "insufficient information is given here to answer this question [i.e., what is the role of repentance in regeneration] fully." [7]

Since Paul was the champion of justification by faith alone, my interpretation of this verse was quite odd. In addition, Paul doesn't mention repentance even once in his defense of justification by faith alone, the Book of Galatians. It only occurs once in Romans, and then not in the justification section. (See below for a discussion of that verse.) As James D. G. Dunn has noted, "Repentance…is a category strikingly absent in Paul."[8]

The most natural way to read this verse is that John's baptism of repentance was part of a ministry whose aim was to get people to believe in Jesus for eternal life. It was not that one had to submit to John's baptism as a precursor to come to faith in Christ. The woman at the well came to faith in Jesus yet she never submitted to John's Baptism. So did Nicodemus, and there is no evidence he was baptized by John the Baptist.

People who were baptized by John were more likely to listen to him when he called for them to believe in Jesus Christ (cf. John 1:7; 5:33-47; see also Luke 20:1-8).

Therefore, this verse is not at all saying that one must repent to be born again.

Romans 2:4. Here Paul addresses the legalist (or moralist, see below), the person who thinks he is free from God's wrath because he is such a righteous person. Paul says to this wrath-deserving individual, "Do you despise the riches of His goodness, forbearance, and longsuffering, not knowing that the goodness of God leads you to repentance?"

The comments by Zane Hodges on Rom 2:4 are very helpful:

> The moralist is trapped in a catch-22! Since he condemns the sin around him and justifies the wrath inflicted on it, how can he himself hope to **escape God's judgment**? After all, Paul's list of vices (1:24-32, especially vv 28-32) includes the failures of the moralist himself. If he justifies, explicitly or implicitly, God's judgment on others, should he not anticipate God's judgment on himself?

---

[7] Ibid., 87.

[8] James D. G. Dunn, "The Justice of God: A Renewed Perspective on Justification by Faith," *Journal of Theological Studies*, New Series, 43 (April 1992): 7.

What is his problem, Paul asks? Just because judgment has not reached *him* as yet, does he in fact **despise** this delay in experiencing consequences as unworthy of his respect? Rather, does not this display of God's **kindness and tolerance and longsuffering** reveal God's desire that the moralist himself should come **to repentance**? Doesn't he realize that God's kind behavior toward him is His way of **drawing** the moralist [= **you**] **to repentance**? (The verb rendered *is drawing* [*agei*] could also be translated "is leading," in the sense of "showing you your proper path"!) How sad it is when man is so self-righteously proud that God's kindly patience to him is regarded as unworthy of his attention or response. By persisting in his sins, even the moralist endangers his own well-being.

The idea of repentance here, of course, refers to the need the moralist has to turn away from his own sins to avoid the "wrath" that God exercises against such things (1:18). It has nothing to do with Paul's doctrine of justification. Indeed this reference to repentance is the only one in the entire book of Romans! Moo (*Romans*, pp. 134-35) writes: "Repentance plays a surprisingly small part in Paul's teaching, considering its importance in contemporary Judaism." But Paul cannot be correctly understood when he is read, as many do today, as though he reflected the thinking of "contemporary Judaism." On the contrary, his gospel came directly "through the revelation of Jesus Christ" (Gal 1:12).[9]

The issue here is temporal wrath, not eternal condemnation. God's delay in punishing our sins should not be seen as a sign that we are pleasing God. Rather, His kindness and patience should lead us to repent of our sins.

2 Peter 3:9. "The Lord is not slack concerning His promise, as some count slackness, but is longsuffering toward us, not willing that any should perish, but that all should come to repentance." This single verse kept me from changing my view on repentance and salvation for several years. I had come around on the verses mentioned above. But this one still seemed as though it clearly and unequivocally taught that one had to repent to escape eternal condemnation. If so, then this verse is a show-stopper for the idea that repentance is not a condition of everlasting life.

---

[9] Hodges, *Commentary on Romans*, s.v. Rom 1:16-17. This has not been published yet. We expect publication in mid to late 2012.

In the mid-nineties, around ten years after I completed my dissertation, I was reading in 2 Peter 3. I came to verse 9 and thought, "I wonder how Peter uses the word *perish* elsewhere in his two epistles." Why hadn't I asked that question while writing my dissertation? It is such an obvious question.

I pulled my Greek concordance off the shelf and found out something quite enlightening and embarrassing. The *only other use* of the verb *perish* (*apollumi*) is in 2 Pet 3:6, just three verses prior. I had just read verses 1-9. When I asked the question about verse 9, I had forgotten or failed to notice that the same word appears in verse 6.

As I thought about verse 6, I had one of those flash of insight moments. Here is how my thinking went:

> Verse 6 says that the world that existed at the time of Noah "perished, being flooded with water."
>
> Clearly *the perishing* mentioned in verse 6 is not eternal condemnation. Peter is speaking of physical death, not eternal condemnation in verse 6.
>
> If the perishing in verse 6 is *physical* death, then isn't it highly possible that it also refers to *physical* death in verse 9, just three verses later?
>
> If verse 9 refers to physical death as well, then the point Peter is making is not about heaven and hell, but about life and death.
>
> That verse 9 is talking about the deadly consequences of not repenting as compared with the life-extending benefits of repenting is supported by the repentance of the Ninevites as recorded in Jonah 3 (cf. Matt 12:41). Clearly God didn't wish for the Ninevites to perish, but for all of them to come to repentance. They did repent and thus Jonah's prophecy of death in forty days was averted.
>
> If 2 Pet 3:9 is not an evangelistic verse, then the biggest support for the idea that repentance is a condition of eternal life disappears.

I called up my friend and mentor, Zane Hodges, and shared my insights into 2 Pet 3:9. "Do you think I could be on to something here?" Zane replied that this way of handling the verse made perfect sense, not only in light of verse 6, but also in light of verses 10-13, which refers to the future *physical* destruction of the current heavens and earth by fiery judgment. Zane went on to point out that Peter's point is that the reason God delays the Second Coming is that billions will die in the Tribulation and He doesn't want that. He doesn't want any to die prematurely. Since repentance is the cure for premature death, as long as the sins of mankind are not filled up, the Tribulation will not come. Repentance forestalls the Tribulation.

Frankly when I look at 2 Pet 3:9 now, I have a hard time even seeing what led me to think it was talking about eternal condemnation. Once everything fell in place, the correct interpretation just sort of emerged. Just as when a jigsaw puzzle piece clicks in place, so this interpretation fit perfectly with all the details of the entire context, before and after.

Repentance and Confession of Sins

As a friend pointed out to me, the words *repent* and *repentance* are not found in First John. Thus, he suggested, would this not mean that repentance is not a condition of fellowship with God, if that indeed is the subject of First John?

He was exactly right. The condition for fellowship with God in First John is confession of our sins, not repentance (1 John 1:9).

However, confession occurs as we "walk in the light" (1 John 1:7). That is, confession occurs when we are living under the teaching and instruction of the Word of God. When God's Word points out sins in our lives, we are to confess them, not deny them.

First John is written to mature believers who are already in fellowship with God (cf. 2:12-14, 20, 27). For the believer who is already in fellowship with God, the way to maintain that fellowship is confession of sins, not repentance.

Luke 15 shows that repentance is the condition *for the prodigal believer* to get back in fellowship with God. But if one is not a prodigal believer, then the issue is confession.

I remember talking with Zane Hodges about this. He said something like this,

> You know, I think a person could go for years or even decades in fellowship with God without ever needing to repent. As long as a person walks in the light of God's Word and confesses his sins, he remains in fellowship. Only when he goes to the spiritual far country would he need to repent.

Now I know that people can get confused. They wonder, *Is confession just a game? Don't I need to want not to do the sin again when I confess?*

One man in his forties told me that when he was a teenager he misunderstood confession. He went out one Saturday night and got drunk with a bunch of his high school friends. Well, he confessed his sin the next morning and went to church.

The next week he kept thinking how it would be fun to go out drinking with his friends again. By Saturday he decided to do it again. Once again on Sunday morning he confessed.

The following week he decided that he would go out drinking and getting drunk every weekend, but that he would only be out of fellowship with God during his Saturday night binge. He thought that "confession" on Sunday morning made his prodigal lifestyle acceptable.

What he didn't understand at the time, but suspected, is that he was not walking in the light. He knew what he was doing was wrong, yet he not only kept doing it, but actually made plans to do it each week. It was something he looked forward to.

The week after his first time getting drunk, he should have thought,

> You know, that was fun, but I was also out of control. I feel guilty for much of what I said and did. If I do that again, then I will start a habit. And I could start doing worse things. I could even become an alcoholic. But even if I don't, I will be running with the wrong crowd, doing the wrong things, and displeasing God. And if my parents knew, they would not be pleased either. Lord, I confess that I'd like to do it again. But I want to nip this in the bud. Please help me to stop this sinful behavior right now. I know that getting drunk is sin. Please keep me from ever getting drunk again. I want to be a man after your own heart.

Then the young man should have followed up his prayer by making different plans for Saturday night, plans that didn't involve being around booze and getting drunk.

After he got deeper and deeper into that lifestyle, he began to miss church on Sunday mornings. Eventually he *was* the prodigal son of Luke 15. He needed to repent, because his confessions each Sunday had become a ritual with no substance. Since he had stopped walking in the light, he needed to repent in order to get back in the light.

Therefore, as odd as it sounds, repentance should not be a regular part of the life of a believer. Confession is what we should be doing regularly. As long as we are in fellowship with God, the issue for us is confessing our sins as God makes them known to us. As long as we do, then God forgives us for the sins we confess (fellowship forgiveness) and cleanses us from all unrighteousness, which includes all of the sins of which we are unaware.

Maybe an illustration will help. A man and woman have been married for ten years. Let's say these are two very well-adjusted and mature believers. So in those ten years they have never been separated. At no time did the husband or wife move out. But there were times in their marriage, as there are in every marriage, in which their fellowship was *strained*. They had arguments. Sometimes they both raised their voices or gave each other the evil eye. But they didn't break fellowship. They stayed together and worked things out.

Now another couple, also married ten years, has a different experience. Both come from very dysfunctional families. Though both are believers, they are not mature. In those ten years they, too, had strains in their fellowship. But unlike the first couple, these strains led to separations that sometimes lasted for months. Man and wife actually lived in different cities and didn't communicate for days or weeks at a time. During those times they were out of fellowship.

Married people know when they are in fellowship with their spouse. They know when the fellowship is strained and something needs to be done to avoid a break in fellowship. And they know when they are out of fellowship.

The same is true in our fellowship with God. Staying in fellowship is not a matter of some sort of legalistic woo-woo. Walking in the light is not legalistic. Confessing our known sins is not legalistic. But if we set up extra Biblical rules in order to maintain fellowship, then we err.

Repentance is not for the believer who is in church every Sunday and who loves God and who confesses his sins and delights in pleasing God. It is for the believer who is away from God.

What Difference Does It Make?

Evangelism. The change is enormous. No longer will we tell someone that to be justified or born again he must *repent and* believe in Jesus. We will simply tell them the message of John 3:16.

In a famous book on evangelism the author tells of a pivotal moment in her efforts to lead a friend to Christ. For some time she'd been witnessing to her friend. Finally one day her friend said, "Okay. I'd like to become a Christian now." The author, knowing that her friend was living with a man to whom she was not married, said, "Well, you aren't ready to become a Christian until you stop living with your boyfriend. God says that is sin. You must turn from that in order to be saved."

I cringed when I read that. The friend was given a false, though well intentioned message. I thought of John 4 in which the Lord, when confronted with the same situation, did not tell the woman she had to turn from her sin to gain everlasting life.

No longer need the evangelist tell people that they must "repent and believe" in order to be born again. Faith alone in Christ alone is the cry of the evangelist who understands what repentance is (and is not).

Rescuing Errant Believers. Believers who are in fellowship with God need to keep on walking in the light of God's Word (1 John 1:7) and confessing their sins (1 John 1:9).

But the believer who is out of fellowship with God desperately needs to repent. He needs to turn from his sinful rebellion and get back in fellowship with God. Repentance is the medicine for the believer who has ceased to walk in fellowship with God (Luke 15).

Let's say your brother is a believer, but he strayed from the Lord in college and ever since has not been walking with the Lord. He has had a series of women with whom he has lived. They have drained all his money and left him heavily in debt. He gets drunk a lot. As a loving sibling, you urge him to repent. But since you know he is already born again, you don't question his standing as a believer. In fact, you start by pointing out that you both know he is born again and eternally secure. You rejoice in that with him. But you tell him that you love him and are concerned about him. You can see that he is ruining not just his finances, but his life. You urge him to turn from his sinful ways and get his life straightened out.

Rescuing Errant Unbelievers. Not only are we to help bring believers back from their sins, we are also to help unbelievers do the same. Let's say your brother is an unbeliever who grew up in a moral home but drifted in college. Same scenario as before, except this time your brother is not born again. You would still call for him to turn from his sinful ways because they are ruining his life. But here you would also remind him what hopefully you've told him before, that all he needs to do to have everlasting life is to believe in the Lord Jesus Christ as John 3:16 shows. You wouldn't simply evangelize him without urging him to repent. You would do both. But you would keep the two distinct.

Conclusion

Repentance is one of the most misunderstood words in the Bible. But once we grasp what it means, it is a wonderful concept. God has made a way for the person who is on the path of death to escape. It is called repentance.

Anyone, believer or unbeliever, who continues down the path of rebellion against God is inviting premature death. Sooner or later, God will take his life. Repentance is the way of escape.

While repentance is not a condition of eternal life, it is the condition for ongoing physical life for the person who is living in the spiritual far country.

Chapter 8
Grace

Common Perception: Grace (*Charis*) Means Unmerited Favor

Most people in Christianity have a general idea of what God's grace is. But their conception is typically quite fuzzy. It lacks sharp focus.

What is *grace*? Most within Christendom would say it is God's favor or His unmerited favor. But they do not realize that the word translated *grace* in the New Testament, *charis*, actually not only does not always mean favor, *it quite often does not mean favor*. Of its 156 New Testament uses *charis* is only translated as *favor* eight times (in the NKJV). While we might suggest that it should be translated as *favor* three or four times that amount, it is clear that *charis* means *favor* well under 25% of the time.

Charis, like most words, has a range of meanings in the New Testament. Since our reception of everlasting life is "by grace [*charis*]" (Eph 2:8), it is certainly important to know what grace (*charis*) is.

The Range of Meanings of *Charis*

The word *charis* is translated in the following ways in the New Testament (NKJV or KJV):

- Grace,
- Favor,
- Thank(s),
- Thankworthy,
- Gift,
- Commendable,
- Benefit,
- Acceptable,
- Pleasure,
- Liberality.

As is easily seen, the word is translated in many different ways. While the most common translation is *grace*, this is not the only way it is translated. And, to make matters worse, it is far from obvious what the English word *grace* means; hence, that translation is less helpful than it could be.

The following are the top six definitions for *grace* according to dictionary.com. The number one meaning of the English word *grace* is, "Elegance or beauty of form, manner, motion, or action." The second meaning is, "A pleasing or attractive quality or endowment." It isn't until the third meaning that we find, "Favor or good will." The fourth is similar, "A manifestation of favor, especially by a superior: *It was only through the dean's grace that I wasn't expelled from school.*" The fifth meaning is "Mercy; clemency; pardon." The sixth: "Favor shown in granting a delay or temporary immunity [a grace period]." Altogether there are a whopping 20 definitions given of *grace*.

The leading dictionary for New Testament Greek (BDAG) lists these major meanings for *charis*: 1) a winning quality or attractiveness that invites a favorable reaction, *graciousness, attractiveness, charm, winsomeness*, 2) a beneficent disposition toward someone, *favor, grace, gracious help/care, goodwill*, 3) practical application of goodwill, (*a sign of*) *favor, gracious deed/gift, benefaction*, 4) exceptional effect produced by generosity, *favor*, 5) response to generosity or beneficence, *thanks, gratitude*.[1]

Note that none of these five definitions is *unmerited favor*. While BDAG sometimes is guilty of reading its theology into its definitions, there is no indication that is going on here.

We would have been better off if the translators had rarely chosen the word *grace* as a translation for *charis* since often the Greek is relatively clear what is meant whereas the resulting English translation—using *grace*—is not.

Basic Definition of *Charis* Is Favor

The basic definition is *favor*, not *unmerited favor*. By *basic definition* I mean the single most common use of the word in the New Testament.

When in doubt, it is safe to start with a guess that *charis* in a given passage means *favor*. For example, consider Luke 1:30. The angel told Mary, "You have found *favor* with God" (emphasis added). This favor

---

[1] BDAG, *A Greek English Lexicon of the New Testament and Other Early Christian Literature* (Chicago, University of Chicago Press, 2000), 1079-81.

was clearly not arbitrary. Mary was specifically chosen because of her godly character (though, of course, she was a sinner).

Luke 2:52 is also instructive: "Jesus increased in wisdom and stature, and in *favor* with God and men" (emphasis added). Jesus was highly regarded by God and man as He grew up. That's the point. And clearly the favor He experienced was well deserved and was not unmerited.

Similarly, Luke tells us that the early believers in Jerusalem were breaking bread from house to house, "praising God and *having favor* with all the people" (Acts 2:47, emphasis added). William Barclay captures the sense of *charis* here when he notes, "In the early Church there was *a winsomeness* on God's people."[2] They were held in high regard by the unbelieving Jews in Jerusalem because of their winsomeness, their love and good deeds.

Other Common Meanings of *Charis*

Gift

Charis is translated as *gift* in 2 Cor 8:4, 19 (as well as in 1 Cor 16:3) and probably should also be translated that way in 2 Cor 8:6, 7, 9. Why did Paul not use one of the more typical words for *gift* in these places? Clearly Paul is playing on the word *charis* in these two chapters (2 Corinthians 8–9), using it ten times here, more than in any other two chapters in his writings. Indeed, he uses *charis* more in Second Corinthians (18 times) than he does in any other of his letters, with Ephesians a distant second (12 times), though because Ephesians is half the length, the emphasis per chapter is actually greater.

Basically Paul is using word plays to make his point. God's *favor* (8:1) is what has allowed the Macedonians to support Paul's ministry. That same favor has been showered on the Corinthians and it makes this *gift* possible, and for that there should be *thanks*.

The Macedonians "implor[ed Paul and his team] with much urgency that [they] would receive *the gift* and the fellowship of the ministering to the saints" (2 Cor 8:4). *Charis* here does not mean *unmerited favor*, or even *favor*. It means *gift*. The same is true in verses 6, 7, 9, and 19.

A more careful look at verses 6, 7, and 9 shows how translators sometimes simply grab for a word's generic translation, when the context actually suggests something else.

---

[2] William Barclay, *The Acts of the Apostles* (Philadelphia, PA: The Westminster Press, 1955), 27, emphasis added.

Second Corinthians 8:6 follows verses 4 and 5 in which Paul used *charis* to refer to the financial *gift* the Macedonians made. Since verse 6 immediately follows, we should expect that *charis* most likely carries the same sense here. However, the NKJV translators simply fell back on a generic translation that misleads the English reader as to what Paul meant: "So we urged Titus…[to] complete *this grace* in you…" (emphasis added). The words *this grace* do not accurately convey the meaning of the Greek. Paul was urging Titus to help the Corinthians complete *this gift*. This was a gift the Corinthians had promised a year before (2 Cor 8:11; 9:2, 5). Now Paul wants them to complete it.

The New Living Translation puts it as "this ministry of giving." Other translations similarly say "this act of grace" (NIV), "this gracious work" (NASB), or "this act of beneficence" (Weymouth New Testament).

In verse 7 Paul expresses his desire that the believers in Corinth would "abound in *this grace* also" (NKJV, emphasis added). Again, that translation misses the point. Paul wants them to abound *in this gift also*. A number of translations show this sense: "in this grace of giving" (NIV), "in this gracious act of giving" (New Living Translation), "this gracious work also" (NASB), and "this grace of liberal giving also" (Weymouth New Testament). Some of the translators are trying to get in both the ideas of gift and grace in their translation, which is surely far better than putting the ubiquitous "this grace."

In verse 9 Paul then speaks of the Lord Jesus Christ, and once again some translations, including the NKJV, put a misleading translation: "For you know *the grace* of our Lord Jesus Christ, that though He was rich, yet for your sakes He became poor, that you through His poverty might become rich." Paul isn't speaking of some vague concept here. He is thinking of *the gift* the Lord Jesus gave us. The incarnation involved His giving up the riches of heaven and the presence of His Father and the angels to come to earth and to live as a pauper. The reason: so that we might become spiritually rich.

Now it is admittedly harder to translate *tēn charin* in verse 9 as *the gift* than it is in verses 4, 6, and 7. The reason is that it doesn't read well in English. But it should be noted that neither does it read well in English to speak of "the grace of our Lord Jesus Christ" in a verse dealing with His giving up His riches in heaven for poverty on earth. English readers come away with some general sense of *His lovingkindness*. But that is not what is in view here. In view is what He has given us, His gift to us. In this verse none of the translations use *the gift* or anything close. I believe that is because *charis* in the sense of *grace* is so often associated with the Lord Jesus in Paul's greetings (e.g., 2 Cor 1:2) and benedictions (e.g., 2 Cor 13:14). However, here I think the preceding context is clear that Paul is using Jesus' gift to us to spur the Corinthians to complete their gift to the churches of Judea.

Second Corinthians 8:19 is widely translated "this gift" (NKJV), "the offering" (NIV, NLT), or "this generous gift" (Weymouth New Testament), though some translations have the ubiquitous "this grace" (KJV, ASV, Douay-Rheims, Darby).

Thanks

The first word in both 2 Cor 8:16 and 9:15 is *charis*. "Thanks (*charis*) be to God..." is a fine translation in both places. Clearly Paul doesn't mean, "Grace be to God" or "Favor be to God" or "Gift be to God."

Now there probably is a play on words here. Paul used this word to subtly convey the idea that our thanks to God is due to His grace, or His favor, which He has shown to us in Christ.

Blessings

The NKJV and most other versions translate *charis* in 2 Cor 8:1 as *grace*: "Moreover, brethren, we make known to you the grace of God bestowed on the churches in Macedonia." However, that translation is a bit misleading since Paul is speaking of what God did in and through the churches in Macedonia, not what He did *to them*. Paul is thinking of the liberal giving of those relatively poor churches (verse 2). The New Living Translation is closer to the sense: "Now I want you to know...what God in His kindness has done through the churches in Macedonia." The NASB translation is along those lines: "Now, brethren, we wish to make known to you the grace of God which has been given in the churches of Macedonia." While *grace* gets the basic idea, I would have preferred a translation like *blessings* or even *favor*: "we make known to you *the blessings* of God bestowed on the churches in Macedonia."

Commendable

Charis is used by Peter in back-to-back verses in which the meaning is not *grace* or probably even *favor*. The NKJV translates *charis* as *commendable* in both 1 Pet 2:19 and 20: "For this is *commendable* [*charis*], if because of conscience toward God one endures grief, suffering wrongfully. For what credit is it if, when you are beaten for your faults, you take it patiently? But when you do good and suffer, if you take it patiently, this is *commendable* [*charis*] before God" (emphasis added).

Of course, if we wanted to use the word *favor* to translate *charis* here, we could. But the translation would be cumbersome: "For this *brings favor*, if because of conscience toward God one endures grief...But when you do good and suffer, if you take it patiently, this *brings favor* before God" (emphasis added). The word *commendable* better conveys the sense of the Greek than the words *brings favor.*

How This Helps Us Understand God's Word Better

By Grace You Have Been Saved Through Faith

Ephesians 2:8-9 is one of Paul's most famous uses of the word *grace*: "By grace you have been saved through faith." What does grace mean there? Unmerited favor? Probably not. It means something like *by God's favor* or *by God's goodwill.*

Of course, eternal life is not merited. But that doesn't mean that the word *charis* means that here. This text is saying that we are saved, which in context means *we are made alive* (2:5), by God's favor or blessing, through faith, and that the *by-favor-through-faith salvation* we receive is not of works, lest anyone should boast. *Not of works* defines the whole idea of verse 8, not simply God's favor.

Here is what Zane Hodges says about the meaning of *charis* in Eph 2:8:

> Grace? It was one of his [the Apostle Paul's] favorite words. Kindness, goodness, mercy, generosity; grace [*charis*] signifies all these things to him [in Eph 2:8].[3]

My point is that Paul is not discussing whether God's favor that brought the Ephesians the message of everlasting life was merited or not. His point is that God did favor them by bringing them the message that they might believe it and be made alive.

Peter said to Cornelius and his Gentile household, "In every nation whoever fears Him and works righteousness is accepted by Him" (Acts 10:35). That certainly makes it sound like in some cases the favor of God in bringing the message of life to people is not arbitrary. Note that Peter speaks of "whoever fears Him" and whoever "works righteousness." The expression *is accepted by Him* does not mean *is born again*, but as Acts 10 shows, it means that God will bring to such a person the message of life, as He did to Cornelius. Of course the gift of everlasting life is never merited (see Rom 4:4 and 11:6 where grace [*charis*] is used in the sense of *gift* or *unmerited favor* and is contrasted with *wages*). But the favor that

---

[3] Zane C. Hodges, *A Free Grace Primer: The Hungry Inherit, The Gospel Under Siege, Grace in Eclipse* (Denton, TX: Grace Evangelical Society, 2011), 35.

results in the message being proclaimed is sometimes given in response to the actions or attitudes of unbelievers like Cornelius.

Many people wrongly assume that the favor of God that led Him to send someone to give us the message of life is arbitrarily dispensed, with no thought on God's part of our attitudes and actions.

Falling from Grace

"You have become estranged from Christ, you who attempt to be justified by law; you have fallen from grace." You can see how a misunderstanding of grace would make Gal 5:4 quite confusing. If receiving God's grace means one has received everlasting life, then this would seem to be teaching some sort of falling from the reception of eternal life. But grace here has its common meaning of favor. The Galatians who were seeking to be justified by works had fallen *from the present experience of God's favor.* People who adopt legalism are not highly regarded by God. They fall under His *displeasure*, not His pleasure.

Charis in the Four Gospels

It may surprise you to learn that the word *charis* only occurs eleven times in the four Gospels. More surprising is that it doesn't appear at all in Matthew and Mark. It only occurs seven times in Luke, and never in the sense of *grace*. And in the only evangelistic book in Scripture, the Gospel of John, the word *charis* only appears four times, all in the prologue (1:14, 16, 17), and never on the lips of the Lord Jesus.

Not once in the recorded words of Jesus anywhere in the Gospels do we hear Him use the word *charis* in the sense of *grace*.[4] In fact, He only utters the Greek word *charis* four times in the Gospels, all in Luke, but in all four cases He clearly means *thanks* or *credit*, not *grace* or *gift* (Luke 6:32, 33, 34; 17:9).

What this means is that *charis* is not something one must understand to be born again. If it were, the Lord would have used it often, as He did the word *believe* (*pisteuō*). It also suggests that we should be careful when using the word *grace* or else we may end up saying things that the New Testament simply does not say. This is particularly important for those of us in the Free *Grace* movement.

---

[4] In 2 Cor 12:9 Paul quotes the Lord telling him, "My grace is sufficient for you, for My strength is made perfect in weakness."

God's Favor May Indeed Be Given in Response to Our Actions or Attitudes

The idea is common in Reformed circles that there is nothing the unregenerate can do to move God to bring the message of everlasting life to him. The unregenerate are seen as totally unaware of and unresponsive to spiritual truth. Indeed, Calvinists often speak of the unregenerate as cadavers. To evangelize an unregenerate person would be like evangelizing a piece of granite. There is no responsiveness there whatsoever.

Thus it is easy to see how in the Calvinist system the favor God bestows on someone that results in the new birth is totally arbitrary. Indeed, within Calvinism the new birth occurs before faith. Thus in Calvinism God arbitrarily causes a given person to be born again. There is absolutely nothing in the unregenerate person that moves God to bring him the message of life and then open his eyes to it (Acts 16:14).

Oddly, those same Calvinists say that one cannot be sure he is regenerate. For the Calvinist, faith is more than believing facts; it is commitment and obedience and perseverance. Thus the only real proof of faith and regeneration is perseverance until death. Prior to death any Calvinist could fall away, and if he did, he would prove he was not really born again.

Of course all this is odd since presumably the unregenerate Calvinist gave every appearance that he understood and believed things within the Word of God. He didn't seem like a stone or a cadaver. Rocks can't believe in the deity of Christ, for example. Yet unregenerate Calvinists can and do. But if a Calvinist falls away, then he supposedly proves he never was a beneficiary of God's unmerited favor. That doesn't make sense.

Non-Calvinists, one would think, would affirm that we can do things (pray, humble ourselves, attend church) that lead God to bring us the message of everlasting life.

However, it is common for Arminians to say that God's favor is unmerited, but that everlasting life requires diligence and hard work. Thus while they normally won't put it quite like this, they believe that God's favor is unmerited, but everlasting life itself is merited. But this does not fit the Biblical picture.

Take Cornelius in Acts 10 as an example. There can be no question but that the reason God sends an angel to him is because of his prayers and his alms giving. The angel said to him, "Your prayers and your alms have come up for a memorial before God. Now send men to Joppa, and send for Simon whose surname is Peter" (Acts 10:4-5). Luke waits until chapter 11 to add that the angel told Cornelius that Peter "will tell you words by which you and all your household will be saved" (Acts 11:14).

Cornelius heard the saving message *because of his prayers and alms*. He heard Peter's message in part because of what he did. But he certainly did not merit everlasting life. As a sinner who until his death fell short of God's glory (Rom 3:23), he could not work any works to gain everlasting life (John 6:28-29). But he could seek God and his seeking did move God to bring him the message he needed to hear and believe to be born again.

But doesn't that contradict Rom 3:11 where Paul says, "There is none who understands; there is none who seeks after God"? Clearly not. Scripture doesn't contradict Scripture. In Rom 3:11 Paul is discussing men *when left to their own initiative*. Apart from God's drawing, no one seeks God. But since God is drawing all men (John 1:9; 12:32), then all men are free to seek God in response. Along with Cornelius, Lydia in Acts 16 and the Bereans of Acts 17 (see Acts 17:11) are examples of unregenerate people who sought God. Paul specifically said in Acts 17:27 that the unregenerate can indeed seek God.

In my estimation, the favor of God that brings unbelievers the message of life is often, though not always, related to their actions and attitudes.[5] But the life of the Lord Jesus, everlasting life, is never given in response to our attitudes and actions. We need to distinguish between those two. God's favor is not the same as the life He gives.

Some people go to great lengths to explain away their own seeking of God before their new birth. They discount their prayers, their church attendance, their Bible reading, and questions they asked. But why? God wants the unregenerate to pray, to attend church and Bible studies, to read His Word, and to seek Him. We need not worry that admitting we may have sought Him somehow robs Him of glory and praise for what He has done for us. He did it all. He gave us His Word. He gave us churches we could attend. He brought believers into our lives to give us

---

[5] Was Saul of Tarsus in a misguided way seeking God before he met Jesus on the road to Damascus? Possibly. See 1 Tim 1:12-16. However, it is very likely that many people do not seek God at all before He confronts them with the message of life. The Philippian jailer of Acts 16:25-34 is not mentioned as a God fearer and unlike Lydia (Acts 16:14), he was not at the place of prayer by the river to hear Paul. Thus it is probably fair to say that in some cases a person did little if anything in the way of seeking God prior to his hearing of the message of life. But that is not only not always the case, it appears to be slightly unusual. More normal is the experience of Cornelius, Lydia, and the Ethiopian eunuch in Acts.

the message of everlasting life. He gave us minds to think and He has set eternity in our hearts. The longing we have for everlasting life is from Him. Thus our seeking of God is only possible because of what He has done and is doing.

What Difference Does It Make?

This may seem a bit esoteric, but it is far from it. Let me show you how an improper understanding of *grace* hinders people.

First, if we think that the favor God grants unbelievers in bringing them the message of everlasting life is arbitrary, then we clearly do not think unbelievers can do anything to aid themselves in hearing or believing that message. Thus we would not encourage unbelievers to pray and ask God to show them the message of life. We would not encourage them to search the Scriptures, for there is nothing they can do. We would not encourage them to turn from their sins,[6] for that would smack of trying to earn God's favor.

So many believers do not treat unbelievers as though they could pray, study, or learn. They do so in great part because of the mistaken notion that people come to faith because of a totally arbitrary bestowal of favor. Thus they want unbelievers to be totally passive.

Second, this misunderstanding causes us to give a less than candid testimony of how we came to faith in Christ. We leave out all the praying we did, all the tears we shed, all the churches we visited, all the longing we had. I know, because for years I left these things out of my own testimony since these things didn't seem to fit with the *by grace through faith salvation* of Eph 2:8-9. A faulty view of grace can lead to a faulty testimony that inadvertently confuses people on how we came to faith in Christ.

Third, many believers think that nothing good that happens in their lives is ever a result of good works they have done. I've heard pastors preach that every blessing believers get from God is totally unrelated to their attitudes and actions. Thus when good things happen, we should thank God for His arbitrary blessings in our life.

---

[6] While repentance is not a condition of everlasting life, God calls all men everywhere to repent (Acts 17:30). God's kindness should lead unbelievers to repentance (Rom 2:4). If an unbeliever repents, it often makes him more open to God and to the message of life. Whereas before repentance, unbelievers might refuse to listen to friends trying to evangelize them; afterwards they might seek those same friends out and ask them to tell them about Christ. They might start going to church, praying, and studying the Bible. Repentance is a good thing, even though it is not a condition of everlasting life.

But that is a contradiction of what God's Word says. God blesses obedience and curses disobedience (Heb 6:4-8). "Whatever a man sows, that he will also reap" (Gal 6:7). While that latter statement primarily looks to the Judgment Seat of Christ (see Gal 6:9), it certainly applies to this life as well.

Of course, in one sense any divine favor, any blessing from God, to sinful humans is undeserved. Even believers "fall short of the glory of God" (Rom 3:23). God alone is good (Matt 19:17). All of our righteous deeds are as filthy rags before Him (Isa 64:6).

However, in another sense God's favor to sinful humans may at times be "deserved." God has promised to bless us if we do certain things or if our attitudes please Him. For example, He guarantees to give grace to the humble (Jas 4:6; 1 Pet 5:5). He promises that He is a rewarder of those who diligently seek Him (Heb 11:6). Searching the Scriptures with an open heart is an activity blessed by God (Acts 17:11). Praying invites His blessings (Acts 10:4).

Since God has chosen to obligate Himself to bless us if we please Him, we ought to stop saying that His favor toward us is always arbitrary and is totally undeserved.

The idea that God doesn't bless us when we obey Him, but only when He feels like it, is a terrible mischaracterization of the truth. Such teaching actually demotivates believers from working hard for God, even though we are called to work hard for Him (cf. 2 Tim 2:6). This borders on true antinomianism.

Fourth, if we think every time our English translation uses the word *grace,* unmerited favor is in view, then we misunderstand and hence misapply many verses. Clearly it is a bad thing to misunderstand what God is saying.

Conclusion: *Charis* Means What the Context Dictates

The bottom line for determining the meaning of *charis*, as well as for any word used in the New Testament, is context. What is the context talking about?

As with most words, *charis* has a range of meanings. Thus the perceptive Christian will look at the context and see what *charis* might mean. The fact that his English translation renders *charis* as *grace* in a given verse should not lead the believer to blindly accept that as the best translation, especially if it results in a sentence that is confusing.

We ought to give thanks (*charis*) to God for the favor (*charis*) He has shown to us in Jesus Christ, God's gift (*charis*) to mankind.

As Free *Grace* people, we should know that God's favor and blessings on our lives are crucial to our daily living. And we should know that when our actions and attitudes please God, His favor is guaranteed to follow.

All of life, from the new birth until the Bema, is about gaining and staying in God's grace.

Chapter 9
Gospel

Introduction

The word *gospel* is part of modern Christianese. "I shared the gospel with my parents this past weekend" means "This past weekend I told my parents how they could be born again." The same truth is conveyed with "I gave the gospel to..."

I quickly adopted that way of speaking once I came to faith in Christ. Everyone I knew who was a Jesus person (we called ourselves *Jesus people* in the early seventies) used the term *gospel* to refer to the message of life, the saving message.

But is that accurate? Is the expression *the gospel* equivalent to the answer to the Philippian jailer's question, "What must I do to be saved?"

It wasn't until long after I received my doctorate that I changed my thinking on the term *gospel*. But once I did, I found the change to be very helpful. I started emphasizing not only the gospel, but also everlasting life, the message of life. The gospel is the means by which someone comes to believe the message of everlasting life. But the gospel is not the message of life.

The expression *the gospel* is never used to refer to the message of life—or, the saving message—anywhere in the New Testament.

Paul told the Galatians, "I marvel that you are turning away so soon from Him who called you in the grace of Christ, to a different gospel, which is not another; but there are some who trouble you and want to pervert the gospel of Christ" (Gal 1:6-7).

What is *the gospel* that Paul preached to the Galatians and which was being perverted by men we now call *Judaizers*?

What does the word *gospel* mean?

What if I'm correct and the term gospel *does not refer to what we might call "the saving message"* (which in itself is potentially misleading) or what the Scriptures call *the word of life* or *the promise of life* (see Acts 5:20, "the words of this life"; Phil 2:16, "the word [or message] of life";

2 Tim 1:1, "the promise of life")?[1] Paul spoke of himself "as a pattern to those who are going to believe *on Him for everlasting life*" (1 Tim 1:16, emphasis added).

My thesis about the term *gospel* is simple: the gospel of Jesus Christ is the good news that He died on the cross for our sins, was buried, rose bodily from the dead on the third day, and appeared to over 500 people over the course of forty days (1 Cor 15:1-11). That is not the precise object of saving faith. Stated another way, a person who believes the gospel may or may not have everlasting life.

The message of Christ crucified and risen is what should lead people to believe in Jesus for everlasting life (John 3:14-16; 1 Tim 1:16). But it is not the same as the message of life.

The term *gospel* means *good news* and most often *gospel* refers to the good news *about Jesus Christ*. It is my contention that that the word *gospel*, and the related word *evangelist*, refer to good news about the Lord Jesus Christ that should *lead to* both justification and sanctification. The expression *the gospel* is not the message of justification by faith alone. Nor is it the message of sanctification by faith working through love. The good news about Jesus Christ should lead unbelievers to faith in Christ and believers to living by faith in Him.

Let me state my thesis again in a variety of different ways so you can clearly understand my point before we go to the Scriptures to see if my point is Biblical.

According to the New Testament, the gospel is a message proclaimed both to unbelievers and to believers. The gospel message to unbelievers is meant to lead them to faith in Christ and the new birth. For those already born again the gospel message is intended to lead them to think and act in ways that are pleasing to the Lord Jesus.

The good news about Jesus Christ looks back to Jesus' birth, sinless life, death on the cross, burial, bodily resurrection, post-resurrection appearances, and even His ascension to heaven. The gospel of Jesus Christ also looks forward to His soon return, including the Rapture, the Second Coming, and His reign forever on the Millennial earth and then the new earth.

---

[1] See Acts 3:15 where Peter calls the Lord Jesus "the Prince of life." Also see the many places in which the Lord Himself indicated He is the source of life: "[I am] the light of life" (John 8:12); "I am the bread of life" (John 6:35, 48); "I am...the life" (John 14:6). The Lord called for people to believe in Him for everlasting life. He never called for faith in the gospel for everlasting life.

We err if we think the New Testament gospel is the message of everlasting life. It is related to it in that belief in the gospel should lead people to believe the saving message.

I realize this is a major paradigm shift for many people, so I expect there will be plenty of questions.

I hope, however, that you don't simply reject what I'm saying if it doesn't fit your understanding at this point. I also hope you won't accept as true what I say simply because I say it is so. You need to examine what is said in light of Scripture, as the Bereans did in Acts 17:11. The Bible alone is God's infallible Word and it is our only way of knowing what He has revealed to us.

This chapter, as is the case with all of the chapters in this book, is essentially a concordance study, in this case of the word *gospel* (*euangelion*, noun, *euangelizō*, verb, meaning "I preach the gospel" or "I preach good news") and the related word *evangelist* (*euangelistēs*).

The first place to start in our concordance study of the words *gospel* and *evangelist* is to see how they are used in the only book in the Bible which is designed to tell the unbeliever what he must believe to be born again.

Let's turn to the use of the word *gospel* in John.

The Word *Gospel* Isn't Found Even Once in the Only Evangelistic Book in the Bible

Neither the word *gospel* nor the word *evangelist* occurs anywhere in the text of the only "evangelistic"[2] book in Scripture, the Gospel of John.[3]

The Lord Jesus did not say to Nicodemus, *He who believes the gospel has everlasting life* (see John 3:14-16).

The Lord Jesus did not tell the woman at the well, *He who drinks the gospel will never thirst again* (see John 4:10-14).

He never told Martha, *He who believes the gospel shall never die* (see John 11:26).

---

[2] In this chapter I will use the words *evangelize* and *evangelistic* to refer to proclaiming the message of everlasting life. However, I do so because otherwise I have to use cumbersome expressions a lot. But to evangelize someone is more than simply sharing the message of life with them. This is discussed further on p. 145.

[3] The term *gospel* does, of course, appear in the title of the book. But the word *gospel*, when referring to the first four books of the New Testament, does not mean *good news*. Rather, it means something like *holy biography*. In this sense *Gospel* refers to a genre or type of literature, a holy biography of Jesus Christ.

When the Lord identified Himself as the bread of life, the water of life, the life, and so forth, He was calling for faith in Himself for everlasting life. He never said that the gospel is the way, the truth, and the life, or that the gospel is the Good Shepherd.

In John's Gospel Jesus always called for faith *in Himself.* He said, "He who believes in Me has everlasting life" (John 6:47; see also John 3:14-16; 4:10-14; 5:24; 6:35; 11:25-26).

The object of faith in John's Gospel is always Jesus and His promise of everlasting life. The object of faith in John's Gospel is never something called *the gospel.*

Of course, we know from Mark 1:15 that the Lord Jesus called upon Israel to repent and believe the gospel. However, as we saw in Chapter 7, Mark 1:14 makes clear that the Lord was speaking about *the gospel of the kingdom.* There *gospel of the kingdom* refers to the good news that Messiah King, Jesus Himself, is present and He is ready to give Israel her kingdom. Even in the Synoptic Gospels (Matthew, Mark, and Luke) the Lord Jesus never said that that the one who believes the gospel (or the gospel of the kingdom) has everlasting life.

As with our discussion about repentance in Chapter 7, this is not an argument *from* silence. This is an argument *about* silence.

This alone should cause us to reject the idea that the word *gospel* is a special word that means the message we must believe to have everlasting life.[4]

Various Uses of the Expression *the Gospel*

To the uninitiated the good news of or about Jesus Christ might simply refer to one thing, like the cross, or two things, the cross and the resurrection. While it is true that the expression *the gospel* often refers (explicitly or implicitly) to the good news of Jesus' death and

---

[4] Some have argued recently that John's Gospel is actually no longer a valid means of determining the saving message. They argue that after Jesus ascended to heaven, the saving message changed. In this Dispensation, it is argued, the Apostle Paul, not the Lord Jesus, tells us what one must believe to be born again. And, in this view, Paul taught that one must believe the gospel to have everlasting life. I have dealt with this argument elsewhere. But it can be noted that John wrote long after the start of the Church Age and he wrote to lead people on this side of the cross to faith in Christ for everlasting life (John 20:30-31). In addition, never once does Paul say that the person who believes the gospel has everlasting life. Rather, Paul says that one must believe in Jesus for everlasting life (e.g., 1 Tim 1:16).

resurrection,[5] there are other truths about Jesus that are also called *gospel* in the New Testament.

Glad tidings about the birth of John the Baptist (Luke 1:19). The word *euangelizō* is used here not about Jesus, but about His forerunner. Zacharias *was told glad tidings*. We should not see this as a specific message about Jesus or His saving message.

Glad tidings about the birth of Jesus (Luke 2:10-11). Here the reference is about the birth of Jesus, but not specifically His saving message.

The gospel of the kingdom. This expression is found twice in Matthew (4:23; 24:14) and once in Mark (1:14). It refers to the good news that the kingdom of heaven is at hand. It is not the message that all who believe in Jesus have everlasting life. The gospel, or good news, of the kingdom is the message that the kingdom has drawn near for Israel. It is a message to Israel. The condition the nation had to meet for the kingdom to come at that time was to believe in Jesus and to repent of their sins (cf. Mark 1:15). This was not a faith-alone message.

The mystery of the gospel (Eph 6:19). The gospel is clearly in the Old Testament. The death of Jesus is spoken of in Psalm 22 and Isaiah 53, as well as in Genesis 22 via typology when Abraham offered up his only begotten son, Isaac. The resurrection of Jesus is also prophesied in the Old Testament (cf. Ps 16:9-11). So what is this mystery? Is this not the mystery of the church, Jews and Gentiles together in one body? Indeed, it is. That is the good news Paul has in mind here. The church was a mystery in the Old Testament.

Your fellowship in the gospel (Phil 1:5). Here Paul is referring to the financial participation of the Philippian church in his ministry. The term *gospel* here refers to all of Paul's ministry, evangelism and discipleship. This is not merely a reference to the times when he shared the saving message with unbelievers.

The everlasting gospel (Rev 14:6). One of the more colorful uses of the term *gospel* is found in the Book of Revelation. John says:

> Then I saw another angel flying in the midst of heaven, having the everlasting gospel to preach to those who dwell on the earth—to every nation, tribe, tongue, and people— saying with a loud voice, "Fear God and give glory to Him, for the hour of His judgment has come; and worship Him who made heaven and earth, the sea and springs of water."

---

[5] See, for example, Acts 15:7 (cf. Acts 10:39-40); 1 Cor 1:17; 15:1-11.

The text goes on to speak of the judgment of Babylon ("Babylon is fallen," v 8) and of the future judgment of all who take the mark of the beast on his forehead or hand (vv 9-11).

The everlasting gospel here relates to Jesus since He is the One who pours out judgment on the wicked. But it is not good news about who is born again and how. It is the good news that all who do not fear God and worship Him will be judged.

It is interesting to see how the otherwise very helpful Nelson Study Bible views this as an offer of everlasting life to all who fear God and worship Him.

> **14:6, 7** The **angel** who preaches the **gospel** to **every nation, tribe, tongue, and people** helps to fulfill God's promise that the gospel "will be preached in all the world as a witness to all the nations" (Matt. 24:14) before Christ returns...[God] continues to offer **everlasting** life to the world (see John 3:16). The gospel message at this point beseeches unbelievers to **fear God and give glory to Him** and to escape **the hour of His judgment.**[6]

Of course the Nelson Study Bible teaches that the sole condition of eternal life is believing in Jesus, not fearing God and worshipping Him, so the note here is confusing.

Similarly, the Ryrie Study Bible has excellent notes, but here follows this same line of thinking: "*An eternal gospel to preach.* God's last call of grace to the world before the return of Christ in judgment."[7]

This comment by the late Dr. John Walvoord is helpful in explaining the issue in Rev 14:6:

> Because of the word "gospel," some have felt that this was a message of salvation or the good news of the coming kingdom. The context, however, seems to indicate otherwise, for the message is one of judgment and condemnation. The angel announced, **Fear God and give Him glory, because the hour of judgment has come.** So the "eternal" message seems to be a message of God's righteousness and judgment rather than a message of salvation (emphasis in original).[8]

---

[6] *The Nelson Study Bible*, Gen ed. Earl D. Radmacher (Nashville, TN: Thomas Nelson Publishers, 1997), 2186.

[7] *The Ryrie Study Bible* (Chicago: Moody Press, 1976, 1978), 1912.

[8] John F. Walvoord, "Revelation," in *The Bible Knowledge Commentary*, New Testament Edition, edited by John Walvoord and Roy Zuck (NP: Victor Books, 1983), 964.

Evangelist Is Related to the Word *Gospel* in Greek

The word *gospel*, *euangelion* in Greek, is used 77 times in the New Testament. The verb form, *euangelizein*, to preach the gospel, is found 55 times in the New Testament. The related word *euangelistes*, *evangelist*, is only used three times in the New Testament (Acts 21:8; Eph 4:11; and 2 Tim 4:5).

We know what the word *evangelist* meant because we have a record of what Philip the evangelist preached.

Look at Philip the evangelist (called thus in Acts 21:8) in Acts 8:5-13. He goes to Samaria and leads many to faith in Christ. But did you notice verse 12: "But when they believed Philip as he preached the things concerning the kingdom of God and the name of Jesus Christ, both men and women were baptized"? His good news preaching included information about the kingdom of God and evidently about baptism too. That is all part of the work of an evangelist.

Note also Philip the evangelist's ministry to the Ethiopian eunuch in Acts 8:26-40. There he also preached Christ, and he must have mentioned baptism and the call to discipleship, for he baptized this man as well. Clearly evangelism for Philip included initial follow up and baptism.

I don't know too many people today who include preaching about the kingdom of God and baptism as part of evangelism. But it was for Philip and it should be for us. A person is not an effective evangelist if he leads someone to faith in Christ and tells them nothing about His soon return, about the Judgment Seat of Christ, about ruling with Christ, about identifying publicly with Him in baptism, about walking in the Spirit, and so on.

Evidence That *the Gospel* Is Not the Precise Object of Saving Faith

It isn't simply John's Gospel that fails to say that the one who believes the gospel has everlasting life or is justified. No verse says that.

That is a show-stopper for the idea that the gospel is the object of saving faith.

Nowhere in the entire Bible are we told that the person who believes *the gospel* has everlasting life, is saved, is justified, will never die spiritually, or anything of the kind.[9]

Repeatedly the Bible says that the person who believes *in Jesus* has everlasting life, is saved, is justified, or will never die spiritually (John 1:12-13; 3:16-18, 36; 5:24; 6:35-40, 47; 11:25-27; Acts 16:31; Rom 4:4-5; Gal 2:16; Eph 2:8-9).

Jesus, not the gospel about Jesus, is the precise object of saving faith. That is why I prefer to call the message one must believe to be born again *the word of life* or *the message of life* (cf. John 6:68;[10] Acts 5:20; 13:46; Phil 2:16; 1 John 1:1) and not *the gospel*.

Many people believe *the gospel* is a technical expression that refers to the content of saving faith. Free Grace people with that understanding say that if someone believes *the gospel* he is born again, no matter what else he might or might not believe,[11] and, of course, regardless of his works. If that is correct, there would be no problem. But if that is incorrect, then it creates tremendous confusion.

Do all who believe that Jesus died on the cross for our sins and rose bodily from the dead have everlasting life? Of course not. Even if we add in belief in Jesus' deity, virgin birth in Bethlehem, and His sinless humanity, people believing all that still are not born again if they believe in works salvation.

The person who is born again is the one who has come to believe that by faith in Jesus Christ he has everlasting life. That is the message of John 3:16 and a host of other verses.

---

[9] It is true that in the Book of Galatians the gospel *points to* the message of justification by faith alone apart from works (cf. Gal 2:14-16; note esp. in v 14 "the truth of the gospel"). And it *points to* the message that all believers have been crucified with Christ and that we are to live by faith in Him who loved us and gave Himself for us (Gal 2:20). The false gospel of the Judaizers was a message that perverted the intended result of the good news message both in terms of justification and sanctification (cf. Acts 15:1, 5). However, even in Galatians we find Jesus, not *the gospel*, the object of justifying faith (e.g., 2:16; 3:6-14).

[10] As this verse shows, the word or message of life that Jesus preached was not merely the message of how one gained everlasting life. Peter and the apostles already were born again and knew it. Peter's words here show that the message of life also included teaching about how to experience this life more abundantly (cf. John 10:10).

[11] Compare Acts 15:1 and 15:5. Two types of Judaizers were bothering the Gentile churches. Both groups said Gentiles must be circumcised and must keep the Law of Moses. The former group, Acts 15:1, said Gentiles must do that to have everlasting life. The latter group said that they must do so to please the Lord, to be sanctified. The latter group Luke calls believers. The former, who required law keeping for everlasting life, he does not call believers. This is quite telling.

Think back on the Judaizers who were troubling the believers in the churches of Galatia. Did they proclaim Jesus' substitutionary death and bodily resurrection? Certainly they must have. In the first place, they never would have received a hearing by the believers in Galatia otherwise. In the second place, if they had failed to proclaim the good news, Paul would have certainly noted that in his epistle to the Galatians.

The Judaizers proclaimed justification by faith plus keeping the Law of Moses, and sanctification by faith plus keeping the Law of Moses. (We derive this by reading Gal 2:14-21.) But they not only did not deny the good news, they proclaimed it. The way in which they perverted the good news was by taking it where God never intended. God intended the good news to lead people to faith in Christ. Instead, the Judaizers were using it to lead people to faith in their own works.

Is this not a concern in Christianity today? Do not Roman Catholics, for instance, proclaim the good news of Jesus Christ, yet use it to lead people to justification by works? The same is true for the Eastern Orthodox Church and the cults and many denominations, too.

Those who suggest that *the gospel* is the object of saving faith, rather than the proof that Jesus indeed is the Guarantor of everlasting life to all who simply believe in Him, inadvertently confuse people on what they must believe to be saved.

The gospel should lead people to faith in Christ. But believing the gospel is not the same as believing in Jesus Christ. Most in Christianity believe the gospel and yet they are still unregenerate since they do not believe in Jesus for the life He promises.[12]

If we know someone who believes the gospel of Jesus Christ, yet who also believes in works salvation, we should share the message of John 3:16 with him. As one friend likes to say when he shares John 3:16 with people, Jesus said that the one who *believes in Him*, not the one who *behaves in Him*, has everlasting life. The issue is believing *in Jesus* for the life He guarantees.

---

[12] Some Free Grace people argue that a person does not *truly* believe that Jesus died on the cross for his sins until he also believes in justification by faith alone. If that were true, then I'd agree that believing that Jesus died on the cross for our sins is the same as believing in Jesus for everlasting life. However, that simply is not true. For one thing, either a person believes something or he does not. There is no such thing as *truly believing*. For another, I personally believed that Jesus died on the cross for my sins long before I believed in justification by faith alone. Nearly everyone I know who believes in eternal security points to a time before that when they believed Jesus died on the cross for their sins.

The Gospel in Galatians

Earlier I said that there is not a single verse in the Bible in which the term *gospel* refers to the message of life. Yet the letter to the Galatians seems to be an exception to that statement. Doesn't Paul say that there were some who were preaching "a different gospel" and who "want to pervert the gospel of Christ" (Gal 1:6-7)? That sounds like the false teachers, called *Judaizers*, were perverting the message of justification by faith alone.

While it is true that the Judaizers perverted the message of justification by faith alone (cf. Gal 2:15-16), that does not mean that the term *gospel* in Galatians means *justification by faith alone*.

The expression *the truth of the gospel* is found twice in Galatians (Gal 2:5, 14). It concerns not only the message of justification by faith alone, but also the unity of Jews and Gentiles in one Body, the Church (Gal 2:14-21; compare Gal 3:28). In Galatians 2, Paul was reporting about a time when he publicly rebuked Peter and Barnabas in Antioch because they "were not straightforward about *the truth of the gospel*" (Gal 2:14, emphasis added). The issue there was that they withdrew from the Gentile believers at the Lord's Supper meal (Gal 2:11-13). Clearly Peter and Barnabas weren't failing to preach justification by faith alone or Jesus' substitutionary death and resurrection. They gave an object lesson when they would no longer eat with the Gentile believers (Gal 2:12). By no longer eating with Gentiles at the Lord's Supper, Peter and Barnabas were implicitly siding with the legalists, the Judaizers.

To bring this into a contemporary discussion, let's say that your church had a luncheon. At that luncheon a group of Jewish believers, led by one of the elders in your church, refused to eat the food served and even refused to sit anywhere near the Gentile believers in the church. Instead, they went off into a different room and ate their own kosher food. This splinter group did not shake hands with the Gentile believers and they left without saying goodbye. How do think that would go over in your church?

Now imagine that Messianic Jewish traveling teachers had recently visited your church and had said that in order to be born again and in fellowship with God, Gentiles must be circumcised and must keep the Law of Moses. Wouldn't the actions of the small group of Jewish believers at your church luncheon be seen as a denial of the very truth of the gospel?

Here is how what Peter and Barnabas did contradicted the truth of the gospel. The gospel teaches that believing Jews and Gentiles, slaves and free, men and women are all equal in the Body of Christ (Gal 3:28).

There are to be no separations based on diet or even based on the Jewish Law (Gal 2:11-21; 4:10-11; Acts 10:9-23). Believers are not under the Law of Moses (cf. Rom 6:14-15; Gal 4:21; 5:4, 18).

Proof of what I'm saying about the actions of Peter and Barnabas is seen in Paul's comments in Gal 2:14-21. Based on Paul's comments, it is clear their actions even brought the message of justification by faith alone into question.

Paul's rebuke of Peter and Barnabas runs from Gal 2:14-21. Note that in Gal 2:15-16 Paul stresses the message of justification by faith in Christ, apart from works of the Law. Three times he mentions that justification is not by the works of the Law. And three times he mentions justification is simply by faith in Christ. He mentions this because the actions of Peter and Barnabas imply the Gentiles must keep the Law to be justified (compare Acts 15:1).

The Apostle Paul also went on to discuss progressive sanctification in one of the greatest verses on that issue in the Bible, Gal 2:20, "I have been crucified with Christ; it is no longer I who live, but Christ lives in me; and the life which I now live in the flesh I live by faith in the Son of God, who loved me and gave Himself for me."

As the Jerusalem Council in Acts 15 also showed, there were actually *believers* who said that it was necessary to circumcise Gentile converts and get them to keep the Law of Moses in order for them to be in fellowship with God and with Jewish believers (Acts 15:5).

The Judaizers preached that Gentiles must be circumcised and must keep the Law of Moses, both in order to be justified and in order to be sanctified (Gal 2:14-21). That is the "different gospel" they preached. That is how they tried to pervert the gospel of Christ.

The expression *the truth of the gospel* is different than the expression *the gospel*.[13] The truth of the gospel includes the fact that Gentile believers are born again and are on equal footing with Jewish believers in the Church, apart from circumcision and apart from keeping the Law of Moses. The gospel itself does not.

The gospel concerns the truth that God became a Man, lived a sinless life, died on the cross for the sins of the whole world (fulfilling the Law of Moses), rose bodily from the dead on the third day, appeared to many people, ascended to heaven, and is coming again soon. The truth of the gospel goes beyond that message to its application in terms of justification and sanctification and church life.

---

[13] Compare Gal 2:14-21 (*the truth of the gospel*) with 1 Cor 15:1-11 (*the gospel*). These two messages are related, but clearly are not identical.

Even in Galatians there is not a single place in which *the gospel* equals the message of justification by faith alone (or *the message of life*).

But What about First Corinthians 15:1-11?

Many people believe that Paul is laying out here, in precise form, *the saving message* he preached to lead the Corinthians to faith in Christ when they were still unbelievers.

I don't agree.

In the January-February, 2008 issue of *Grace in Focus* newsletter, I wrote an article on this passage. I urge you to look there for more details.[14] I will here only summarize my points.

If this is Paul's exact saving message, then where is justification by faith alone in Christ alone in 1 Cor 15:1-11? That it isn't in this passage shows this isn't the entire message he wants believers to share with unbelievers.

Why do people always add to and take away from these eleven verses if this is what one must believe to be born again? The answer is that they recognize that these verses do not give enough information for an unbeliever to be born again.

Paul's good news message should have kept the Corinthian believers from dividing into cliques (see 1:12-13). His good news message should have directly impacted their *sanctification*.

Paul determined only to know Christ crucified among them (1 Cor 2:2), a vital sanctification message (Gal 2:20).

First Corinthians 15 is the great resurrection chapter and it culminates in a reference to the Bema (v 58). Clearly the good news of our own personal future bodily resurrection must be held onto (v 2) if a believer is to rule with Christ in the life to come.

What does Paul say he is defining in this passage? Does he not say he is speaking about "the gospel which I preached to you, which also you received, in which you stand"? He is defining the gospel he preached, not the saving message he preached.

Only if we think those two messages are one and the same can we possibly see 1 Cor 15:1-11 as Paul's explanation of the message one must believe to be born again.

It is telling that the only reference to salvation in 1 Cor 15:1-11 is a present tense salvation, which is conditioned upon continuing to hold fast to Paul's gospel: "by which also you are saved, if you hold fast the word which I preached to you..." The present-tense salvation Paul mentions

[14] Available online at http://faithalone.org/news/index.html#2008.

there is being spiritually healthy (cf. 1 Cor 5:5). Believers are presently in a state of spiritual health (being saved) as long as they hold fast to Paul's gospel. Obviously Paul is not saying that if one simply continues to believe the gospel message he is guaranteed to be spiritually healthy. Paul is thinking here of holding fast to that message and its intended results, which includes sanctification by faith working through love.

When we compare the tense of the verb *sōzō* in 1 Cor 15:2 with that in the famous verse Eph 2:8, we see a radical difference. Ephesians 2:8 uses a perfect passive: "you have been saved." However, in 1 Cor 15:2 Paul uses a present passive, literally, "you are being saved." The former is looking at regeneration truth (cf. Eph 2:5). The latter is looking at sanctification truth.

What is interesting is that people who say that the gospel message found in 1 Cor 15:1-11 is the saving message nonetheless almost always supplement it with truths not found there. Ephesians 2:8-9 is a case in point. People feel compelled to go there because 1 Cor 15:1-11 doesn't speak of past tense salvation ("you have been saved"), nor does it say that salvation is "by grace through faith," or that it is "not as a result of works, lest anyone should boast." If they feel the message of Eph 2:8-9 must be believed as well, then they add it to the message of 1 Cor 15:1-11. Sometimes they also add in the message of John 1:1, that Jesus is God. Some add the message of 2 Cor 5:21, that Jesus never sinned and that His righteousness is imputed to the believer and that our sins are imputed to Him. But if the message of 1 Cor 15:1-11 is the saving message, then it needs no additions. A person who believed that would be born again.

What Difference Does It Make?

All believing parents long to know that their children are born again. This leads them to evangelize their children.

If the parents don't know precisely what their children must believe to be born again, then they will not know if their children are born again.

If the parents are wrong about what one must believe to be born again, then they will not be able to lead their children to the new birth.

Let's say the parents think that all who believe the gospel as laid out in 1 Cor 15:1-11 are born again. They teach their children this passage. They have their children memorize it. They are convinced that their children believe it. So they are happy that their kids are born again. But they never share with them the message of John 3:16 and Eph 2:8-9.

It makes a big difference what message we tell someone they must believe in order to be born again. Whether we are witnessing to our own children, our parents, our siblings, our neighbors, friends at school or work, or total strangers, we must get the message right. If we tell people that anyone who believes X is born again, and that isn't true, then we are misleading people whom we care about. And we are misleading them on the most important issue in life.

It is my experience that this is the reason why many parents entrust the evangelization of their kids to someone else. They hope the youth pastor knows what to tell them. After all, he went to Bible college or seminary.

Many people don't evangelize their friends, but instead invite them to church where they hope the pastor will tell them how to be born again.

The main reason people shirk evangelism is not, as is often taught, that people don't care or are unwilling to risk persecution. The reason is because they don't know what to say and they believe that it is best not to evangelize people unless they know what to say.

The Gospel of John is written to tell the unbeliever what he must believe to be born again. It shows us how to lead people to faith in Christ. John 3:16 is simple.

Many tracts hop all over the Bible and include lots of seemingly unrelated teachings. Thus people conclude that evangelism should only be done by the professionals.

Confusion about the meaning of the word *gospel* greatly contributes to people not knowing if they are born again and not knowing how to tell others how they can be sure that they are born again.

If we know that the good news of Jesus Christ is meant to lead people to faith in Christ for everlasting life, then we need to be clear what that good news means.

Many people who say they believe that Jesus died for everyone (unlimited atonement) actually say the opposite when they evangelize. Many say something like this:

> "You are a sinner and your sins separate you from God. See Rom 3:23. But the good news is that Jesus Christ, God's Son, died on the cross in your place, paying for all your sins, past, present, and future. If you believe that He died on the cross for your sins, then He will take away your sins so that they are no longer a barrier to you being saved. You see He *potentially* paid for your sins at the cross. But His blood is not effective until you apply it to your life (like the Jews applying the blood of lambs on the doorposts in Exodus 12). If you do

not believe that He died on the cross for your sins, then you remain separated from God due to your sins."

In reality we should say just the opposite:

"You and I are both sinners. Indeed, every living human being is a sinner. See Rom 3:23. But the good news is that Jesus Christ, God's Son, "[took] away the sins of the world," as John the Baptist said in John 1:29. The Apostle John said the same thing in 1 John 2:2. So neither of us is blocked from God and from His kingdom because of our sins. He has removed the sin barrier so that now we are all savable. All we need to do to have everlasting life, life with God that can never be lost, is to believe in Jesus Christ. Look at John 3:16. There Jesus says that whoever believes in Him will not perish but has everlasting life. Because of the cross and the resurrection of Jesus, all who simply believe in Him have everlasting life and will one day be raised from the dead to live physically forever in perfect, glorified bodies. I am now sure I have everlasting life and I know it has nothing to do with how good or bad I am. It is all about Jesus' faithfulness to His promise."

Those two messages are radically different. The second message proclaims true unlimited atonement. Jesus didn't *potentially* die for the sins of the whole world. He *actually* did that. No one will be condemned because of his sins. Revelation 20:11-15 shows that the basis of condemnation is that a person is not found in the Book of Life, and people get in that Book by believing in Jesus. So unbelievers are not in the Book. Believers are.

The Gospel Is the Good News That Runs from Eden to the New Earth

In one sense everything from creation to the New Earth is part of the good news. That is how many in New Tribes Mission evangelize people who've never heard about Jesus. While I would suggest telling people each time that Jesus guarantees eternal life to all who simply believe in Him, and I wouldn't wait until the last of scores of messages to tell the message of John 3:16, I do agree that it is all part of the good news.

A person, of course, need not know every aspect of the good news to be born again. A person could be born again and not know about Mary anointing Jesus for burial (Matt 26:13), or Judas betraying Jesus for thirty pieces of silver, or Jesus being buried in a rich man's tomb, or Jesus being born in Bethlehem. But that is all part of the good news.

The aim of the gospel is what it should lead to. Once a person believes that Jesus died on the cross for his sins and rose bodily from the dead, he is a great candidate to believe that simply by faith in Him he has eternal life (John 3:16) and is justified (Gal 2:16). The gospel message should lead people to believe in Jesus for eternal life.

But that's not all. The gospel message should also lead a person to live for Christ in light of His soon return. Because He died for us, we ought to love Him and seek to please Him in all we say and do so that when He returns we might hear, "Well done, good servant" (Luke 19:17a) and might be given the privilege of ruling with Him (Luke 19:17b).

Of course, once a person comes to faith in Christ for eternal life, there is certainly much more of the good news that everyone needs to learn and apply. The longer we live with and for Christ, the more precious the good news of Jesus Christ should become to us.

Conclusion

The gospel is the good news about Jesus Christ. The Messiah has come and He is coming again soon.

One intended result of believing the gospel is that people believe in Jesus for everlasting life. The other intended result of believing the gospel is that people would live for Christ, seeking to please Him. The gospel is intended to lead to both justification and sanctification.

In America a high percentage of people already believe the gospel and almost everyone has heard about Good Friday and Resurrection Sunday. That makes it easier to lead them to faith in Christ. Since many already believe that Jesus died on the cross for our sins and rose bodily from the dead, it is logical for them also to believe His promise of life. However, they need to *hear* the promise of life to believe it. Sadly most people in America today have never heard a clear explanation of John 3:16 or related verses.

Let's say you are speaking with someone and you say that Jesus said, "He who believes in Me has everlasting life" (John 6:47). Let's say they then object: "If that were true, then bad people could and would go to heaven."

Recently I had just that experience. I was in the Phoenix airport awaiting a flight back to Dallas. I was talking to a pastor friend, Dan, about this very issue. We were discussing precisely what a person had to believe to be born again.

Two women were listening to our conversation, one about thirty and one about sixty. The thirty year old asked, "You aren't talking about once saved, always saved are you?"

We said yes and I pointed her to Jesus' promise in John 11:26, "Whoever lives and believes in Me shall never die."

Then she said, "But my former husband is no good. He was messing around with another woman and he gets drunk a lot. But he claimed that he was saved once and for all. That doesn't make sense."

With that the sixty year old woman chimed her agreement: "That's right. Bad people can't go to heaven."

With that Dan said, "But we are *all* bad. 'For all have sinned and fall short of the glory of God' (Rom 3:23)."

Then I added, "That's the point of the cross, is it not? John the Baptist said, 'Behold! The Lamb of God who takes away the sin of the world' (John 1:29). He has taken away *all our sins, past, present, and future.* Our sins are no longer a barrier to our having everlasting life."

Then she responded, "Well sure, sinners can be saved. But you can't be *really* bad."

With that Dan said, "So how bad can you be? How would you know how good was good enough and how bad was too bad?"

I had to go off and check with the gate agent since I was flying standby. The conversation kept right on going and was very fruitful. The issue was not whether Jesus died on the cross for our sins. The issue was whether a person who simply believes in Jesus is saved once and for all. The two women's concern about sinners being saved led us back to talk about Jesus' substitutionary death on the cross. But we did so to get them to believe the promise of life, not to get them to believe that Jesus died on the cross as our substitute.

Sometimes you can even ask the person you are talking with what they think the point of the cross is. If Jesus wasn't taking away the sin of the world as John the Baptist said (John 1:29; cf. 1 John 2:2), *what was He doing*? And if He did take away the sin barrier, so that our sins no longer keep us from having eternal life, then why focus on how good or bad a person might be who goes to heaven (or, better, has everlasting life)?

There are many ways such conversations could go. But they do come back to the gospel, for the gospel is the proof that John 3:16 is true.

Chapter 10
Judgment

Introduction

Justice is often pictured as a blindfolded woman holding a set of balancing pans. Justice is blind in the sense that it is not prejudiced by race, color, gender, age, or any other factor. Justice simply weighs the evidence and renders the final verdict.

When I was a young man in a sinless-perfection group, I don't recall any of the leaders speaking about *final judgment*. I simply recall the fact that we were taught that there were two hurdles we needed to clear to go to heaven and not hell. First, we had to give our lives to Christ when our moment of opportunity came. That meant we also had to prepare ourselves to be ready for that time by repenting and following Christ daily. Second, if we were ready and did give our lives to Christ and were saved, then we had to live a sinless life until death in order to stay saved. Only people who remained perfect from their new birth until death actually get into heaven. So, as long as you never sinned after being saved, you'd make it.

I broke free of such legalistic and hopeless thinking my senior year in college through the ministry of Campus Crusade for Christ staff member Warren Wilke. The issue Warren stressed wasn't judgment. The issue he emphasized was eternal salvation. Warren used Eph 2:8-9, which does not mention judgment, to persuade me that all who simply believe in Jesus are saved once and for all, apart from works.

Only later did I learn that most Christians talk about something called *final judgment*. I found it was common for people to say that after this life is over, everyone will appear before God and have his works judged. This will be a *final judgment* of works to determine where each one will spend eternity. Those whose works are good enough will avoid the lake of fire. Some say that the works are *a condition* of escaping eternal condemnation. Others say that works are not a condition, but that they are necessary nonetheless since good works *confirm* that we were truly born again in the first place.

I was amazed that people who called themselves *Christians* and who read their Bibles would say that there will be a *final judgment* of our works *in order to determine our eternal destiny.* That is completely foreign to the message not only of Eph 2:8-9, but of the entire Bible, the way I see it.

I found then, and I find now, that such a view of judgment is terribly flawed. It results in a sort of works-salvation mentality. No matter how you explain it, if our ultimate destiny is determined by whether our works tip the scales in our favor, then Eph 2:8-9 is a lie, eternal salvation is of works, and people will be able to boast.

The Myth of Final Judgment

It is common in Christian books, sermons, and Christian education (Bible colleges and seminaries) to be taught this idea of *final judgment.* Many people have heard this expression long before they have come to faith in Christ.

The teaching on final judgment has become so prevalent that even the word *judgment,* by itself, is often understood as referring to a coming day when the Lord will judge all of humanity and determine who will spend eternity with Him and who will be cast into the lake of fire. Recently I heard Dr. Robert Jeffress, Pastor of First Baptist Church of Dallas, say on the radio that anyone who bails out on his ministry or marriage will soon face *God's judgment.* While he surely was talking about the *temporal* judgment of born-again people and not the *eternal condemnation* of unbelievers, it struck me that some might have misunderstood his point. I know that I personally make a habit to speak of *temporal judgment,* rather than merely *judgment,* when I am speaking of God's judgment of believers in this life, for fear that people will misconstrue my words.

Sadly, confusion about judgment can actually keep someone from being born again, or can result in born-again people losing assurance of their eternal destiny.

Matthew Easton writes:

> As the Scriptures represent the final judgment as certain [Eccl. 11:9], universal [2 Cor. 5:10], righteous [Rom. 2:5], decisive [1 Cor. 15:52], and eternal as to its consequences [Hebrews 6:2], let us be concerned for the welfare of our immortal interests, flee to the refuge set before us, improve our precious time, depend on the merits of the Redeemer, and

adhere to the dictates of the divine Word, that we may be found of Him in peace.[1]

In this way of thinking believers must go through life uncertain of their eternal destiny. They must "adhere to the dictates of the divine Word," if they hope to "be found of Him in peace."

The great American theologian and preacher Jonathan Edwards, in a sermon entitled, "The Final Judgment," similarly said:

> If God has appointed a day to judge the world, let us judge and condemn ourselves for our sins. This we must do, if we would not be judged and condemned for them on that day. If we would escape condemnation, we must see that we justly may be condemned. We must be so sensible of our vileness and guilt, as to see that we deserve all that condemnation and punishment which are threatened. And that we are in the hands of God, who is the sovereign disposer of us, and will do with us as seemeth to himself good. Let us therefore often reflect on our sins, confess them before God, condemn and abhor ourselves, be truly humbled, and repent in dust and ashes.[2]

I am reminded of a conversation I had in the Summer of 2000 with a five-point Calvinist pastor and seminary professor. Over breakfast I asked him if all those who are born again persevere in faith and good works. He said, "Yes." I then asked, "Doesn't the Bible say that it is impossible to be sure that we will persevere while we are still in this life?" He said, "Of course. If even the Apostle Paul was unsure that he would persevere as he indicated in 1 Cor 9:27, then we certainly can't be sure we will either." I then asked if that meant that we couldn't be sure of our eternal destiny until after we died. His answer was honest and alarming. He said:

> *Well, I see in my life what I think are the works of the Spirit. However, I must admit that it is possible that I could fall away. If I did, then I would prove that I was really never born again in the first place, and I would go to hell.*

That man is very warm and gracious. I like him. But I am concerned about him because he lives each day in uncertainty. I myself struggled

---

[1] http://www.christiananswers.net/dictionary/judgmentthefinal.html. Accessed April 29, 2010. The title of the article is "The Final Judgment."

[2] http://www.biblebb.com/files/edwards/final-judgment.htm. Accessed April 29, 2010.

with uncertainty from ages six to twenty and was tormented nearly daily by the thought of spending eternity in torment. Likewise, the mistaken doctrine of final judgment contributes to a lack of assurance and a works-salvation mentality.

In a December 31, 2007 post, Dr. John Piper expresses his confidence as well as his lack of certainty as to how he will fare at *the final judgment*. In his conclusion he is referring to the Great White Throne Judgment of Rev 20:11-15:

> Therefore, when I say that what is written in the books is a public confirmation of our faith and of union with Christ, I do not mean that the record will contain more good works than bad works. I mean that there will be recorded there the kind of change that shows the reality of faith—the reality of regeneration and union with Christ. There will be enough evidences of grace that God will be able to make a public display of what is in the books to verify the born-again reality of those written in the Book of Life. No one is saved on the basis of his works. But everyone who is saved does new works. Not perfectly, but with humble longing for more holiness. That is how I enter 2008, confident that my condemnation is past (Romans 8:3), and that my name is in the Book of Life, and that the one who began a good work in me will bring it to completion at the day of Christ. I pray for you, that you are with me.
>
> —Pastor John [3]

It is true that Piper says he is "confident that [his] condemnation is past [and] that [his] name is in the Book of Life." However, confidence is not the same as certainty. Within the Reformed thought of Pastor John Piper, confidence means hopefulness. Like the Reformed pastor I spoke with in 2000, he thinks his works are the real deal. But notice that in order for that to be true, his works must be "brought to completion." That is, he must persevere.

What Piper is saying is that if there is insufficient evidence in our works to prove the reality of our faith, then we will go to the lake of fire. Indeed the title of the article suggests as much: "What Will the Final Judgment Mean for You?"

---

[3] http://www.desiringgod.org/ResourceLibrary/TasteAndSee/ByDate/2007/2550_What_Will_the_Final_Judgment_Mean_for_You/. Accessed April 29, 2010. The title of the blog post is "What Will the Final Judgment Mean for You?"

But how can anyone have enough works to prove he is regenerate? No one can. Besides, even if someone was extremely confident that he was okay right now, he could not be sure he would not fall in the future. Any one of us can fall. The New Testament is filled with warnings to believers about the danger of falling.

For years I had grave concerns about my eternal destiny. Every day I carried around the fear. Maybe you did as well. If so, we can and should be very sympathetic toward those who still face those struggles. Maybe you are struggling with fear of final judgment even today. If so, you don't need to.

You don't need to worry about final judgment. We are accountable to the Lord Jesus Christ, of course. And everyone, believer and unbeliever, will be judged after this life is over. However, no one will be judged to determine his eternal destiny, as we shall see from Scripture.

How can you be sure of your eternal destiny? The Lord Jesus repeatedly says how you can be sure in the Gospel of John. Let's look at one verse, John 5:24, that summarizes the message Jesus gave in the Fourth Gospel.

Believers Shall Not Come into Judgment

The statement by the Lord in John 5:24 is one of the most magnificent statements of the eternality of the life that Jesus gives to the believer. The Lord uses three different verb tenses, present, future, and past, to make His point. All three tenses are dealing with one issue: the one who believes in Jesus has everlasting life that can never be lost.

The future tense statement is that the one who believes in Jesus "shall not come into judgment." In context this means no believer will come into judgment *regarding his eternal destiny.* We know from many other texts that believers will indeed be judged by Jesus one day to determine their degree of reward in the kingdom (e.g., Matt 16:27; Luke 19:11-27; Rom 14:10-12; 1 Cor 4:1-5; 9:24-27; 2 Cor 5:9-10; Jas 5:9; 1 John 2:28). But here the Lord is speaking of a different judgment, the judgment of eternal condemnation.

The Lord is unequivocally saying that there is no *final judgment* of the believer. Believers will only be judged to determine degree of reward, not to determine where they go. All believers are secure forever, even those who are not watchful (cf. 1 Thess 5:10).[4]

---

[4] It should be noted that Dr. John Piper does comment on John 5:24 in the blog previously cited. He says: "When Jesus says, 'Whoever hears my word and believes him who sent me has eternal life. *He does not come into judgment,* but has passed

Yet Believers Will Be Judged

In 2 Cor 5:1-11 Paul speaks of the future judgment of believers. He says that believers will be judged for "the things done *in the body*" (emphasis added) in verse 10. He does so because in verses 1-8 Paul emphasizes the pain and suffering we experience in *these decaying bodies* as compared with the pain-free glorified bodies we anticipate receiving at the time of the Rapture. Our eternal rewards will be based on what we do in service for Christ in these fallen bodies, not with what we will do in the future in glorified bodies.

It hit me recently, however, that there is another reason why verses 1-8 help explain verses 9-11. Paul makes it clear that we are certain that we will receive these glorified bodies (vv 1-5). There is no doubt of the eternal destiny of his readers, or of any believer.

The Judgment Seat of Christ truth found in verses 9-11 is built on *certainty* of our glorified bodies and hence our certainty of our eternal destiny. In other words, assurance of our eternal destiny underlies Paul's teachings on the Judgment Seat of Christ.

Paul says that "we must all," meaning all born-again people, "appear before the judgment seat of Christ." The reason is "that each one may receive the things done in the body, according to what he has done, whether good or bad."

Tying this in with Paul's remarks in his first epistle to the Corinthians, we know that only those believers who persevere will be approved (*dokimos*). Paul feared disapproval (*adokimos*, 1 Cor 9:27). But by the end of his life he could say, "I have fought the good fight, I have finished the race, I have kept the faith" (2 Tim 4:7). Thus he could joyously say, "Finally, there is laid up for me the crown of righteousness, which the Lord, the righteous Judge, will give to me on that Day [the Bema], and not to me only but also to all who have loved His appearing" (2 Tim 4:8).

In his first letter to the Thessalonians Paul urges the believers there to be *watchful* regarding Christ's soon return, a theme from the Olivet Discourse (cf. Matt 24:42-44; 25:13). But Paul encourages them that in any case, they will not go through the Tribulation: "For God did not

---

from death to life,' I take him to mean that we will not be *condemned* in the final judgment, because our sentence has already been passed—not guilty. So why are we there at the last judgment?" (emphasis his). He goes on to answer that we are there to show that God's grace indeed transformed our lives. But he does not see John 5:24 as teaching that there is no judgment to determine the eternal destiny of believers. Note that even when discussing John 5:24 he speaks of "the final judgment." In his view all will be judged there, and only those whose works prove they are regenerate will escape the lake of fire.

appoint us to wrath [i.e., the Tribulation], but to obtain salvation [i.e., deliverance from the Tribulation via the Rapture] through our Lord Jesus Christ, who died for us, that whether we wake [literally, *whether we watch*] or sleep, we should live together with Him" (1 Thess 5:9-10).

The Destiny of Unbelievers Is Based on Their Unbelief, Not Their Works

It might be accurate to speak of the judgment of unbelievers at the Great White Throne Judgment (Rev 20:11-15) as their *final judgment*. After all, it is judgment, and it is final.

However, the Bible never specifically calls it *final judgment*,[5] and the basis of condemnation is not the judgment of the works of the unbelievers. The basis of condemnation is not being found in the Book of Life. After the books (plural) containing the works of all people are examined, then a separate Book, the Book of Life is opened. Notice what we learn about this Book: "And anyone not found written in the Book of Life was cast into the lake of fire" (Rev 20:15).

Opening the Book of Life to see who is in there is not called a judgment. And it doesn't seem that it is judgment in any normal sense of that term.

Therefore, I would say that it is a bit misleading even for unbelievers to speak of final judgment as though that judgment is where their eternal destinies will be decided. Those destinies are decided before the Great White Throne Judgment. That is simply where their destinies *will be announced*.

Even a casual reading of Rev 20:11-15 shows that there are two separate issues. The judgment concerns the books, plural, that are opened. These are books containing the works, good and bad, of all people.

While the text does not specifically say the reason for opening the books, we know from other Scripture that every person will be recompensed according to his works (e.g., Matt 16:27). That includes unbelievers. Unbelievers will receive degrees of suffering in the lake of fire depending on their works in this life.

Possibly a second reason why the books are opened is to show that no one present is sinless. Someone might claim, absent the books, that he never once sinned. The books will refute such a claim and show that no one present is worthy of entering the kingdom on the basis of his works.

But after the books are opened and examined, a separate Book, singular, is opened. This Book is the Book of Life. It is this Book which

---

[5] Indeed, the expression *final judgment* doesn't occur anywhere in the Bible.

reveals who goes to the new earth and who goes to the lake of fire. Anyone not found written in the Book of Life is cast into the lake of fire.

The basis of condemnation is found in the Book, not in the books.

Will there be believers *present* at the Great White Throne Judgment? Quite probably there will be. In the first place, when will Millennial saints be judged? Possibly they will be judged at this occasion to determine their degree of reward for the new earth.

In the second place, it is likely that Old Testament and Church Age believers will be present *as witnesses*.

In the third place, the fact that the text says "anyone not found written in the Book..." suggests that there will be people present who are written in the Book.

What about Matthew 7:21-23?

Matthew 7:21-23 is one of the more famous sayings in the Sermon on the Mount. There Jesus says "Not everyone who says to Me 'Lord, Lord,' shall enter the kingdom of heaven, but he who does the will of My Father in heaven." This has been used to promote Lordship Salvation, the view that one must not only believe in Jesus to have everlasting life, but must also yield to His Lordship and persevere in that yieldedness to death.

While Matt 7:21-23 is indeed dealing with the Great White Throne Judgment, it is not teaching Lordship Salvation and it is not teaching *final judgment*. The text makes this clear if we look at it carefully.

The first issue is what the will of the Father is. What did Jesus mean? Was He warning His legalistic Jewish listeners that they had to be better Pharisees and more legalistic to escape eternal condemnation? Hardly. He repeatedly explained to the legalists that the sole condition of eternal life is faith in Him, not works (cf. John 6:28-29).

The will of the Father is to believe in His Son for the promise of everlasting life. This is borne out by the uses of the expression *the will of the Father* in the Gospels. See especially John 6:39-40:

> "This is the will of the Father who sent Me, that of all He has given Me I should lose nothing, but should raise it up at the last day. And this is the will of Him who sent Me, that everyone who sees the Son and believes in Him may have everlasting life; and I will raise him up at the last day."

The will of the Father is that all who believe in the Son have everlasting life now and guaranteed bodily resurrection (with glorified bodies) when the Lord Jesus returns.

The second issue is what is meant by the words, "Have we not prophesied in Your name, cast out demons in Your name, and done many wonders in Your name?" Note the repetition of *in Your name*. These are all good works they claim to have done in Jesus' name.

What they mean is obvious. "That day" refers to the Great White Throne Judgment. On that day many will point to works they did in Jesus' name as proving they should be permitted to enter the kingdom. This claim is unmistakable.

The third issue is what was wrong with what they said. Many assume the problem is that they didn't really do these works. Others assume they did these works, since even unregenerate people can be priests, pastors, missionaries, and so forth, but that they did not have enough good works to prove that they were recipients of grace, as Piper suggests.

But that is not borne out by Jesus' response in verse 23. Jesus does not deny their claim. His response strongly suggests that their claim is true, but irrelevant, or worse yet, damning.

On what basis do these people argue that Jesus should let them into the kingdom? On the basis of their works. Not on the basis of their faith in Jesus. They do not even mention believing in Him. They only appeal to their works.

The second Kennedy question in Evangelism Explosion is this: "If God were to ask you, 'Why should I let you into My Heaven?' what would you say?" The correct answer is: "You should let me in because the Lord Jesus said, 'He who believes in Me has everlasting life.' I believed in Him for everlasting life, so I have it." The wrong answers all revolve around works: "I try to follow the Golden Rule." "I'm better than most." "My good works outweigh my bad works." "I pray and read my Bible daily and go to church each week."[6]

The answer of verse 22 is the type of answer that anyone trained in Evangelism Explosion would say reveals a works-salvation mindset.

Rather than *teaching* Lordship Salvation—the view that in order to be born again one must not only believe in Jesus, but must also yield to His Lordship until death, Matt 7:21-23 *refutes* Lordship Salvation.

When Jesus opens the books of deeds at the Great White Throne Judgment, it will be clear who did what and for what reason. But no matter how many good deeds a person did in Jesus' name, if he did not believe in Him for everlasting life, then he will not be found in the Book of Life and Jesus will announce that He never knew the person.

---

[6] See http://EvangelismExplosion.org/resources/steps-to-life. Accessed Mar 1, 2012. EvangelismExplosion.org does not specifically give the answers to the question. However, these are what many of us were taught are the right and wrong answers.

There will likely be no false posturing at this judgment, for the evidence will be clear. Only a fool would claim to have done works in Jesus' name if he did not, since the evidence is irrefutable. The problem with these people will not be that they failed to do the works. The problem will be that they failed to do the will of the Father. They failed to believe in His Son.

The fact that they say they did these works *in Jesus' name* strongly suggests these people were "Christians." By that I mean that these are unregenerate people *from within Christianity*. These are not Buddhists, Hindus, Muslims, Animists, Atheists, or the like.

Finally, if we compare verses 21-23 with the preceding context, we see that these people are on the broad road of destruction (Matt 7:13-14). After all, the first thing they claim is to have prophesied in Jesus' name. They are representatives of the false prophets of verses 15-20. Those false prophets are known "by their fruits." The fruits there do not speak of their works, for they look good on the outside (they come in sheep's clothing, verse 15). The fruits in question are their words, their teachings (cf. Matt 12:33-37 in which the Lord links trees and their fruit with words spoken). We know false prophets by what they teach about Jesus and particularly about the condition of everlasting life.

Matthew 7:21-23 does not teach that there will be a final judgment of all people, regenerate and unregenerate. Only unregenerate people are mentioned here. And it does not teach that the basis of their condemnation is their works. It teaches just the opposite. The basis of their condemnation is their reliance on their works and their concomitant failure to have believed in Jesus for everlasting life during this life.

What Difference Does It Make?

Unless we know that believers will never be judged to determine where they spend eternity as Jesus promised in John 5:24, we can't be sure we have everlasting life that will never be lost.

What is sweeping Evangelicalism today is the idea that there is a coming final judgment of our works to determine who gets in and who does not.

Anyone who believes in Jesus for everlasting life has that life, shall not come into judgment, and has already passed from death into life. By believing that promise, we know with certainty that we are saved once and for all (once saved, always saved), that we are eternally secure in Jesus.

By believing the promise of life, we know with certainty that we will not come into judgment concerning our eternal destiny. We will not be judged at the Great White Throne Judgment. We are already in the Book of Life. It is a done deal and we cannot mess it up, no matter what we do or do not do.

Does this move us to rebellion? Does the promise of eternal security promote lawlessness and wickedness? No way. While it is certainly *possible* to abuse grace, one can only do so by neglecting the powerful motivation of gratitude that eternal security provides. And to walk in the darkness requires one to live contrary to the knowledge that one day we will appear at the Judgment Seat of Christ and have our works evaluated and recompensed. Do we not long to hear our Lord, Savior, and Judge say, "Well done, good servant" (Luke 19:17)?

In addition, if a believer foolishly rebels against God, he will reap *temporal* judgment. The prodigal son (Luke 15:11-32) found poverty, famine, and pain when he left the fellowship of his father (Luke 15:14). "No one gave him anything," we are told (Luke 15:16). The son came to his senses and returned to his father, not because his eternal destiny was at stake, but because his temporal well-being hung in the balance.

A failure to distinguish between temporal judgment and eternal condemnation is a terrible error. It is one that can actually keep people away from faith in Christ because as long as a person thinks he must persevere in good works in order to succeed in "the final judgment," he does not believe the promise of John 5:24.

When I was a senior in college I came to believe in Jesus for everlasting life and thus to know I was secure forever. This knowledge transformed me. I changed from pre-Med to pre-Ministry. I devoted the rest of my life to telling others this wonderful news.

Having grown up in an alcoholic family and having struggled with perfectionism all my life, I'm not confident that my works will prove to myself, others, or the Lord Jesus, that I've received the grace of God. While I'm not what I used to be, I'm also not what I'm going to be (1 John 3:2). I'd be scared to death if I thought I would one day face some final judgment of my works to see if I'm going to the lake of fire. This isn't because I have some secret life of immorality. It is because I fall short of the glory of God all the time (Rom 3:23) and because of the fact that I have lots of flaws in my thinking, speaking, and acting.

I close with a candid article from leading Reformed scholar R. C. Sproul, the head of Ligonier Ministries. He expresses the same kind of concerns I would have if I believed what he believes. While he doesn't mention the expression *the final judgment*, it is clear that he is concerned precisely about that. He wrote:

There are people in this world who are not saved, but who are convinced that they are. The presence of such people causes genuine Christians to doubt their salvation. After all, we wonder, suppose I am in that category? Suppose I am mistaken about my salvation and am really going to hell? How can I know that I am a real Christian?

A while back I had one of those moments of acute self-awareness that we have from time to time, and suddenly the question hit me: "R.C., what if you are not one of the redeemed? What if your destiny is not heaven after all, but hell?" Let me tell you that I was flooded in my body with a chill that went from my head to the bottom of my spine. I was terrified.

I tried to grab hold of myself. I thought, "Well, it's a good sign that I'm worried about this. Only true Christians really care about salvation." But then I began to take stock of my life, and I looked at my performance. My sins came pouring into my mind, and the more I looked at myself, the worse I felt. I thought, "Maybe it's really true. Maybe I'm not saved after all."

I went to my room and began to read the Bible. On my knees I said, "Well, here I am. I can't point to my obedience. There's nothing I can offer. I can only rely on Your atonement for my sins. I can only throw myself on Your mercy." Even then I knew that some people only flee to the Cross to escape hell, not out of a real turning to God. I could not be sure about my own heart and motivation. Then I remembered John 6:68. Jesus had been giving out hard teaching, and many of His former followers had left Him. When He asked Peter if he was also going to leave, Peter said, "Where else can I go? Only You have the words of eternal life." In other words, Peter was also uncomfortable, but he realized that being uncomfortable with Jesus was better than any other option![7]

Doesn't your heart break when you hear something like that? Don't you want to talk with him and explain that he doesn't need to worry about final judgment? If, like me, you dealt with such fears for years, then you want to help such people out of the fog that they are in.

I find it very sad that someone believes that "being uncomfortable with Jesus" [that is, being unsure whether he is going to hell or not] is

---

[7] R. C. Sproul, *TableTalk* (Nov 6, 1989): 20.

"better than any other option." Isn't the option of being comfortable with Jesus a better option? Isn't taking Jesus at His word a better option? Doesn't God want His children to be certain that they are His children? Human parents don't keep their children in the dark as to their parentage. Why would God?

However, I understand why Dr. Sproul speaks this way. Being a Calvinist, he doesn't know if Jesus died for him (the L in TULIP) or if he is unconditionally elect (the U in TULIP). Only his *perseverance* in faith and good works until death (the P in TULIP) will show what his destiny is. But since he can't be sure he will persevere in faith and good works, then he naturally fears the so-called *final judgment*—something that believers will not even face. "Being uncomfortable with Jesus" is thus probably the best option for someone, Calvinist or Arminian, who believes that he must persevere in faith and good works until death in order to escape eternal condemnation. By keeping busy, one can hopefully keep these "moments of acute self-awareness" to a minimum. But one will always carry around fear of hell if he believes that he will not discover his eternal destiny *until the final judgment.*

As the Lord said in John 5:24, the one who simply believes in Him has, present tense, everlasting life. That is, he has life that can never be lost.

And the one who simply believes in Him has already, past tense, passed from death into life.

Indeed, the one who simply believes in Him shall not, future tense in the negative, come into judgment concerning his eternal destiny.

You don't need to worry about final judgment since there is no final judgment to determine the eternal destiny of believers. And you won't worry about a so-called final judgment as long as you remember the promise of the Lord Jesus Christ that the one who believes in Him shall not come into judgment.

Conclusion

These Ten Words Are Vitally Important

Words are the building blocks of sentences and ideas. Without words, communication is impossible. Even sign language and gestures communicate words.

Words only communicate correctly if they are understood. When I hear someone speak any language other than English, at best I only catch a few words I think I might understand. I do not grasp the meaning of what someone is saying in a foreign language.

The same is true with the words used in the Bible. If we bring to the Bible misunderstandings of words like heaven, hell, faith, repentance, everlasting, judgment, and so on, then we will miss what the Bible is saying in many passages because those words occur often in the Bible.

Faith

Most people from within Christianity today and over the centuries reject and have rejected justification by faith alone apart from works. Yet these same people have to admit that John 3:16 refers to "whoever believes in Him," not to "whoever behaves in Him." Thus they have to find a way to explain verses like John 3:16.

The solution for most people within Christianity is to define faith as including commitment, obedience, and perseverance. Yet that "solution" is really an evasion of the clear meaning of Scripture. The result is that justification is no longer truly by faith. Justification becomes by commitment, obedience, and perseverance.

Faith really is believing what God has said. Faith is persuasion.

Faith is not like getting in a wheelbarrow, or in a boat, or on a plane. Those are well-intentioned illustrations that fall flat. They are illustrations of commitment, obedience, and perseverance.

Saving faith is believing the promise the Lord Jesus makes concerning everlasting life: "He who believes in Me has everlasting life" (John 6:47). It is not commitment to Jesus. It is not obeying the Lord. It is not persevering in faith and good works. It is simply believing Him concerning the message of everlasting life.

Everlasting

The first battle with the word *everlasting* is simply to use it. This is a very common word in John's Gospel and in the Bible. It is a vitally important word. We dare not let this word become some rarely used word in our churches and in our conversation. *Everlasting* is a beautiful word and it is the heart of John 3:16, the Gospel of John, and evangelism.

What God gives the believer, at the very moment of faith, is everlasting life. Everlasting life is ever-lasting life. It is life that never ends. "And whoever lives and believes in Me shall never die," the Lord promised (John 11:26).

Everlasting life begins at the moment of faith. The idea that everlasting life is awarded at "the final judgment" to those whose works measure up to God's standard is a sad misrepresentation of Scripture. Believers gain everlasting life the moment they believe. Perseverance is not a condition of everlasting life.

Saved

In my opinion, an incorrect understanding of this one word creates more problems than any of the other words. We have turned the word *saved*, and its noun form, *salvation*, into words that refer to one's eternal destiny. Yet *saved* is never used that way in the Old Testament and only about one-third of the time is it used that way in the New Testament.

Most of the salvation in the Old and New Testaments is conditioned upon good works. That is because the salvation most often found in the Bible is some sort of deliverance from enemies, from illness, from persecution, and from death. Rarely is salvation from eternal condemnation discussed in the Bible using the word *saved*.

Context is the key to understanding anything in the Bible and that is especially true of understanding the meaning of *saved* in any given verse.

Lost

The word *lost* is not used in Scripture the way it is used in most churches. Christians use the word *lost* to refer to being spiritually dead. The lost are the unbelievers, the unregenerate, as far as most people are concerned.

But that is not the way the word *lost* is used in Scripture. To be lost is to be lost. The believer who departs to the spiritual far country is lost. That is, he is out of fellowship with God.

In Greek the verb form of the word *lost* is *apollumi*. That word translates into English with the word *perish*. Of course, *perish* doesn't look like it is related to *lost*. But they are the verb and noun form of the same word in Greek. *To perish* is thought by most to mean *to be eternally condemned*. While *apollumi* is used with that meaning a few times in the New Testament, that is not its usual meaning. It is typically used to refer to physical death or destruction.

Heaven

Heaven is not where believers will spend eternity. In fact, heaven is not "a place." Heaven is three different places.

The first heaven is the air around the world where the birds fly and the clouds drift. The second heaven is outer space, the stars and the galaxies. The third heaven is the place where God's glory is especially manifested. The third heaven might be outside our universe spatially. Or, it might be a different dimension all together.

Prior to Jesus' ascension to the third heaven, believers who died went to Hades, also called Sheol, which is in the center of the earth. Believers were in a good part of Hades. Unbelievers were in a bad part.

After Jesus' ascension to the third heaven, believers who died went to the third heaven. However, that is not their final destination.

Believers will spend eternity on the new earth, not in the third heaven.

The idea that physical matter is bad comes not from the Bible, but from Greek philosophy. God created Adam and Eve to live on earth with physical bodies and a physical existence. The reason He will raise us from the dead is because He will fulfill that purpose. We will have physical bodies and we will have a physical existence forever.

As the song says, "Heaven is a wonderful place." But you and I were not created to live there. We were created to live on earth.

Hell

Hell is not where unbelievers will spend eternity. Hell is where unbelievers who have died are now. But that will not be their eternal home.

The eternal home for unbelievers is called the lake of fire (Rev 20:15). After the Millennium unbelievers who have died will be transferred from hell (Hades/Sheol) to the Great White Throne Judgment. At that judgment it will be shown that they are not found in the Book of Life. Hence their departure will be swift and sure.

Contrary to popular opinion, we know very little about what hell is like now, or about what the lake of fire will be like in eternity. We know hell and the lake of fire are hot places where torment occurs. But beyond that, we know very little. We do not know if the level of pain fluctuates or is constant. We do not know how high the level of pain rises. We have reason to believe that the torment is and will be tolerable.

What we know for sure is that hell and the lake of fire are not good places. No sane person would desire to live there, in a place of torment.

Since there is not a single reference in the Gospel of John to Hades, Sheol, or the lake of fire, we can be sure that the preaching of hell is not essential to clarity in evangelism. In fact, a medieval picture of hell may actually hinder evangelism since many people today are turned off by such a picture.

If your view of hell fills in lots of details not found in Scripture, then it is time you pull back and only say what the Scriptures say. If you wish to speculate, make sure you are clear when you share your speculations that they are just that.

Repentance

Repentance is turning from sins. Many people in Christianity see repentance that way. So in a sense this misunderstanding is a different type of misunderstanding.

The big issue in repentance is recognizing what its purpose is. Why does God command all men everywhere to repent (Acts 17:30)? What is at stake?

Repentance is not a condition of everlasting life. The only condition of everlasting life is faith in Christ (e.g., John 3:16).

Temporal judgment, judgment here and now, is what unrepentant people receive from God. That thieves end up in jail is not the only consequence of their unrepentant actions. They also become corrupted in their souls. Their personalities change for the worse.

All sinful paths lead to pain and suffering for the unrepentant and for those closest to them. That is why people go to rehab and twelve-step programs. They realize that unrepentant sin is bad for them and those they love.

Repentance is God's way for you to straighten out your life and to get back on the right path. Repentance is primarily for the born-again who have lost their way. But repentance is good for unbelievers too. Fortunately God rarely hardens peoples' hearts. Thus even unbelievers can turn from their wicked ways and extend and improve their lives.

Justification is by faith alone, apart from works. But a full and meaningful life is only found by abiding in Christ and in His Word. The believer who strays needs to repent if he wishes to get back on track. His eternal destiny is not the issue. His well-being is the issue. (Of course, his *eternal* well-being, but not his eternal destiny, is also related. See 1 John 2:28.)

Grace

Grace is one of the most beloved words in Christianity. However, it is also one of the most misunderstood.

Grace (*charis*) carries a range of meanings including *favor, thanks, gift, commendable, benefit, pleasure, grace, goodness, generosity,* and *liberality.*

The favor (grace) God bestows in bringing the message of life to people is not merited or earned. But it may be in response to God-pleasing actions and attitudes on the part of unbelievers. Cornelius is an example.

Context must be consulted to determine the meaning of this word, as with any other word. Of course, translators try to do this for us. But translators are not inspired. Often translators fail to give the context sufficient study and they simply use a default translation like *grace.*

Gospel

What does *gospel* mean? Most people know that it means *good news.* But most have two misconceptions about this word. First, they wrongly think it always refers to the good news about Jesus Christ (His birth, His substitutionary death on the cross for our sins, His burial, His bodily resurrection on the third day, His post-resurrection appearances over forty days, His ascension, His soon return). Often it does. But it sometimes refers to other good news as well.

Second, many wrongly think that the gospel of Jesus Christ is the message of life. In other words, many think that all who believe the gospel of Jesus Christ are born again. Yet the truth is that the gospel of Jesus Christ is the good news which *points to* the message of life. It is not the message of life.

One searches John's Gospel in vain for the term *gospel.* The Lord Jesus repeatedly said that whoever believes *in Him* has everlasting life. Not once did He say that the one who believes *the gospel* has everlasting life.

Nearly everyone in Christianity believes the gospel of Jesus Christ. But most people in Christianity do not believe the message of life. That is, most in Christianity do not believe that all who simply believe in Jesus have everlasting life that can never be lost.

Judgment

People in Christianity know that there is a coming judgment. In that sense, they understand this word. However, they terribly misunderstand the number of judgments and the purpose of those judgments.

Most think that there is only *one* coming judgment for all people, believers and unbelievers. They call this *the final judgment*. That is wrong. There will actually be *two separate judgments*, one for believers before the Millennium, and one for unbelievers after the Millennium.

These two judgments have related but not identical purposes. The judgment of believers, the Judgment Seat of Christ, will determine the degree of reward each believer will experience in the life to come. That judgment will not at all determine or even announce the eternal destiny of those judged. That was settled the moment each one believed. The Lord promised that believers "shall not come into judgment" concerning their eternal destiny (John 5:24).

The judgment of unbelievers, the Great White Throne Judgment, has three purposes. First, as the books of works are opened and examined, unbelievers will be shown that they were not perfect and are not qualified to enter into Christ's kingdom on the basis of their imperfect works. Second, the unbelievers will be told, in light of their deeds, what their degree of suffering will be in the life to come. They will reap what they sowed. Third, the Book of Life will be opened, and since no unbelievers will be found there, every unbeliever will be cast into the lake of fire.

Even for unbelievers the judgment of their works is not to determine or even announce their eternal destinies. The Book of Life is the determining factor in who gets into Christ's kingdom, not what is found in the books of deeds.

The idea that believers will undergo some *final judgment* to determine their eternal destinies is a tragic contradiction of the message of everlasting life. Assurance is destroyed by such a caricature of Christ's promise. There will not be a final judgment to determine the destiny of believers. Believers are secure whether they persevere or not. The Lord Jesus guarantees it.

Take Heed How You Hear

The Lord applied the Parable of the Sower and the Four Soils to His listeners saying, "Therefore take heed how you hear" (Luke 8:18).

It is not enough to shout "Amen" and "Hallelujah" as you hear God's Word read and preached. You need to understand it correctly and then apply it correctly. It is the doers of the word and not the hearers only who will be blessed (Jas 1:22, 25).

My desire with this book is to get people to read the Word of God more carefully, especially concerning these ten vital words. Even if people do not agree with my conclusions on each word, if they would ask themselves what these words mean each time they see them, I will feel that I've accomplished much of what I set out to do with this book.

Lordship Salvation is tragic, not because it has bad intentions. It is tragic because it distorts the promise of everlasting life into a sort of probation. Eternal security, even if it is formally taught, is reduced to conditional security if it is based on the need of the believer to persevere.

The same is true with all the ten words. Tragic consequences occur for assurance, evangelism, and discipleship when one misunderstands these words.

Take heed how you hear. The Bible is the most important book in the universe and its message is contained in words. We must grasp the meaning of key words if we wish to understand and correctly apply God's Holy Word.

Appendix 1:
Eleven Additional
Misunderstood Words

Overcomer

The word *overcomer* means what it sounds like. An overcomer is person who overcomes adversity. In the New Testament an overcomer is a believer who overcomes the world, the flesh, and the devil by persevering in faith and good works until the end of his life (whether by Rapture or death).

The Greek word translated *he who overcomes* (e.g., Rev 2:11) is the verb *nikaō*, used as a verbal noun (an articular participle, *ho nikōn*). The noun associated with *nikaō* is rather famous in our culture today: *nikē* (the noun is only found once in the New Testament, in 1 John 5:4, though a related noun, *nikos*, is found four times). *Nike* was the Greek goddess of victory. That is the reason why a sports company chose that name.

To be an overcomer is to be a victor, a winner.

It is common in Christian circles for pastors and theologians to equate the term *overcomer* with the term *believer*. In the minds of most Christian educators all believers overcome in their Christian lives.

Many would say that failure is not really possible in the Christian life because God guarantees that all truly born again people will persevere in faith and good works. Those are Calvinists. But non-Calvinists typically say something similar: those who fail in the Christian life go to hell because only those who overcome in their Christian experience retain their salvation.

One group speaks of *proving* you are truly born again. The other group speaks of *not losing* your born-again status. But both argue that only overcoming Christians will escape the lake of fire.

The expression *overcomer* only occurs in 1 John 5 and Revelation Chapters 2, 3, and 21. It should be obvious that winning in the Christian life is not a condition of spending eternity with Jesus. Winning is a rewards concept, not a by-grace-through-faith-not-of-works-lest-anyone-should-boast (Eph 2:8-9) concept.

Are all Christians victors in life? Well, if the New Testament epistles are to be believed, then the answer is clearly no. While there may have been a few overcomers in the church of Corinth, it is clear that most were not (e.g., 1 Cor 3:3; 5:1-11; 6:1-11; 11:30).

James speaks of believers who stray and who might or might not return to the Lord before death (Jas 5:19-20).

Paul called Demas one of his beloved fellow workers in several of his epistles (Col 4:14; Phlm 24), yet later Paul says of him, "Demas has forsaken me, having loved this present world" (2 Tim 4:10). We hear no more of Demas. Surely if all believers are overcomers, then Paul would need to explain why Demas is an exception, or that he later stopped loving the present world. But Paul doesn't do that because Paul never taught that all believers are winners. Indeed, he, like all the New Testament authors, warned believers of the danger of failure in the Christian life (e.g., 1 Cor 9:24-27).

In Jesus' seven letters to the seven churches of Revelation 2–3, He challenges those believers to be overcomers, but He holds out the very real possibility that some or even many of them may not be (cf. Luke 19:16-26).

Many pastors and theologians start with 1 John 5:4-5 and conclude it is saying that all born-again people are overcomers. Then they read that understanding into the references to overcomers in the Book of Revelation. That is, however, poor exegesis.

Does 1 John 5:4-5 really say that all believers are overcomers? I would say it does not. What John says is that our faith overcomes the world. As long as a believer keeps on living by faith in Christ, he remains an overcomer. But, of course, not all believers live by faith in Christ.

In my view John is saying that living by faith in Christ is powerful and results in a victorious experience as long as we walk by faith. However, it is also possible to understand 1 John 5:4-5 in another sense. Possibly he means that those who have come to faith in Christ are victorious *in their position*. Either way, John is not saying in 1 John 5:4-5 that all believers are winners in their experience.

Victory in the Christian life is possible. Not only that, God expects us to be victorious. But, and this is vitally important, victory is not automatic. It takes effort. In light of all that the world, the flesh, and the devil throw at us, it is quite a challenge to keep looking to Jesus. Keep your eyes on Him. Live by faith in Him and His soon return. In this way

God will transform your life and make you an overcomer who will one day hear, "Well done, good servant" (Luke 19:17; Rom 12:1-2; 2 Cor 3:18).

Baptism

Questions abound about baptism. For example, Should we sprinkle or immerse? Do we baptize babies? Is baptism a condition of everlasting life?

If we simply looked to Scripture, instead of tradition, these and other questions about baptism would be quickly answered.

John the Baptist immersed those he baptized (e.g., Mark 1:9-10). So did Jesus' disciples (cf. Acts 8:38-39). We have not a single New Testament example of anyone who was baptized by sprinkling. All were immersed.

There is no record in the New Testament of babies being baptized. Those who were baptized were believers (cf. Matt 28:18-20; Acts 10:47).

Since believers are to be baptized, it doesn't matter how many times a person was baptized before he came to faith in Christ. None of those count for anything. Once a person comes to faith in Christ, he should be baptized, whether this is his first time or his tenth time.

Baptism is clearly not a condition of everlasting life (cf. John 3:16; 6:35; 1 Cor 1:14-17). Cornelius and his household were born again before they were baptized (Acts 10:43-48). So was Saul of Tarsus, who came to faith on the road to Damascus and was baptized three days later (Acts 9:1-19).

In the Gospel of John, the only evangelistic book in the Bible, the sole condition of eternal life is stated as believing in Jesus Christ (e.g., John 3:16; 4:10-14; 5:24; 6:35, 47; 11:25-27; 20:30-31).

Since the kingdom is for children (Matt 19:14), then surely children can be baptized. As long as a person is a believer, he is old enough to be baptized as a first step of discipleship (Matt 28:18-20).

Just as we should not look at the quality of someone's life to determine if he is born again or not (1 Cor 3:1-3), we also should not look at one's lifestyle to see if he is ready to be baptized. New believers obviously are babes in Christ (1 Cor 3:1). They may need to grow a lot before they will overcome their ungodly habits. But if they have come to faith in Christ and wish to follow Him in baptism, we should not stand in their way. To do so is almost like saying we doubt whether they are born again because their lifestyle doesn't seem up to par to us.

Election

This word would be in the top ten for sure if most people in Christianity were Calvinists. But most are not. Most are Roman Catholic or some flavor of Protestant that does not believe in the Reformed doctrine of election. Therefore, I moved this word to the other eleven.

I was taught in seminary that in eternity past, before God created man or the universe, God chose, or elected, those who would spend eternity with the Lord Jesus Christ. From the mass of humanity, illustrated as a basketball-sized lump of clay, God arbitrarily pulled off a small piece of clay. The small lump represents the elect. These people will be born again and will spend eternity with God. No matter what. Free will played no role in who would be born again. Those not chosen were doomed to hell. They had no opportunity to come to faith and be born again.

According to most Calvinists, the situation is worse than I just described. Not only are 99 percent of humanity doomed because they were not elected by God, but Jesus didn't even die for the basketball-sized lump of clay. He only died for the small lump that was chosen. Everyone else is unable to be born again because Jesus didn't take care of their sin problem.

Thus no five-point Calvinist could say to someone, "Jesus Christ died on the cross *for your sins.*" They can't say that because they do not know if the person they are talking to is one of the elect.

The doctrine of election, even minus limited atonement, didn't make too much sense to me. But most of my professors taught that this was a mystery which we could not fully understand. All are able to believe in Jesus, I was taught (contrary to the strict Calvinist understanding of election), since Christ died for all (DTS taught unlimited atonement). However, only the elect will believe. It is not that God forces the elect to believe, or keeps the non-elect from believing, it is simply that all who freely believe happen to be the elect and all who freely reject Christ happen to be the non-elect.

That eliminated some concerns I had. But it still didn't make a lot of sense. I remembered thinking something like, *Well, this makes the most sense of anything I've heard until now. However, I'll keep studying and will remain open. Possibly there is a better explanation of what this doctrine of election is.*

Over the past ten to fifteen years I've been studying the actual Biblical references to God's choosing and electing people. What I have found is far different from what I was taught.

Jesus chose twelve men to be His disciples and His apostles (Luke 6:13; John 6:70; 13:18; 15:16, 19; Acts 1:2). When one of those, Judas, betrayed Jesus, his place was taken by another man chosen by God, Matthias (Acts 1:24-26).

Saul of Tarsus was later chosen by God to be an apostle as well (Acts 9:15; 13:2; 22:14-15).

Peter was chosen by God to be the one to take the gospel to Cornelius and his household, the first Gentile converts (Acts 15:7).[1]

None of these elections were to everlasting life. These were elections *to service*. And guess what? Almost all of God's choosing of people is to service, not to everlasting life.

The Old and New Testaments both make it clear that the Jews are God's *chosen people* and *the elect* (Deut 14:2; 1 Kgs 3:8; Pss 33:12; 106:5; Isa 43:10; 45:4; 65:9, 22; Matt 24:22, 31; Mark 13:20; Luke 18:7; Rom 11:28; 2 Tim 2:10). They were chosen to be the line through which Messiah came.

God chose Moses to lead His people out of Egypt and to the Promised Land (Num 16:5-6, 28-30).

God chose Aaron and the tribe of Levi to be the priestly line (Num 17:5; 1 Sam 2:28; 2 Chron 29:11). God chose that priests from the tribe of Levi would minister before Him in the temple and would be paid by the tithes of the people (Deut 18:5-8; 21:5; 1 Chron 15:2).

Specifically God chose Abraham (Neh 9:7), Isaac, Jacob (Ps 135:4; Isa 41:8; Ezek 20:5), and Judah (1 Chron 28:4; Ps 78:68) to be in the line of Messiah. He chose David to replace King Saul and to be in the line of Messiah (2 Sam 6:21; 1 Kgs 8:16; 1 Chron 28:4; 2 Chron 6:6; Ps 89:3). God chose Solomon over David's other sons to be king (1 Chron 29:1).

All of these selections, of course, were to ministry, not to eternal destiny. Many of those not chosen were born again. Many of God's chosen people did not come to faith in Messiah and hence were not born again. But they were God's chosen people. Indeed, the Jews still are God's chosen people today. One day soon, during the Tribulation, the Jewish people will come to faith in Jesus *en masse*; and then He will return and establish His rule from Jerusalem.

Over and over again God reminds His people that Jerusalem was and will forever be God's chosen city (e.g., Deut 15:20; 16:2, 15; 1 Kgs 8:44;

---

[1] Regarding the Ethiopian eunuch of Acts 8, in the first place, he was an individual, not a group. In the second, he was at least a proselyte who kept the feasts and read the Old Testament. In the third, it can be argued that he may have been born a Jew in Africa.

11:13; 14:21; 2 Kgs 21:7; 23:27; 2 Chron 6:6, 34; 12:13; 33:7; Neh 1:9; Ps 132:13; Zech 3:2).

Even Jesus was chosen by God the Father to be the chief cornerstone (1 Pet 2:4, 6), to be the Messiah (Isa 42:1-4; 49:7; Matt 12:18), and to die on the cross for our sins (cf. Matt 26:42, 56; Rev 13:8).

You may think, *why all this talk about God choosing cities and peoples to various tasks?* Shouldn't we be getting around to the Biblical doctrine of election?

But that is the point, isn't it? Everyone and everything God chose or elected is part of the Biblical doctrine of election. It is a major error to think that the Biblical doctrine of election is merely His choosing who would be born again and who would not.

In fact, there is not a shred of incontrovertible evidence that shows that God chose or elected *anyone* to have everlasting life. While there are some verses that I cannot yet explain to my own satisfaction (e.g., Rom 8:33; 11:5; Col 3:12; 1 Thess 1:4; Titus 1:1; 1 Pet 5:13; 2 John 1, 13), the number is small and shrinking all the time. And none of them clearly says that God chose someone for everlasting life.

Indeed, one of the strongest verses meant to prove this doctrine, Acts 13:48, actually undercuts it when you read the preceding context. In verse 46 Paul did not say, "God did not elect you unto everlasting life."

Instead, he said, "you...*judge yourselves unworthy* of everlasting life" (emphasis added). Clearly the reason why they lacked everlasting life fell squarely on them, not at all on God. They are the reason they didn't have everlasting life.

And the context is clear what they did to judge themselves unworthy. They did not believe (compare Acts 13:48). They were not like the Bereans of Acts 17:11 who searched the Old Testament Scriptures to see if what Paul was saying was true. They rejected it as out of hand without any searching of the Scriptures, prayer, or openness. Since what Paul said conflicted with their tradition, they rejected it without giving Paul a serious hearing.

If we read Acts 13:48 in light of what Paul already said in Acts 13:46, we gain a much different picture than what the Calvinist paints. The Calvinist ignores verse 46 and ignores that verse 48 does not use any of the words for election or choosing, and then reads it as though it said, "As many as had been elected to eternal life believed."

But that doesn't fit the context at all, nor is that in any sense a legitimate way to translate or interpret verse 48.

"As many as had been appointed to eternal life believed" means "As many as judged themselves worthy of eternal life believed." We know this because verse 48 is saying the opposite of verse 46. Note that Paul introduces the expression *everlasting life* in verse 46 and then Luke comments on that same expression in verse 48. There is no question but that the verses are directly linked and are making statements about those who did not believe as compared with those who did believe.

Indeed, the word typically translated *appointed* in verse 48 also can mean "as many as *devoted themselves to* everlasting life," or we might even paraphrase, "as many as *aligned themselves with* everlasting life believed."[2]

Those who came to faith were open. Those who did not were not. No one lacks everlasting life because Jesus didn't die for them (He died for all) or because God isn't drawing him (God is drawing all) or because God did not elect him (since there is no evidence Biblically that God ever elected anyone to everlasting life).

I encourage you to take out your concordance and look up every use of the words *choose* and *elect* and *election*. Study each and every one. See if you can find a single one that clearly refers to election to eternal life. See if instead you see verse after verse after verse that refers to people and places that are chosen for various tasks. In my view the only reason this notion of election to everlasting life emerged is because someone misunderstood a few texts and then they created a doctrine and that doctrine caught on, at least within the Reformed branch of the Church. Reformed theology continues to promote this doctrine even though the evidence is not there to prove it.

I really don't care one way or the other. What I mean by that is that I realize that what God says is true and just and good. Thus if God elected certain people to everlasting life and the rest He did not, I would be fine with that even if I couldn't get my mind around it now. Indeed, I believed that for a decade or more, from the start of my seminary training until years after I received my doctorate.

God is God and can do what He wants. Who are we to question what He does? But since He never says He does that, to create and perpetuate such a doctrine ends up actually contradicting what God has said.

Of course, if God did that, then the moment we believed in Jesus for everlasting life, we would know that we are elect. That was actually my

---

[2] The Greek word is *tetagmenoi*, from *tassō*, which means *to arrange, put in place, determine, appoint* (BDAG, p. 991). This is a perfect middle-passive participle, which I believe should be taken here as middle voice. For further discussion see, Bob Wilkin, "A New View on Acts 13:48: 'As Many As Were Prepared for Eternal Life Believed,'" *Grace in Focus*, Jan-Feb 2007, 1, 4.

view until I came to see that the whole doctrine of election to everlasting life is bogus.

The Reformed doctrine of election is linked to the Reformed doctrine of perseverance, which says that only those who persevere to the end of their lives will escape eternal condemnation. All other believers will be sent to hell since their faith was *merely intellectual* or was not *heart faith*. Thus the Reformed doctrine of election is sadly tied to the Reformed idea that no one can be sure of his eternal destiny until he dies. No consistent Calvinist will say he is sure he is born again since he cannot be sure he will persevere or that he is elect.

While most of the Calvinists I have met are very well intentioned, they follow an unbiblical, man-made theology that is logical, but wrong, wrong, wrong.

Practically speaking, if you believe in election to everlasting life the way it is taught by Calvinists, you are beset daily with fears about going to hell, for you cannot and will not know where you are going until you die, or until you are set free from this insidious teaching.

Hallelujah

The word *hallelujah* is really multiple words compressed into one. The ending, *jah*, is actually short for Yahweh. The beginning, *hallelu*, is an imperative that commands people to *praise*. Thus *hallelujah* actually means *praise the Lord* or *praise God* or even *praise Yah*(weh).

So many people today think that the way we praise Yahweh is by saying the word *hallelujah* over and over again.

Let's say someone said, "Praise the President." Then the way to do that would not be to say or sing, "Praise the President" over and over again. The way to do it would be talk about the great things the President has done, to speak about his great character, his great acts, and so on.

The way to praise God is to speak about His goodness, His eternality, His justice, His love, His grace, and so on. Or we might speak about His great works: His creating us, His setting Israel free from Egypt, His giving them the Promised Land, His sending His Son to die on the cross for our sins, His giving us eternal life by faith in His Son, His promising us a glorious future, etc.

Christianity is not Hinduism. We do not chant mantras. God doesn't want that. That dishonors God. He wants mindful praise.

Consider the shortest chapter in the Bible, Psalm 117. You can memorize it in a few minutes. It speaks of praising the LORD and it gives specific praise: "For His merciful kindness is great toward us, and the truth of the LORD endures forever."

There is a genre of psalms called *praise psalms*. The last five Psalms, Psalms 146–150, are all praise psalms. When you look at them you find that they do much more than say *praise the Lord*. They actually praise Him. Psalm 146, for example, recounts creation, the fact that God "keeps truth forever," that He "executes justice for the oppressed," and "gives food to the hungry." It says He "raises those who are bowed down" and that "the LORD shall reign forever."

The next time you sing *Hallelu, Hallelu, Hallelu, Hallelujah*, try actually thinking of some attribute or action of God as you sing. You might think about His immutability, His truthfulness, His glorious creation of the universe, and so on. But to blithely sing one word over and over again with an inactive mind is not pleasing to God.

Justification

The level of confusion on the doctrine of justification by faith alone is very sad. Much of this confusion has arisen in the past two to three decades as scholars and pastors have adopted the New Perspective on Paul and its belief that there are two justifications before God, one by faith in this life, and the other by works, that will occur at *the final judgment* after this life is over.

The word *justify* means *to vindicate* or *to declare righteous*. The sense of vindication is found in the New Testament, though it is rare. Declaration of righteous standing by God is the normal usage.

From the time I was born again in 1972 until I completed my seminary training in 1985, there were really only two widely held views of justification. Some held that justification before God was by faith *alone*. Others held that justification before God was by faith, but not by faith alone. In this view justification before God required faith plus perseverance in good works.

It should be noted that among those who taught justification by faith alone, there were two understandings of that. Most Calvinists would say justification is by faith alone, but that all who are truly justified will persevere in faith and good works until death, though there might be short times away from the Lord before the ultimate perseverance. Thus in this view justification is formally by faith alone, but in reality, it is by faith plus works.

The other understanding of justification by faith alone is that it is indeed by faith alone. In this view the moment one believes in Jesus for everlasting life, he is not only regenerated and eternally secure, he is also justified and guaranteed that he is permanently righteous in his standing before God. Good works play no role in this. Thus failure is possible for the justified person. A person might be once-for-all justified and yet fail to persevere in faith and good works.

What has happened over the past few decades is that many Calvinists have adopted a two-stage understanding of justification before God. Stage one is past justification by faith alone. Stage two is future justification, also called *final justification*, by works. According to this understanding, believing in Jesus results in initial justification, but without perseverance in good works there will be no final justification. The believer who fails to persevere ends up in the lake of fire since at the *final judgment* some believers will find that their works are not good enough to lead to final justification.

If that sounds odd to you, I share your perspective. Theology is becoming like politics, with more and more doublespeak going on. Now people can with a straight face proclaim that justification is by faith alone and justification is by works.

The Bible knows nothing of a final justification or of a final judgment to determine everyone's eternal destiny. Remember that Jesus promised that the believer "shall not come into judgment" concerning everlasting life (John 5:24). Once a person is justified by God by faith alone (Rom 4:4-5), he is justified forever (Rom 11:29). There is no double jeopardy with God.

Worship

Most churchgoers today think that worship is a feeling that one gets when he sings reverently, when he speaks in tongues (if he is Charismatic), when he raises his hands while singing, or when he hears a moving sermon. Yet Biblical worship is not a feeling.

It would surprise most people to learn that the word *worship* primarily refers to *bowing down to* someone or something. That is why Daniel would not bow down to the idol that Nebuchadnezzar built. God forbade such worship in the Torah.

When the man born blind in John 9 learned that the One to whom he was speaking was the Messiah, "He said, 'Lord, I believe!'" Then John adds, "And he worshipped Him" (John 9:38). What does that mean? What did the man do? Did he start singing? Did he perform a sacred dance before Him? No. He fell at Jesus' feet.

Do you remember a recorded incident in the Book of Revelation when John bowed down before a majestic being? John says, "And I fell at his feet to worship him. But he said to me, 'See that you do not do that! I am your fellow servant, and of your brethren who have the testimony of Jesus. Worship God!'" (Rev 19:10). John *fell at his feet to worship him.* Worship is falling down before someone. It is bowing to someone.

When we are told that one day every knee will bow to Jesus, what that means is that one day even unbelievers will worship Him. When they bow the knee to Him at the Great White Throne Judgment, they are acknowledging His sovereignty over them and His deity.

When we kneel in prayer, we are worshipping God. When we even bow our head (or heart) in prayer, we are worshipping God.

Jesus told the woman at the well that God is seeking those who "worship in spirit and in truth." What did He mean?

Clearly true worship in not found in a location, whether Mt. Gerazim, as the woman and other Samaritans thought, or the temple in Jerusalem, as Jews of the day thought. Jesus' point is that true worship is a matter of the heart.

Thus we might suggest that the mere act of falling before someone or kneeling or bowing is not, absent of heart involvement, complete worship. Full worship engages the whole person.

Worship is when we bow ourselves internally (and often externally) to the Lord. We may or may not feel good while doing this. Worship is not pleasing to God simply because we feel lifted up, nor is it necessarily displeasing if we do not. Indeed, if we are seeking a feeling, then what we are doing is self-serving and is defective worship.

Christian

Most people think that *Christian* is a synonym for a professing believer or a person who professes to be born-again. Others would say that it is a synonym for a born again person.

Actually neither of those is correct, but the former is closer than the latter.

Most people are surprised when they learn that the word *Christian* only appears a total of three times in the Bible. *Three.* It is a rare word.

The first use appears in Acts 11:26, which reads, "And the disciples were first called Christians in Antioch." Notice that Luke does not say, "And the disciples first *called themselves* Christians in Antioch." A passive voice is used, which means that someone else was calling them by this name.

The most natural understanding, one taken by many commentators, is that it was *the unbelievers* in and around Antioch that called them *Christians.* And this was surely a derisive term, meaning something like *little Christs* or, more charitably, *followers of Christ* (who was viewed negatively by the unbelievers).

When I came to faith in Christ, unbelievers referred to me and other devoted believers as *Jesus freaks* or *Jesus people*. That is probably the way the term *Christians* was first meant.

The second use appears in Acts 26:28 in which King Agrippa says to Paul, "You almost persuade me to become a Christian." This is normally understood to mean, "You almost persuade me to believe in Jesus for everlasting life." But that is not at all what is meant, as the context shows.

In the previous verse Paul says, "King Agrippa, do you believe the prophets? I know that you do believe." Note that Paul knows that Agrippa believes the Old Testament prophets. About what? About the coming Messiah.

What did Agrippa believe about the coming Messiah? Did he believe that Jesus is the Messiah who fulfilled the Old Testament prophesies?

Looking back in the sermon, we see that Paul preached Jesus to Agrippa (Acts 26:12-15, 23, 26). Therefore, when Paul says, "I know that you do believe [the Old Testament prophets]," he means *about Jesus*.

What Agrippa meant was thus, "You almost persuade me to openly confess faith in Jesus Christ" or "You almost persuade me to publicly identify myself as a follower of Jesus Christ."

The third and final use of the word *Christian* occurs in 1 Pet 4:16: "If anyone suffers as a Christian, let him not be ashamed, but let him glorify God in this matter." To suffer *as a Christian* means to suffer *as a follower of Christ*. It does not mean merely to suffer *as a believer*. A person can believe and yet not confess Christ. Nicodemus in John's Gospel is a prime example (cf. John 12:42).

In seminary I met a young man who was from a Muslim family. He came to faith in Jesus and told his parents. They told him not to tell anyone and to forget about it. Nevertheless, he told his parents he planned to be baptized.

His parents, being devout Muslims, told him that if he was baptized, they would hold a funeral for him and never speak to him again. He thought about it and decided it was best to do what Jesus said. He counted the cost and then acted. He was baptized. Unlike many stories with happy endings, his parents did not come to faith in Christ. They didn't even back down from what they had said they would do. His own parents indeed had a funeral for him. They stopped speaking to him or having anything to do with him. It had been years since this happened when I met him. The pain was still evident when he told the story. Yet there was also in his eyes the conviction that he did not regret what he did since identifying himself as a Christian was a vital step in his spiritual growth and development.

He was born again before he identified himself a Christian. We might say that first he was born again and then later, when he submitted to baptism, he became a Christian.

There are people who are following Christ but who are not born again. In a sense, those people are Christians. That is, they are following Christ, even though they do not yet understand and believe the promise of life. There are also people who are born again yet who are not following Christ. These people really are not Christians.

A Christian is a person who is following Christ.

Paradise

Paradise is commonly understood as a synonym for heaven. As you might guess, that is wrong.

The word *Paradise* also only appears three times in the New Testament. Two of the three uses show that it is not identical with *heaven*.

When Jesus was on the cross, one of the two thieves said, "Lord, remember me when You come into Your kingdom" (Luke 23:42). Most people wrongly think he is asking Jesus to allow him into His kingdom. But look more carefully at what he asks.

The thief clearly now believes that Jesus is the Messiah. He believes that Jesus is going to rise from the dead and will come again as King of Israel and will rule and reign. The man believes that he will be in that kingdom with Jesus and he wants Him, at that time, to *remember him*. What would that mean? That would mean that the man would be honored in some way by Jesus in His kingdom.

Imagine you worked in Congress as a lobbyist and you had a friend running for the U.S. Senate whom you were convinced was going to win. If you said, "Remember me when you come to Congress," you would be asking for him to give you a hearing in your lobbying efforts once he arrived. You would be asking for some reward for your friendship with him. The same was true with the thief on the cross.

Though he only confessed Jesus publicly for three hours, he was the only one at the cross who confessed Jesus as the Christ prior to His death. Jesus promised that all who confess Him He will confess before His Father (Matt 10:32).

How did Jesus respond to his question? He didn't talk at all about what He would say to the man, or what He would do for him, when

He came in His kingdom. Instead, He gave a much more immediate answer: "Today you will be with Me in Paradise."

Well, where did Jesus go after He died? He did not go to heaven. Instead, He went to Sheol, to the place of the dead. For three days He was in the saved part of Sheol (cf. Matt 12:40; Luke 16:19-31). The thief was *with Jesus* in the saved part of Sheol that very day. The key is the phrase *with Me*. That means that Jesus would honor this man by having Him close by Him that very day. Certainly there were millions of people in the saved part of Sheol. This man would not be off on the periphery. He would be close to Jesus. This implies, of course, that he would be *with Jesus* also when Jesus comes in His kingdom.

Paradise in Luke 23:43 is Sheol, not heaven. That is certain.

The second use of Paradise is found in Paul's second canonical letter to the Corinthians. Speaking of himself he says, "I know a man in Christ who…was caught up to the third heaven…into Paradise" (2 Cor 12:2-4). Paul here does identify the third heaven as Paradise.

It should be noted, however, that this is after Jesus' ascension. Before His ascension Paradise was the saved part of Sheol. At this point it is the third heaven.

What the first two uses have in common is that Paradise is where Jesus and the saints are.

The third use clinches that Paradise is where Jesus and His saints are. That use is found in Rev 2:7. It reads, "To him who overcomes I will give to eat from the tree of life, which is in the midst of the Paradise of God." When we compare this with Rev 22:1-2, we know with certainty that the Paradise of God in this case refers to the New Jerusalem and the entire new earth. In eternity future Paradise will be where Jesus and His saints are. It will not be in heaven, for Jesus and His saints will not be there, but will be on the new earth.

Interestingly, in the Greek Old Testament the word used for *Garden* in *the Garden of Eden* is the Greek word for Paradise (*paradeisos*). Thus the Garden of Eden before the Fall was Paradise, where Jesus and Adam and Eve were.

Paradise is heaven right now. But it wasn't heaven before and it won't be heaven in the future. Paradise always is where Jesus and His saints are.

Approval

This word is much misunderstood and the misunderstandings rob people of assurance of everlasting life.

The underlying Greek word is *dokimos*. Every believer should long to be approved by Christ (2 Tim 2:15) and should fear that he might be disapproved by Him (1 Cor 9:27, using the antonym *adokimos*).

Sadly most in Christianity today think that *dokimos* refers to approval to spend forever with Jesus. In this view only those approved by Christ will spend eternity in Paradise. All believers who are disapproved will go to the lake of fire.

A failure to recognize this as a rewards concept is tragic.

Maslow in his hierarchy of needs lists *approval* (especially concerning parents, spouse, and those closest to us) as the second-highest need any human has.

All who come to faith in Christ are in the family of God, also called "the household of faith" (Gal 6:10). But not all in the family are approved. Only those who are walking by faith and who continue to do so are approved (cf. 1 Cor 9:27; 2 Tim 2:15).

While I am certain I am eternally secure, I am uncertain I will hear the Lord tell me, "Well done, good servant" (Luke 19:17) at the Judgment Seat of Christ. I cannot know I will have His approval, since I cannot be sure I will persevere (1 Cor 9:27).[3]

I realize that my life will be a success if the Lord approves of me at His Judgment Seat. Of course, my life would be partially successful if I lay up treasure in heaven and receive at least some measure of authority in His kingdom (Matt 6:19-21; Luke 19:19). But I want to hear Him say, "Well done, good servant." Don't you want Him to say that to you? Wouldn't that be the greatest thing that will ever happen to you other than the time you received everlasting life by faith in Christ?

Living for His approval is a wonderful motivation as long as we realize that the issue here is how well we will be able to glorify Him forever, not whether we will be with Him.

Anathema

Anathema is a relatively rare word in the Bible. It is only found six times (Acts 23:14; Rom 9:3; 1 Cor 12:3; 16:22; Gal 1:8, 9).

---

[3] Paul says in 1 Cor 9:27 that he would be disapproved—*adokimos* (*dokimos*, approved, plus the alpha prefix, which negates it)—if he fell away after having preached to others.

Most people think that *anathema* in the Bible refers to eternal condemnation. This is certainly aided by translations like the NIV, which translates *anathema* in Gal 1:8-9 as "let him be eternally condemned!"

Actually, the word never means that. The word refers to an oath or a curse in Acts 23:14. A group of forty Jews bound themselves to an oath (NKJV reads *great oath*, but literally it could be translated "with a curse we have cursed ourselves" or "with an anathema we have anathematized ourselves") that they would eat nothing until they killed the Apostle Paul. They are clearly not talking about eternal condemnation.

Romans 9:3 is the one verse which seems most like it might refer to eternal condemnation. Paul is saying that he could wish that he were *anathema from Christ* on behalf of his Jewish brothers if it would result in their conversion. The sense is something like *cut off from Christ*.

Here is what Zane Hodges says about the idea that *anathema* in Rom 9:3 refers to Paul's willingness to be eternally condemned:

> But how, one might ask, could Paul even bear the thought, much less desire it, that he could be eternally separated **from Christ** for the good of Israel? This, however, is the wrong question and proceeds on a false assumption about what is meant by the term *accursed* (*anathema*).
>
> Jewett (p. 561) is not correct to say that "in some sense Paul offered his own damnation on behalf of his fellow Jews and that his prayer was rejected." There is nothing in the general usage of this word, either in the NT or the LXX, to suggest that Paul's expression had the theological nuance that Jewett and others have given it...
>
> Paul himself used the term *anathema* only here in Romans and only elsewhere in the NT at 1 Cor 12:3; 16:22, and Gal 1:8-9. It would be entirely gratuitous to read "damnation" into any of the Pauline passages. There seems to be no evidence in the Greek Scriptures for the idea that the word *anathema* implies that Paul was willing to go to hell for Israel. Summary destruction (e.g., execution) appears to be the worst implication that can be linguistically supported, but the term *anathema* itself is not specific and might be expected to be realized in diverse ways. [4]

First Corinthians 12:3 says that "no one speaking by the Spirit of God calls Jesus accursed." The word *accursed* (*anathema*) there does not mean *eternally condemned*, but rather, *cursed by God*.

---

[4] This quotation is taken from his soon to be published commentary on Romans.

Similarly, 1 Cor 16:22 says, "If anyone does not love the Lord Jesus Christ, let him be accursed." Clearly believers might not love the Lord Jesus. If they do not, then they fall under this curse. This is not eternal condemnation. It is temporal judgment which might culminate in premature death if repentance does not occur.

Galatians 1:8-9 not only is a curse on the Judaizers, who were likely all unregenerate, but on *anyone* proclaiming a false gospel. That could include born-again people. Paul actually says in Galatians 2 that Peter and Barnabas were for a time not straightforward about the truth of the gospel (Gal 2:11-14ff.).[5] Certainly a believer can be duped into believing and teaching justification and/or sanctification by works and not by faith in Christ, and if so, that born-again person falls under this curse, which is temporal judgment.

Anathema does not refer to eternal condemnation. It refers to a curse, that is, temporal judgment from God.

Inherit

This word seems simple enough. We all know what it means to inherit something. Many of us who are older have already received some sort of inheritance from our parents or grandparents or from aunts or uncles. So why is this word in the list?

It is here because people do not think of Biblical inheritance like they do everyday inheritance. They read the concept of eternal destiny into the Biblical expression *inheriting the kingdom.*

Actually to inherit the kingdom is *to possess it, to rule in it,* not simply to be in it (cf. 1 Cor 6:9-11; 15:50; Gal 5:19-21; Eph 5:5-7).

Romans 8:16-17 is a powerful passage that few understand. There Paul speaks of two inheritances. See if you can notice more than one inheritance here:

> The Spirit Himself bears witness with our spirit that we are children of God, and if children, then heirs—heirs of God and joint heirs with Christ, if indeed we suffer with Him, that we may also be glorified together.

The punctuation in the NKJV (above), as with most modern translations of Rom 8:17, is confusing. Actually it should be punctuated this

---

[5] Paul stops short of saying that Peter and Barnabas preached a false gospel. He does not say or imply that they were under God's *anathema*. But not being straightforward about the truth of the gospel was very bad and was a step in that direction.

way: "and if children, then heirs—heirs of God; and joint heirs with Christ, if indeed we suffer with Him…"

The first inheritance is being "heirs of God." All believers are heirs of God. Note that the only condition given here is to be a child of God. All children of God are heirs of God. I call this *passive inheritance* since a believer need do nothing to get it.

Included in this automatic inheritance are things like being in God's family forever, being in the kingdom forever, reception of the Spirit, and possession of everlasting life.

The second inheritance is being "joint heirs with Christ." I call this inheritance *active inheritance* since being a believer does not guarantee this inheritance. To get this inheritance one must actively "suffer with Him." Peter expressed the same idea in 1 Pet 4:13. Both Paul and Peter received this teaching from the Lord (cf. Matt 16:24-28).

Included in being joint heirs with Christ are things like being His partners (*metochoi*) in the life to come (cf. Heb 1:9), ruling with Him (Luke 19:17, 19; 2 Tim 2:12), and receiving special rewards that will enhance your ability to glorify Jesus forever (e.g., the right to the fruit of the tree of life, the hidden manna, special white garments).

My own family illustrates this well. One of my relatives was the rebel in her family. She used to literally hit her father. She would fight with him verbally all the time as well. She married before she was eighteen as an added act of rebellion.

You might think that rebellious girl was disowned by her parents. But she was not. Her parents loved her in spite of her rebellion against them.

That daughter was included in all the family gatherings. Her parents always spoke of their deep love for her.

Yet her parents were deeply hurt by her rebellion. They did not approve of her or of the way she acted. This impacted her inheritance.

While that girl had all the passive inheritance her family could give (name, love, family gatherings, etc.), she was written out of the will. She did not receive an active inheritance.

Like Esau, this rebellious child lost her inheritance.

If you are a believer in Jesus Christ, then you are a child of God and hence an heir of God. Your eternal destiny is set. You are in God's forever family.

However, to be a joint heir with Christ, you must live for Him, which involves suffering. You must deny yourself, take up your cross, and follow Christ on the path He took if you wish to share in His coming rule (cf. Matt 16:24-28).

Being an heir of God is a free gift received by faith alone. But to become a joint heir with Christ will cost you your very life (Matt 16:25-26). But since He gave His life for us, does it not make sense for us to give our lives in service to Him, especially when He is coming back soon to "reward each according to his works" (Matt 16:27)?

Appendix 2:
The Analogy of Faith

The Analogy of Faith Explained

The analogy of faith is a principle of Biblical hermeneutics, that is, of interpreting passages in the Bible. Since the Bible is the Word of God, it has no errors in it. That means that no passage in the Bible contradicts any other passage in the Bible.

Therefore, if one or more clear passages establish that "A" is true, no other passage can be correctly interpreted to say that "A" is false. For example, John 20:28 clearly shows that Jesus Christ is God. Thus whatever John 1:1 means, it does not mean that Jesus is not God.

The analogy of faith technically applies to doctrines, not passages *per se*.[1] So in the example just given, once we know that Jesus is God, we know that no text says Jesus is not God. But once we go to a specific text like John 1:1 and use the analogy of faith to say that it doesn't question the deity of Christ, we are using a principle within the analogy of faith called *the analogy of Scripture*.[2] However, for our purposes we will use the expression *the analogy of faith* even when technically we are applying the narrower concept of the analogy of Scripture.

The analogy of faith only works when you are comparing two passages that discuss the same exact point. We call such passages *parallel passages*. Of course, this can be tricky since in the case of the Gospels, the Lord taught many things on more than one occasion, often using different words and sometimes even making different points.

The Analogy of Faith Illustrated

Consider two related, but not identical, parables, the Parable of the Minas in Luke 19:11-27 and the Parable of the Talents in Matt 25:14-30.

---

[1] See H. Wayne Johnson, "The 'Analogy of Faith' and Exegetical Methodology: A Preliminary Discussion of Relationships," *Journal of the Evangelical Theological Society* (March 1988): 69.

[2] Ibid.

Both deal with the future judgment of Jesus' servants. Both focus on three servants. The third servant in each case received a bad judgment.

The two parables have some significant differences too. In the Minas the Lord discusses His citizens who hated Him and didn't want Him to reign over them. Not so with the Talents. There the Lord only discusses His servants. In addition, in the Minas all ten servants receive the same sum to invest (one mina), whereas in the Talents they each receive different amounts (five, two, and one talents). There is also a difference in the rewards of the first two servants in the Minas (cf. Luke 19:17, 19), but not in the Talents (cf. Matt 25:21, 23).

We must apply the analogy of faith carefully in a case in which the two passages are clearly parallel *in some ways*, but not in other ways. In my opinion it is legitimate to say that since the third servant in the Parable of the Minas is not slain (compare Luke 19:26 and 19:27), he represents an unfaithful *believer*, and by extension, so does the third servant in the Parable of the Talents. This would lead us to rethink the meaning of the "outer darkness" in Matt 25:30.

Consider Heb 6:4-8 and the doctrine of eternal security. Since many passages establish eternal security as true (e.g., John 5:24; 6:35; 11:26), then we can be certain no other passage denies it. When we come to a text like Heb 6:4-8, which some interpret to teach loss of everlasting life, we can confidently reject that interpretation as impossible in light of the analogy of faith. Even if you don't know what a text means, you can be sure that it cannot contradict other passages of Scripture (see below).

The Analogy of Faith and Understanding Our Ten Misunderstood Words

I used the analogy of faith often in discussing the ten words. For example, when discussing *everlasting*, I pointed out that many texts clearly establish that everlasting life cannot be lost, making the same point I made in the previous paragraph.

When discussing the word *faith*, I pointed out that faith in Scripture is not commitment, obedience, and perseverance, but is always a conviction that something is true.

John 5:24, I pointed out, clearly establishes that believers "shall not come into judgment" regarding their eternal destinies. Thus I used the analogy of faith to debunk the idea of a *final judgment*, a *final salvation*, or a *final justification*.

I first believed in Christ for everlasting life in the Fall of 1972. At that time I could have given a fairly accurate explanation of three of our ten words: faith, repentance, everlasting. But I would have misunderstood all of the other seven in significant ways. That led me, for example, to be uncertain about the meaning of many passages speaking of salvation, since they clearly spoke of salvation by works. Until I learned that salvation is merely deliverance and that it rarely refers to deliverance from eternal condemnation, I had a lot of passages I simply admitted I did not yet understand. But I did use the analogy of faith even then, before I'd learned the expression. Since I knew that John 3:16 was true, I knew that no other passage could contradict it.

Using the Analogy of Faith, You Can Often Determine What a Passage Can't Mean

I mentioned this above regarding the interpretation of Heb 6:4-8. You may not know what it means, but you rule out with certainty the idea that it is teaching the possible loss of everlasting life.

I also mentioned that early in my Christian experience someone taught me this principle without telling me its name. For years I could not explain Heb 6:4-8 or Jas 2:14-17 to my own satisfaction, but I knew neither taught regeneration by works or by perseverance.

The Bible has millions of truths in it. None of us can understand everything in the Bible. Even things we once knew we can forget. I remember once asking Zane Hodges his view on a certain passage. His answer made me smile since I'd had the same experience: "I can't recall how I understand that passage. I know I discuss it in one of my books, but I'd have to go back and check to see how I handle it." But one thing Zane never did was forget the fundamental truths of Scripture and their supporting texts. He regularly used the analogy of faith, even when he couldn't remember what a given passage meant.

Avoid Misusing the Analogy of Faith

It is possible, of course, to misuse this principle. That is called *reversing the analogy of faith*. The true analogy of faith says that we understand unclear passages of Scripture in light of the clear. Thus we should understand John 8:30-32 in light of John 3:16, and not the other way around. Sadly many commentators, however, do just the opposite. They suggest that John 8:30-32 shows that one can "believe in Him" (the Lord Jesus) and yet not have everlasting life unless they abide in His word and become His true disciples. They then understand John 3:16 in that light, saying that "whoever believes in Him" does not refer to those who merely believe in Him, but to those who abide in Him.

As I mentioned in the body of this work, one pastor actually said that he never preached John 3:16 because it was such a difficult text. Well, it is only a difficult text if you reverse the analogy of faith.

You must always make sure that the two passages you are comparing are both talking about the same subject. And you must also be sure which of the two is clearer than the other.

The Analogy of Faith Helps Us with Assurance and Evangelism

If you are fairly new to the faith, you may not know much. But that should not stop you from sharing your faith. It is often new believers who share their faith with the most gusto. How can that be when new believers often can't explain any of the difficult texts in the Bible? It is because they know the principle behind the analogy of faith even if they don't know its name. They may realize that they don't know much about the Bible. But they know that they grasp the meaning of John 3:16 and they share that message boldly and enthusiastically.

I heard a story, which I think was an actual account, of a ten-year-old newsboy around 1900 in a major U.S. city. Back then there were no child labor laws and young boys would sell papers in the downtown areas for many hours each day. The boy was led to faith in Christ by one of his customers. He began to tell his customers that he was now saved because he believed in Jesus.

One of his customers, a middle-aged man, gave him a condescending smile and asked, "Isn't it possible that you only *think* you've been saved?" The man came from a Lordship Salvation perspective in which any profession is suspect until a person has shown years of subsequent perseverance in good works. (And even then, the profession is still possibly false in the Lordship Salvation view, since anyone could later fall away.)

The little boy got a very troubled look on his face. For a moment, he experienced doubt. But then he thought and replied, "No sir. I'm sure I'm saved. Jesus said, 'the one who comes to Me I will by no means cast out' (John 6:37). I came to Him and therefore He will never cast me out!"

The boy didn't realize it, but he was applying the analogy of faith. He had been led to faith by means of John 6:37 (and possibly the entire passage, John 6:35-40). When challenged, he thought it through again and realized John 6:37 left no room for doubt about his eternal destiny, even if a man, one much older and more experienced, was challenging his assurance.

Don't Leave Home Without It

The analogy of faith is better than American Express. We should even teach unbelievers the analogy of faith. We should certainly make this interpretive principle known to all new believers we are privileged to follow up.

Every believer needs to know and apply this principle regularly. It clears up much confusion. It allows us to build on what we've learned thus far in the Christian faith, without having to question clear passages every time we hit a tough text.

No other book on earth is inspired and without errors and without inconsistencies. Since the Bible is the Word of God, we can and should apply the analogy of faith regularly.

Appendix 3:
Blessings and Curses

The Doctrine of Blessings
and Curses Explained

The Pentateuch has two entire chapters devoted to this theme. Leviticus 26 and Deuteronomy 28 both concern blessings for Israel if she obeys the Lord and ever-increasing curses for Israel should she forsake Him. The blessings and curses in those chapters concern *temporal* blessings and curses.

We know from Hebrews 11, the Hebrews Hall of Fame (or Hall of Faith), that at least some Old Testament believers understood that the theme of blessings extended to the life to come. Moses, for example, chose "rather to suffer affliction with the people of God than to enjoy the passing pleasures of sin, esteeming the reproach of Christ greater riches than the treasures in Egypt; *for he looked to the reward*" (Heb 11:25-26, emphasis added). Abraham likewise "waited for the city which has foundations, whose builder and maker is God" (Heb 11:10). Old Testament martyrs "were tortured, not accepting deliverance, that they might obtain a better resurrection" (Heb 11:35). The *better resurrection* is the eternal reward of ruling with Messiah and having special fullness of life with Him (cf. Heb 1:9).

The New Testament has more to say about the doctrine of eternal rewards, a part of the doctrine of blessings and curses, than does the Old Testament. In it we learn of the Judgment Seat of Christ (Rom 14:10-12; 2 Cor 5:9-11), also called the believer's "day of judgment" (1 John 4:17-19). Likewise, the Beatitudes, which start the Sermon on the Mount, are all about eternal blessings, that is, eternal rewards (Matt 5:3-12).[1]

---

[1] For further information see Robert N. Wilkin, *The Road to Reward* (Irving, TX: Grace Evangelical Society, 2003).

How This Doctrine Reduces and Eliminates Misunderstandings

Sadly many Old and New Testament passages which deal with blessings or curses are misunderstood by pastors and commentators as dealing with where people will spend eternity. Ezekiel 18, for example, says, "the soul who sins shall die" (Ezek 18:4, 20) and "'Do I have pleasure at all that the wicked should die?' says the LORD GOD, 'and not that he should turn from his ways and live?'" (Ezek 18:23; see also Ezek 18:31-32). Those are direct warnings of premature death to Israelites who walk away from the Lord, whether believers or unbelievers. The issue there is not eternal destiny, but temporal well-being. Repentance is the way to extend one's life: "'For I have no pleasure in the death of one who dies,' says the LORD GOD. 'Therefore turn and live!'" (Ezek 18:32).

Concerning Ezekiel 18, Charles Feinberg said, "The subject of justification by faith should not be pressed into this chapter; it is not under discussion."[2] Later, commenting on verse nine (which refers to obedience to the Law of Moses) he writes, "This statement, we must caution again, does not have eternal life in view, but life on earth. Eternal life is not obtained on the grounds mentioned in this portion of Scripture."[3]

The ten most misunderstood words are much more easily understood if one already understands the blessings and curses motif found in both testaments. Take, for example, the words *save* and *faith*. If one understands the concept of blessings and curses, then a verse like Jas 2:14 is simple to understand: "What does it profit [an indication the blessings and curses motif is in view], my brethren [= believers], if someone says he has faith but does not have works [i.e., he does not apply what he believes]? Can faith save him [from temporal judgment from God]?" People who read the question, "Can faith save him?" as though it referred to salvation from eternal condemnation, totally miss James's point, especially since the Greek is actually better translated in this way: "Faith cannot save him, can it?" James is saying that if we believe something that God says and don't put that faith into action, we won't be saved from temporal curses. Note that the illustration James gives proves that understanding to be true and even ends with the exact same blessings and curses expression, "what does it profit?" (Jas 2:16).

We need not go through gymnastics to try to explain why Jas 2:14 doesn't contradict John 3:16 or Eph 2:8-9. That is like comparing apples

---

[2] Charles Lee Feinberg, *The Prophecy of Ezekiel* (Chicago: Moody Press, 1969), 99.

[3] Ibid., 101.

and oranges. People who miss this create a new meaning for faith and force their regeneration understanding of salvation upon Jas 2:14-17. Assurance ends up being annihilated and evangelism is eviscerated due to a simple misunderstanding that is easy to clear up.

Imagine a carpenter who only had a saw. He'd have to try to pound down nails using his saw. He'd have to try to use the saw to make a line that he guessed was level. The saw would be used to take out or put in screws. Even the most inventive carpenter would be a lousy carpenter without at least having a hammer and a screwdriver along with a saw and a level.

Many church people lack an understanding of the blessings and curses motif and hence that tool is not in their hermeneutical (interpretive) toolbox. They are like the carpenter without the hammer. Understanding this motif is vital if we are to understand what God means in both the Old and New Testaments, including especially the meanings of these ten words in context.

Failure to Understand Which Passages Deal with Eternal Destiny Distorts the Message of Life

Think again about Jas 2:14. If I think that it concerns one's eternal destiny, then I must conclude that *faith* apart from works cannot *save* anyone from eternal condemnation. But that is a contradiction of the message of life as found in John 3:16 and many other verses.

If a person thinks that Phil 2:12 concerns some final *judgment*, then he most likely distorts the promise of everlasting life to all who simply believe in the Lord Jesus.

If Ezekiel 18 was intended to tell Israelites what they must do to have *everlasting* life, then the Old Testament taught justification by repentance and works, not by faith alone.

The blessings and curses motif is not the message of life. Those are two completely different topics. A person is blessed or cursed based on works. But he receives everlasting life solely by faith in Christ.

Study Guide

Chapter 1
Faith

1. What is *intellectual assent*?
2. Agree or disagree: faith in the Bible is intellectual assent.
3. What is *saving faith*?
4. Why do many people say that saving faith includes commitment, obedience, and perseverance?
5. What does it mean to "believe in Him" in the Fourth Gospel? Defend your answer from more than one passage.
6. What is the relationship between faith and assurance of everlasting life and what is the Scriptural support for your answer?
7. What specifically must a person believe to be born again?
8. Is it possible to believe that Jesus is the second member of the Trinity and yet not be born again? Why or why not?
9. If a person's view of faith in Jesus includes obedience, yet they say that saving faith is a gift of God, are they "believing in Him" in the sense that the Lord means in John 3:16?
10. You have to translate John 3:16 into a language that is just like English except that it does not have the words *faith* or *believe*. How would you translate the phrase "whoever believes in Him" using some words other than *believes in*?

Chapter 2
Everlasting

1. Do you agree that people in Christian circles are much more likely to speak of *salvation* than they are to speak of *everlasting life* when they evangelize?
2. The author suggests that everlasting life is ever-lasting life, life that cannot be lost. Do you agree or disagree, and why?
3. Is there another aspect of everlasting life besides its *duration*? If so, what would that be and what passages show that?

4. How does John 6:35 inform our understanding of everlasting life even though it doesn't specifically mention it?
5. Let's say that diamonds could not be destroyed or damaged or cut up. We might speak of everlasting diamonds. But you might sell them, lose them, or have them stolen. Some people say that everlasting life is like that. It is indeed everlasting, but it can be lost. What does the Lord say about that?
6. Let's say you don't know what Heb 6:4-8 means. Someone points you to it and says, "See, this passage shows that everlasting life can indeed be lost." How would you answer them? (See Appendix 2 for help.)
7. Did Old Testament believers have everlasting life?
8. What is "the promise [or message] of life"? Cite several passages that use that expression.
9. Let's say a person has not yet heard the expressions *eternal security* or *once saved, always saved*. Is it possible that he might believe that he is indeed eternally secure and saved once and for all, even though he doesn't know those words? Defend your answer.
10. What does "will...reap everlasting life" mean in Gal 6:7-9? Defend your answer.

Chapter 3
Saved

1-3. Name three major ways in which the word *saved* (or the noun *salvation*) was used in the Old Testament and give at least one passage illustrating each use.
4-6. Name three major ways in which the word *saved* (or the noun *salvation*) was used in the New Testament and give at least one passage illustrating each use.
7. What does the word *saved* mean in the epistle of James (see 1:21; 2:14; 4:12; 5:15, 19-20)?
8. What does the word *salvation* mean in the epistle of Hebrews (cf. 1:14; 2:3, 10; 5:9; 6:9; 9:28; 11:7)?
9. Name five passages in which *saved* is equated with having everlasting life.
10. What does Paul mean by *deliverance* (or *salvation*; the word is *sōtēria*) in Phil 1:19? Note that this is the same word translated *salvation* in Phil 2:12.

Chapter 4
Lost

1. What does the word *lost* mean in the Old Testament? Give at least two passages illustrating that meaning.
2. What is the main meaning of lost in the New Testament? Give at least two passages illustrating that meaning.
3. Does the word *lost* ever mean *unregenerate* in the New Testament? If yes, defend your view with two passages.
4. Agree or disagree: the prodigal son of Luke 15:11-32 is meant by the Lord to illustrate *a believer* who departs from the Lord for a time and then repents and returns to fellowship.
5. Does it strike you as reasonable or unreasonable that a believer who was out of fellowship with God might be called *lost* in Scripture? Explain your answer.
6. Explain 2 Pet 3:9.
7. In what sense does gold *perish* (1 Pet 1:7)?
8. Do you think that all of the people who *perished* in the flood (2 Pet 3:6) were eternally condemned? Defend your answer.
9. Explain *perish* in Heb 11:31.
10. What did Peter mean when he told Simon Magus, "[May] your money perish with you, because you thought that the gift of God could be purchased with money!" (Acts 8:20)?

Chapter 5
Heaven

1. What is the first heaven and what passages tell us about it?
2. What is the second heaven and what passages tell us about it?
3. What is the third heaven and what passages tell us about it?
4. What is "the new heaven" mentioned in Rev 21:1?
5. What percentage of people in Christianity would you guess believe that the eternal home of the regenerate is heaven?
6. Has your focus been on the new earth or on heaven? Why?
7. How do you think people who are now in the third heaven experience time? That is, do you think they experience it like we do, or do you think that they experience it more like God does (cf. 2 Pet 3:8)?
8. Where did King David go when he died?
9. What are believers who are now in heaven doing?
10. What will believers do in eternity future?

Chapter 6
Hell

1. What is hell?
2. What is the lake of fire?
3. Describe the current suffering people are experiencing in hell.
4. Describe the future suffering people will experience in the lake of fire.
5. Agree or disagree: The torment in the lake of fire will be worse than any suffering any human ever experienced on earth. Defend your view.
6. What evidence is there that the suffering in the lake of fire will be conscious suffering?
7. What evidence is there that the suffering in the lake of fire will go on forever?
8. Do you agree or disagree with the author's suggestions regarding the lake of fire being a *tolerable* experience because of what the Lord said about the day of judgment being "more tolerable" for notoriously bad Gentiles as compared with seemingly good Jews? Why or why not?
9. Do you believe that discussing hell and the lake of fire is a helpful thing to do in evangelism? Why or why not?
10. What will unbelievers do forever in the lake of fire?

Chapter 7
Repentance

1. What is the change-of-mind view of repentance?
2. When the Ninevites repented as a result of Jonah's preaching, what did they do? (Jonah 3:5-10; Matt 12:41; Luke 11:32)?
3. What is *repentance* in 2 Pet 3:9?
4. Do you buy the argument that since the words *repent* and *repentance* are not found in John's Gospel, thus repentance must not be a condition of everlasting life? Why or why not?
5. Explain Luke 13:3, 5, "unless you repent you will all likewise perish."
6. What did the Lord mean when He said, "I did not come to call the righteous, but sinners, to repentance" (Matt 9:13; Mark 2:17; cf. Luke 5:32)?
7. Explain Ezek 18:30-32.

8. What did Paul mean in Rom 2:4 when he said, "the goodness of God leads you to repentance"?
9. Is a person justified before God by faith alone, or by faith and repentance? Defend your answer.
10. In light of First John, is repentance a condition for remaining in fellowship with God? Why or why not?

Chapter 8
Grace

1. What is *grace* (*charis*) in the Old Testament?
2. What is *grace* (*charis*) in the New Testament?
3. Explain Eph 2:8-9 with special attention to the phrase "by grace."
4. Is grace always, sometimes, or never *unmerited* favor? Defend your answer.
5. Were the works of Cornelius a factor in God choosing to send Peter to him to tell him what he must do to be saved (cf. Acts 10:1-8, 35; 11:12-14)? Support your answer from Scripture.
6. Does God normally bless people apart from their works, or are His blessings normally tied to their works? Defend your answer.
7. Cite three passages in which *charis* is translated as *thanks* and explain whether you agree or disagree with the translation in those places.
8. What do you think of Zane Hodges amplification of the meaning of the grace of God when he was discussing Eph 2:8-9 (see p. 132)?
9. What does *grace* mean in Titus 2:11? Use the context to explain your answer.
10. What did the songwriter mean when he says that "grace [is] greater than all our sin"?

Chapter 9
Gospel

1. The word *gospel* in the New Testament refers to what events? List at least four.
2. Why is the death of the Lord Jesus on the cross *good news*?

3. Did the death of Christ on the cross actually or only potentially take away the sin of the world (John 1:29; 1 John 2:2)? Defend your answer.
4. What is "the truth of the gospel" in Galatians?
5. Who were "the Judaizers" and how did they relate to Paul's gospel?
6. What is Paul's gospel according to 1 Cor 15:1-11?
7. How is the gospel related to Old Testament prophecies?
8. Is it possible to preach the gospel and yet not tell a person what he must do to be born again? Explain your answer.
9. Agree or disagree: Racism within the Church is a denial of the truth of the gospel. Why or why not?
10. Is *the message of life* the same message as *the gospel of Jesus Christ*? Defend your answer.

Chapter 10
Judgment

1. What is *final judgment* according to many theologians today?
2. Do you believe that you will experience *final judgment*? Why or why not?
3. Name the two major end-times judgments and give a passage in which each is discussed.
4. What is the basis of being cast into the lake of fire?
5. How does Luke 19:11-27 help us understand more about eschatological judgment?
6. How do you harmonize John 5:24 ("shall not come into judgment") with 2 Cor 5:9-10 and Jas 5:9 (which say believers shall be judged)?
7. Should we fear our coming judgment? Why or why not?
8. What is *temporal judgment*? Give three passages which speak of temporal judgment.
9. Will the results of the judgment of believers (e.g., rulership, treasure) last for 1,000 years or forever? Defend your answer.
10. Are you comfortable thinking of the Lord Jesus as your Judge (e.g., Jas 5:9)? Why or why not? *Should* you be comfortable thinking of Him in that way?

Scripture Index